ROUTLEDGEFALMER STUDIES IN HIGHER EDUCATION

Edited by
PHILIP G. ALTBACH
Monan Professor of Higher Education
Lynch School of Education, Boston College

RoutledgeFalmer Studies in Higher Education
Philip G. Altbach, *General Editor*

SAVING FOR COLLEGE AND THE TAX CODE
A New Spin on the "Who Pays for College Education?" Debate
Andrew P. Roth

TECHNOLOGY TRANSFER VIA UNIVERSITY-INDUSTRY RELATIONSHIP
The Case of the Foreign High Technology Electronics Industry in Mexico's Silicon Valley
Maria Isabel Rivera Vargas

TENURE ON TRIAL
Case Studies of Change in Faculty Appointment Policies
William T. Mallon

FROM HERE TO UNIVERSITY
Access, Mobility, & Resilience Among Urban Latino Youth
Alexander Jun

SCHOLARSHIP UNBOUND
Assessing Service as Scholarship for Promotion and Tenure
Kerry Ann O'Meara

BLACK STUDENT POLITICS
Higher Education and Apartheid from SASO to SANSCO, 1968–1990
Saleem Badat

RESOURCE ALLOCATION IN PRIVATE RESEARCH UNIVERSITIES
Daniel Rodas

A DREAM DEFERRED?
Examining the Degree Aspirations of African-American and White College Students
Deborah Faye Carter

STATE GOVERNMENTS AND RESEARCH UNIVERSITIES
A Framework for a Renewed Partnership
David Weerts

FEDERALISM AND LÄNDER AUTONOMY
The Higher Education Policty Network in the Federal Republic of Germany
Cesare Onestini

RESILIENT SPIRITS
Disadvantaged Students Making it at an Elite University
Latty Lee Goodwin

I PREFER TO TEACH
An International Comparison of Faculty Preferences for Teaching over Research
James J.F. Forest

THE VIRTUAL DELIVERY AND VIRTUAL ORGANIZATION OF POSTSECONDARY EDUCATION
Daniel M. Carchidi

BARELY THERE, POWERFULLY PRESENT
Thirty Years of U.S. Policy on International Higher Education
Nancy L. Ruther

A CALL TO PURPOSE
Mission Centered Change at Three Liberal Arts Colleges
Matthew Hartley

A PROFILE OF THE COMMUNITY COLLEGE PROFESSORATE, 1975–2000
Charles Outcalt

POWER AND POLITICS IN UNIVERSITY GOVERNANCE
Organization and Change at the Universidad Nacional Autónoma de México
Imanol Ordorika

UNIVERSITY AUTONOMY IN THE RUSSIAN FEDERATION SINCE PERESTROIKA
Olga B. Bain

THE CALL FOR DIVERSITY
Pressure, Expectation, and Organizational Response in the Postsecondary Setting
David J. Siegel

SCIENTIFIC COMMUNICATION IN AFRICAIN UNIVERSITIES
External Assistance and National Needs
Damtew Teferra

PHILANTHROPISTS IN HIGHER EDUCATION
Institutional, Biographical, and Religious Motivations for Giving
Gregory L. Cascione

THE RISE AND FALL OF FU REN UNIVERSITY, BEIJING
Catholic Higher Education in China

John Shujie Chen

LONDON AND NEW YORK

First published 2004 by RoutledgeFalmer

Published 2018 by Routledge
2 Park Square, Milton Park, Abingdon, Oxon, OX14 4RN
52 Vanderbilt Avenue, New York, NY 10017

First issued in paperback 2018

Routledge is an imprint of the Taylor & Francis Group, an informa business

Copyright © 2004 by Taylor & Francis.

All rights reserved. No part of this book may be reprinted or reproduced or utilised in any form or by any electronic, mechanical, or other means, now known or hereafter invented, including photocopying and recording, or in any information storage or retrieval system, without permission in writing from the publishers.

Notice:
Product or corporate names may be trademarks or registered trademarks, and are used only for identification and explanation without intent to infringe.

Library of Congress Cataloging-in-Publication Data

Chen, John Shujie, 1968–
 The rise and fall of Fu Ren University, Beijing : Catholic higher education in China / John Shujie Chen.
  p. cm. — (RoutledgeFalmer studies in higher education)
Includes bibliographical references and index.
  ISBN 0-415-94816-9 (hardcover : alk. paper)
 1. Fu ren da xue (Beijing, China)—History. 2. Catholic Church—Education--History. I. Title. II. Series.

  LG51.P25C44 2003
  378.511'56—dc22
                                                          2003021145

ISBN 13: 978-1-138-98545-2 (pbk)
ISBN 13: 978-0-415-94816-6 (hbk)

Contents

List of Tables	vii
List of Abbreviations	ix
Chapter One: Introduction	1
Chapter Two: Critical Literature Review and View Points	19
Section I: Overview of Chinese Higher Education	20
Section II: Existing Literature on Fu Ren University	26
Section III: Analysis	30
Chapter Three: Establishment of Fu Ren University	41
Chapter Four: Finance and Structural Development of the University	63
Chapter Five: Development: Curriculum, Faculty and Student Growth	85
Section I: Curriculum	86
Section II: Faculty	99
Section III: Student Growth	107
Chapter Six: Extra-curricular Activities	123
Section I: Sports	125
Section II: Social Services	131
Section III: Religious Activities	137

Chapter Seven: Political Entanglements	147
Chapter Eight: Conclusion	171
Appendix A: Letter to Pope Pius X	195
Appendix B: Exhortation to Study By Vincent Ying, K.S.G.	199
Appendix C: Terminology	209
Notes	211
Bibliography	249
Index	261

List of Tables

Table I	Faculty Statistics over the Years	106
Table II	Student Distribution Geographically (1938–1939)	109
Table III	Statistics Concerning Catholic Students at Graduation (1931–1939)	112
Table IV	Student Enrollments at Fu Ren University (1925–1951)	113
Table V	Graduating Students Over the Years (1931–1951)	117
Table VI	Competing Universities	118

List of Abbreviations

ABNU	Archives of Beijing Normal University, Beijing, China
ABC	Archives of Beijing City, Beijing, China
ASBC	Archives of Saint Benedict's Convent, Minnesota, USA
ASJA	Archives of Saint John's Abbey, Minnesota, USA
ASVA	Archives of Saint Vincent Archabbey, Latrobe, Pennsylvania, USA
ASHS	Archive of Sisters of the Holy Spirit, Techny, Illinois, USA
ADWM	Archives of Divine Word Missionaries, Techny, Illinois, USA
SJS	Saint John's Seminary, Brighton, Massachusetts, USA

CHAPTER ONE

Introduction

This book intends to be a thorough study of the rise and fall of Fu Ren University in Beijing[1], and provides a description of a key Catholic higher education institution in China. Established in 1925 and closing in 1952, Fu Ren University only existed for 27 years. It was the youngest among all private higher education institutions in Beijing and was the first university in the nation to be taken over by the Chinese Communist Party in 1950. Unlike any other Christian college or university that was initiated and established by missionaries, Fu Ren University in Beijing was started by two prominent Chinese Catholic scholars, Vincent Ying Lian-zhi and Ma Xiang-bo. Knowing the political and cultural needs of China, they felt the Catholic Church needed to have a good Catholic university in Beijing. They were motivated, first of all, by the fierce attacks on the traditional Chinese culture from progressive scholars; secondly, by the aggressiveness of the Protestant missionaries in China who attracted many intellectuals. They wrote a joint petition *Letter to Pope Pius X* in 1912[2] to ask the Pope to establish a Catholic University in Beijing to introduce Western Science and to revitalize Chinese culture. Because of many reasons, their petition to establish such a university was delayed for some years. In 1925, however, Fu Ren University was finally established in Beijing. The pioneers were the American Cassinese-Benedictine monks from Latrobe, Pennsylvania. At the invitation of the Pope, they came to establish and to staff the university with Vincent Ying as the first dean.

It is to be noted that Fu Ren University was first established only for Chinese young men with an emphasis on Chinese culture. Later as the political and cultural situation changed in Beijing, the university expanded and a separate Women's College at Fu Ren was established. Fu Ren University did not become a co-educational institution as many public universities did in Beijing.

Fu Ren was unique in its nature and structure among all higher education institutions in China. It was established first as a preparatory school. The name was taken as *Gong Jiao Da Xue*, which means Catholic University, later was called Fu Ren. The preparatory school was named *MacManus Academy for Chinese Studies* or *Fu Ren She* in Chinese. The university had two names for two reasons: First, Mr. MacManus donated a lot of money to the university as an endowment for the school to secure the best professors in China. Therefore the school was named after him. Secondly, the Chinese name for this academy was *Fu Ren She* because the Chinese founder Vincent Ying used this name before the university was established and because this name appealed to the Chinese. The duality of the university was seen in its title as well as in its nature as both Chinese and Catholic.

Fu Ren University was the only *Pontifical* Catholic University out of three Catholic universities (Aurora in Shanghai and Heutes Études in Tianjin) in China because it was sponsored by the Pope and was administered by the Catholic religious priests who were accountable to the Holy Father. Fu Ren University was first administered by the Congregation of the American Cassinese-Benedictines from 1925–1933, and later administered by the Divine Word Fathers from 1933–1950. During those years, many religious priests, secular priests and lay people were on the faculties. From 1950–1952 however, Fu Ren University fell under the control of the Chinese Communist Party. As a result, all Catholic priests were expelled from the university. During these two years, the university changed drastically in terms of curriculum, faculty, administration and student enrollment.

In an effort, this university was established as both Western and Chinese in nature from its very beginning by both Chinese scholars and Catholic missionaries. The Chinese founders intended to make this place be a center where Western Christian and Chinese cultures could meet. The Catholic missionaries cooperated to achieve this end. Its development and expansion were basically along the line of enculturation. All university structures were built in the Chinese traditional palace style. Curriculum was designed and developed with an emphasis on Chinese studies, as well as on Western sciences that could be useful for the students and for China as well. Fu Ren eventually attracted students from all over China. There were some students from other countries as well.

As the university developed and expanded, student enrollment kept increasing rapidly until the academic year 1947–1948, which had the highest enrollment according to available records[3]. With a student enrollment of 2348, Fu Ren University became the second largest university in Beijing. Only Beijing University was larger. Faculty numbers also grew throughout the years. In the academic year 1948–1949, the university had 282 members on the faculty.[4] This number was the highest in Fu Ren's history and declined dramatically in the following year. The reasons will be discussed in relevant chapters.

For instance, the Men's Section at Fu Ren University: School of Arts and Letters developed out of *MacManus Academy of Chinese Studies* or *Fu Ren She,* which emphasized Chinese studies. The Chinese government required such a school for all universities. The Ministry of Education made it a requirement for universities to have a School of Natural Sciences in the late 1920's. Scientific studies became very important in China at that time because of the battles in the country. The School of Education was established with an emphasis on methodology and psychology to train teachers for elementary and middle schools at first, and eventually broadened its mission. The Benedictine Sisters established the Women's College initially at the high school level in 1932. It developed rather quickly into a college level institution. In 1936, the Benedictine Sisters transferred the college to the Sisters of the Holy Spirit. At that time, the college was ready to accept college level students. The Sisters of the Holy Spirit designed a special curriculum for the young women who were from well-to-do families. Their prestigious status in China required special attention from the Sisters and the university. Saint Albert's College strongly emphasized that its priests should study Chinese literature and Western sciences. The last established College of Agriculture intended to help Chinese farmers by exploring better means of cultivation through study of related elements such as weather and seeds and soils from all over China.

In this book, I discuss the theme of Fu Ren University as both Western Catholic and Chinese in nature and how Fu Ren developed into such a university. All aspects that were related to its development will certainly be analyzed in this writing. Fu Ren University indeed became a place where the Western scientific knowledge and Chinese traditional culture could meet. All who came to study at Fu Ren University benefited from this cultural duality.

It is, therefore, necessary to discuss all aspects of the university, and meanwhile, provide a broad historical analysis so that the importance of the university will be apparent. Although some research has been done, those researchers only studied certain periods or certain aspects of the university. Its whole history is far from complete. This book intends to discuss the newly discovered materials. I have found that the entire history of Fu Ren University can reveal to the academic world the three-fold aims of this university: the preservation and elevation of Catholic ideals, the cultivation of the intellect by means of literary studies and pursuits, and the imparting of useful knowledge which would fit the students as educated, cultured and courteous gentlemen for any walk of life.[5] Any particular period of history can certainly reveal some of these, yet not clear enough to show the dual nature of Fu Ren distinctively. More importantly, those researchers have not mentioned this special, unique characteristic of Fu Ren University in their scholarly works. What I intend to discuss in this book are the threefold aims of Fu Ren and how the university managed to achieve its mission to be Western Catholic and Chinese during the turmoil in Beijing till the year 1952.

With the realization that many good universities[6] had been established in Beijing for a long time, such as Beijing University (1898), Yan Jing (1875), Qing Hua (1907), Beijing Normal University (1902), the American Benedictine Fathers knew well the competition that would lie ahead of them. Encouraged by the zeal to provide education for Catholic youth as well as for non-Catholics who wanted to be educated in the Catholic way, the Benedictines knew their responsibilities in advance. Knowing the possibilities to train Chinese native priests to appreciate Chinese classical culture in order to earn the respect from the Chinese literati and therefore making the Catholic Church more appealing to the Chinese intellectuals, the American Benedictine Fathers decided to take upon the challenges to come to Beijing to establish the Pontifical Catholic University in the old capital at the request of Pope Pius X. It was their determination to make Fu Ren University a first-class university in China when they were asked by the Holy Father to take upon the responsibility:

> 'It must be fully recognized that American Benedictines are faced with a task of great magnitude and responsibility in the work they thus entered upon. It is obvious that there is here no opportunity for economy in the shape of an at all second-rate or mediocre institution; on the contrary, both the honor of Catholicity in China and the great educational problems to be met make the provision of a really first-class and adequately endowed university essential.'[7]

It was both the Benedictine Fathers' and the Vatican's intention to make the future university a first-class and adequately endowed higher education institution. Rome showed its competitive nature in this future project in China. Cardinal Van Rossum, the head of the Propagation of the Faith[8] whom the first Rector O'Toole talked to in Rome in 1920, also said that this Catholic university should be a place,

> 'Of transcendent importance that the new Benedictine Foundation in China should become a great educational institution, a university capable of upholding the best traditions of Catholic culture and of doing for Chinese literature, art, history and civilization...'[9]

Thus far, it is necessary for me to explain briefly the nature of the university as both Western Catholic and Chinese which is the theme of this book. First of all, from the Church's point of view, the Benedictine Fathers and the Vatican both wanted to make the university a Chinese one. The Benedictines were convinced that this university would be "the honor of Catholicity in China and the great educational problems to be met."[10] The Vatican also insisted that it be "a university capable of upholding the best traditions of Catholic culture and of doing for Chinese literature, art, history and civilization."[11] Secondly, the founding Chinese scholars also insisted on this aspect rather decisively, as shown in the petition letter to the

Holy Father.[12] Three parties from three different places: Rome, the American Benedictines and China, came together and had a consensus of the same nature of the university in Beijing before they even actually started the work.

Historically, the early part of twentieth century China was a transitional period for the nation. China was under going a rapidly modernization. The study of Western sciences was on the rise and the study of Chinese classics was on the decline. China was at the crossroads of redefining itself and of seeking its own identity. Western sciences and democracy were most welcomed in China in those days. Many intellectuals and university students who were influenced by Western culture had raised slogans to welcome the Western ideas and sciences. The slogans were written as *Mr. Science* and *Mrs. Democracy*. These intellectuals thought that Confucian culture prevented China from developing which caused the invasion of many countries in China. In order to change the destiny of China, they also raised high other slogans, *Down with Confucian Classis* and *Welcome Mr. Science and Mrs. Democracy*. These slogans expressed the attitudes of the intellectuals at the time. In their minds, the Westernization of China was the only road leading to the survival of China and eventual prosperity. However, many other intellectuals thought differently. They wanted to have a combination of both Western and Eastern cultures. To be Western was to be science-oriented and to be Chinese was to be Chinese classics-oriented. Fu Ren University and its founders were on this path. The curriculum and development of Fu Ren University proved that this was a good approach and its dual nature prevailed. Fu Ren became a unique and first-class university because of this. Under the leadership of the American Cassinese-Benedictines, Chinese scholars such as Vincent Ying and four other eminent scholars who were the first faculty members made this university a center of Chinese learning. Government's influences eventually led to a rapid incorporation of Western sciences into the core curriculum of the university. In contrast with all other Christian universities were initiated, administered and financed by non-Chinese, Fu Ren was the only private one in China that was initiated by Chinese scholars and administered and financed by non-Chinese.[13] Specifically, the American Benedictine Fathers were the administrators and Vincent Ying was the first dean with all Chinese professors at the beginning.

Historical and Political Background of Fu Ren

A sketch of the historical and political background of Fu Ren University at this point can certainly enhance the understanding of the importance of book. How Fu Ren came to be, and the kind of environment under which Fu Ren was established, as well as a brief history of the university will help the readers understand the general situation of Fu Ren University and how it made its history in an ever-changing political movement. It is impossible to write on Fu Ren University without making references to the petition of the Chinese scholars and to the politics of the time both within the Catholic Church and in China because these two were intrinsically related to its vital life as an institution.

As I mentioned, Mr. Vincent Ying and Mr. Ma Xiang-bo petitioned the Pope in 1912 to establish the Catholic University in Beijing. Vincent Ying, a convert, was one of the well-known scholars in China. He was the founder of a well-known newspaper in Tianjin, which was called *Da Gong Bao (The Imperial)* and the lay co-founder of Fu Ren University. The details will be discussed more in Chapter Three. He was an educator, journalist and reformer of Chinese culture.[14] Ma Xiang-bo,[15] the co-founder of Fu Ren, was another well-known Chinese scholar in China. For a period of time, he was the president of Beijing University. He had contacts with many famous scholars in China. They were the only two Catholic Scholars enjoyed national reputation. Because of their love for the Catholic Church, their appreciation of the Chinese classics, and their understanding that Catholic missionaries in China were not making the Church more attractive to the intellectuals, they decided to be more proactive and sent a petition to the Pope to establish a Catholic university in Beijing.

This very action was indeed a criticism to the Catholic missionaries in China, especially the French Jesuits who did not respect Chinese culture. However, it also was a catalyst to revitalize the missionary spirit of the early Jesuits. The Catholic Church indeed benefited from this. For those who are unfamiliar with the Jesuits in China, they were the in fact the pioneers. The first Jesuits, such as Matteo Ricci's group, came to China in the late seventeenth century to convert the Chinese intellectuals. They learned Chinese and tried to converse with them. Unfortunately, the new generation of Catholic missionaries which dominated by the French Jesuits limited their contacts to farmers and people who were considered low-class people, such as criminals of law which despised by the intellectuals. Though there were many converts, Vincent Ying and Ma Xiang-bo did not think that was an appropriate method for the Catholic Church to do evangelization in China. They were convinced that converting intellectuals was the way because all Chinese looked up to them. In the petition letter, they fully expressed their concern and eagerness to have a good Chinese Catholic University in Beijing. This will be addressed later when I discuss the establishment of the university.

The politics within the Catholic Church of the time were rather complex. The French government managed to control the Pope and the Catholic missions.[16] Since French missionaries formed the majority of missionaries in China, they were able to keep the Holy Father out of the land. Therefore the Holy Father could not setup a direct relationship with China for a long time. The Pope, therefore, could not execute the petition during those years because of the strong protest from France.

Introduction

Rome's interest in China did not stop because of France. After many tries and visits on part of the Church,[17] the proposal to establish the university in Beijing finally became a reality when the American Benedictine Fathers first came to Beijing in 1924 under the direction of the Pope. The Benedictines decided to stay and started the process[18] of erecting the university immediately under the leadership of Rome. It took them only one year to do the necessary preparations before they began to recruit students. The university was officially opened in 1925 with only a small Chinese faculty and only a few students specializing in Chinese literature. When the university was first opened, it had a sizable endowment and had four well-known Chinese professors on the faculty. Every student in the school had a scholarship. The details will be discussed in later relevant chapters. After two years of development, Fu Ren University was officially registered with the government in 1927. Therefore it became the first private university in the city of Beijing,[19] and nationally, it was the only Catholic university among three in total with a recognized university status.

Shortly after the establishment, the university experienced some turbulence that actually speeded up the development of the university within a short period of time. However, this rapid development put Fu Ren University deeply into debt. In 1929 two rather dramatic incidents affected the university. First, the Great Depression in the United States affected the finances of the university. The Congregation of the American-Cassinese Benedictines lost almost all their investments in the crash of the Stock Market. This Congregation, with more than ten abbeys, was on the verge of filling for bankruptcy. They were unable to support Fu Ren University any longer. The university was in financial crisis. Secondly, the Nanjing Nationalist Government decided to reorganize all higher education institutions in China in 1928. The order from the Education Ministry did not reach Beijing until 1929 because the Warlord Zhang Zuo-lin controlled Beijing at the time. It was after Zhang's death, Beijing came under the control of the Nanjing Nationalist Government. This mandate from the Education Ministry again threatened the university because according to its requirements, a university should have at least three different schools. Article Five from the Mandate has this:

> 'Only those institutions that already have a college of Arts and a college of Science, together with a third college, may be called university. Those institutions that comprise but one school, or even if more than two, schools not in conformity with the program...'[20]

As of the time when the mandate was made effective, Fu Ren only had one School of Arts, which was far away from meeting governmental requirements. These issues will be discussed later. In order not to lose its university status that was crucial to university, the administration spared no effort to carry out its programs to meet the requirements. These efforts cost the Benedictine Fathers tremendously. In order to build a spacious building for offices and classrooms, auditorium, etc., the chancellor had to borrow money for the university. The Great Depression of 1929 left the Benedictine abbeys in a terrible financial situation. Aurelius, the archabbot of Saint Vincent and the chancellor of Fu Ren had to borrow every penny to erect this new building for expansion. Four years later, Fu Ren University still could not pay its debt because the Benedictines could not recover from their financial downfall. Moreover, the untimely death of Archabbot Aurelius left Fu Ren University financially unguarded for he single-handedly handled the finances of the university. After his death, no other abbot wanted accept this extra responsibility, except for the abbot from Saint John's Abbey in Minnesota. He tried to raise some money and pleaded for all other abbots to make an effort at fund raising for Fu Ren University. Unfortunately he failed to achieve this.

For the sake of the university, the university was transferred to the hands of the Society of the Missionary of the Divine Word (SVD) in 1933 at the request of the Pope. Fu Ren continued as usual and developed into a rather prestigious university in the following years. The Women's College that was established by the Benedictines Sisters continued to grow into a good college. More property was bought, student enrollment increased and graduate programs were inaugurated. The faculty was strengthened during the following years as well.

The political turmoil and the wars in China prior to the Communist period affected the university's growth. However, Fu Ren survived them all. The anti-Christian, anti-foreign movements were constant during those years but did not slow down the university's progress of which I discuss in Chapter Seven. In 1936, Fu Ren University had a new rector, a German priest, who indeed helped Fu Ren University tremendously during the Sino-Japanese War. After the First World War, the Japanese became an ally of many Western countries, such as, Germany, Italy, France, and the United States as well. Because of the treaties that these governments signed with China, each of the countries took a designated geographical part of China, each with its own autonomy into which the Chinese government could not interfere. When the Sino-Japanese War was declared in 1937, many universities moved out of Beijing and went to the Southwest of China, the so-called "free China," *Chong Qing*, where the Nationalist capital was newly established. Fu Ren University stayed in Beijing along with Yan Jing University despite the fact that the Japanese soldiers constantly threatened them. Fortunately when the United States declared war with Japan in early 1942, Fu Ren University once again made history. It became the only operating private university that remained in Beijing without changing much of its structure and staff. The rest of the schools in Beijing were controlled either by the Japanese completely, or were sponsored by the puppet government of Beijing which obeyed Japanese orders. Meanwhile, all other Christian higher education institutions under the administration of the American Protestant Churches in China, including Yan Jing University in

Beijing had to move inland to join other universities. Fu Ren University could stay simply because the rector was a German priest.[21] The administration of the university already was under the German and Dutch Divine Word Fathers' hands in 1936 while most of the American Fathers remained in the university and stayed away from administrations. The Japanese tried to harass the university, in particular, the Chinese priests and some progressive lay professors at the beginning. The American priests were involved after 1942. Some were jailed and some had to flee to inland. The Japanese tried to make sure Fu Ren University would not become a threat to its rule in Beijing. Overall, there was no serious damage to the university. In addition, the Japanese forced all schools in Beijing to fly Japanese flags and enforced the students to bow to the flag before they entered the school gates. Most of the schools complied with this during the Sino-Japanese War. However, Fu Ren University did not. Fu Ren escaped punishment from this defiance due to its German rector and its emphasis on Chinese Confucian culture, which the Japanese respected. Fu Ren kept developing despite the political difficulties.

During the eight Sino-Japanese War years from 1937–1945, Fu Ren persevered and developed into a well-respected and nationally known university. In a way, the Sino-Japanese War made the university famous because of its dual nature and administration. The university not only accepted students from other universities who did not want to go inland, but also took in many famous professors from the closing universities. In the meantime, many high school students in Beijing area who did not want to go to Japanese-run universities were trying to enter Fu Ren. Some had to wait for a long time because of a limited number of students that Fu Ren could accept yearly. Eventually Fu Ren University attracted students from all over China. The competitive nature of the selection process yielded higher qualified incoming students. By the year 1947, Fu Ren University became the second largest university in Beijing, just behind of Beijing University. By 1948, Fu Ren developed into a university with graduate and undergraduate programs, middle schools, elementary schools and kindergarten. This all-encompassing aspect of educational levels was unique to Fu Ren University. By 1949, Fu Ren University curriculum began to change slightly because of the influence of the Chinese Communist Party.

In October 1950, the Catholic Church lost her battle to maintain Fu Ren University because of political differences with the Communists. One of the causes that triggered the battle was the government's appointment of five professors on the faculty without the university approval, of which three were appointed with one specific purpose to attack religion in their lectures. This was a direct confrontation with the university's administration and its Catholicity, which was impossible to compromise. After many unsuccessful bargains with the government, the rector refused to pay these professors' salaries. This action irritated the Beijing government and led to the Communist government's decision to take it over. In 1952, within less than two years after the Communists took over Beijing, Fu Ren University was dissolved and amalgamated with other universities: the Philosophy Department was taken over by *Bei Da* (Beijing University); the Economics Department was taken by *Ren Da* (People's University); the Sociology Department was taken by *Jing Mao Xue Yuan* (College of Trade and Finance) and the Department of Western Languages and Literature was taken by *Wai Guo Yu Xue Yuan* (Foreign Languages College). The rest, and indeed the major part of Fu Ren became part of *Bei Jing Shi Da* (Beijing Normal University). Since then, Fu Ren University disappeared from the list of higher education institutions.

Historically, the early part of the twentieth century was rather chaotic. China was searching for a new model of government and a new model of education. Nationalism and Westernization also were on the rise. This was a period of modernization in China. The Chinese Education Ministry looked to Western countries as model systems for Chinese higher education. The U.S. model became dominant, and its characteristics can still be seen in Chinese curriculums and administration structures.

It is obvious that politics played an important role in the rise and fall of Fu Ren University. It is necessary, therefore, to explore some of the political background, specifically the various governments in Beijing that Fu Ren had to deal with throughout the years. From its establishment in 1925 until its demise in 1952, Fu Ren had gone through, namely: the Warlord era (1925–1928), the Nationalist era (1928–1937; 1945–1949), the Japanese era (1937–1945), and finally the Communist era (1949–1952). These will be discussed specifically in Chapter Seven. Certainly, these dramatic changes made Fu Ren University worthy of research all the more. Each time when power transferred from one to the other, the young university had to make some adaptations in order to survive. Actually during the lifetime of Fu Ren University, neither the university nor China itself enjoyed much peace. Any scholar who knows a little about the modern history of China certainly understands the chaotic situation of that time. It was in that environment that Fu Ren was established and developed into a nationally known university.

Research Proposition

This book explores the original idealized intentions of the Catholic Church, especially the Benedictine Fathers' and the Divine Word Fathers' efforts to make this Catholic university a meeting place for Chinese culture and Western scientific knowledge. The mission and the establishment will be specified; Curriculum and structural development, faculty and student growth and activities, as well as the characteristics of faculty and students will be fully discussed. The internal and external interactions of Fu Ren University were certainly important to understand this institution. Finally, the accomplishments of Fu Ren University, from its establishment in 1925

Introduction

until its demise in 1952, will be laid out systematically in relevant chapters. It is not to be confused that some issues of the university, such as its conception, birth, rise and fall were too complicated to be categorized individually simply because the university was in the midst of an international crisis and the national struggles within China. The very nature of Fu Ren as a Catholic and Chinese attracted a lot of people's attention throughout those warring years. Especially in the final years of its life, Fu Ren became a focal point in the eyes of the Beijing Communist government because of the political issues. As a result of the conflict, Fu Ren became the first private university in China to be taken over by the Communist government. For this, the government announced to the entire nation, "On October 12, 1950, an official announcement broadcast from Peiping declared that the Communist authorities there had taken over the Catholic University of Peiping."[22] Fu Ren University in Beijing, which was the best known among schools of higher learning in China, especially during the Sino-Japanese war years, "comprised a striking group of buildings in Chinese style, gained a high reputation for its courses in literature and science; while its school of arts spread the knowledge and ideas of Christian culture throughout the nation" was forever changed.

In order to discuss the complicated issues of the university systematically, I simply discuss them in answering the following propositional questions:

A) Why was Fu Ren University built as Western Catholic and yet a Chinese University at the same time? Subordinate questions arise:
 1) How did Fu Ren University come to be and achieve its goals?
 2) What was the driving force behind it?
 3) How did the curriculum, faculty and students developed in the years?

B) How did politics affect Fu Ren University? Again,
 1) What were the environment and the necessity of founding a Catholic university?
 2) How did the changes of governments affect the university?
 3) Why did Fu Ren not survive during the Communist era?

In the process of answering these questions, I will analyze as thorough as possible how Fu Ren University tried to adapt the different political currents and continued its expansion, as well as to educate the Chinese youth without compromising the principles of the Church. These examinations certainly help the readers understand the details of the rise and fall of Fu Ren University, as well as the Catholic higher education in China. This book has a twofold purpose: first, to present to the readers the history of Fu Ren Catholic University as both Western Catholic and Chinese in nature. Second, this book intends to stimulate future scholars' interests to think and write more on Catholic higher education in China because this aspect of study has been lacking in the field of higher education for so long in comparison with the studies on Protestant higher education in China. For centuries in the West, Catholic higher education always impacted culture. It has always been an inseparable part of the Catholic mission. Due to the narrow-mindedness and arrogance of the French missionaries who dominated the Catholic mission in China, this impact on Chinese culture was not seen. It was the Protestant Church in China and especially the American Protestant Church missionaries that tremendously influenced Chinese higher education. Many scholars, both inside and outside of China, have done extensive research on this Protestant influence. Unfortunately, the topic of Catholic higher education in China largely has been ignored. In general, China has proved that it was impossible for the Catholic Church, as well as other Christian Churches to do so after 1949 when the Communists took control of China. All private Christian universities and independent universities disappeared in 1952 after the nationwide reorganization of all higher education institutions. The success of taking over Fu Ren University, led a rapidly taking over of all Christian universities by the Chinese Communist government.

Design, Sources and Limitations of this Book

This book is an in-depth study of the history of the Catholic Fu Ren University. In creation of knowledge, I intend to discuss the issues of the university which other researchers either ignored or unexplored as thorough as possible. In some cases, I dispute the issues that I think were misinterpreted for the sake of an authenticity of the history. In a systematic way, a more complete history of Fu Ren University is written. After researching available materials on the university, I find that many works are either chronologically incomplete or are one-sided in their views on the university. Professionally, I feel the urgent need to make the history be more complete and to rectify certain issues of the Fu Ren University.

Fu Ren Catholic University in Beijing had only a short history in comparison with all other higher education institutions in the country. Though the university survived only 27 years, it has a significant history which deserves its own telling. This in fact is the effort I intend to make. Because of the unavailability of archival materials in China[23] and the complex nature of the Catholic Church at the time, no Chinese scholar to date has done research on the entire history of Catholic Fu Ren University. However, one Chinese author, He Jian-ming wrote one essay entitled *Fu Ren Guo Xue he Chen Yuan* (Fu Ren's Chinese Literature and Chen Yuan). This essay simply emphasizes on part of the department of Chinese Studies. My own research has discovered the lacking of the archival materials China, namely, Beijing Normal University Archive and Beijing City Archive. Yet, there are enough archival materials in the United States that can be utilized to write the history of Fu Ren University.

I will also analyze the interactions between Fu Ren University and the various governments, as well as university relations with the Catholic Church. In the concluding chapter I will analyze the effects of these interactions. I will use both chronological and thematic methods in writing this book. Since the university was closed in 1952, I am not able to perform interviews because of difficulties in contacting alumnae. Therefore, the relevant books and the available documents in various archives will be mentioned following will constitute my sources. Two major resources will be relied on in the process of writing: A) the primary sources which are original archival works from China and the United States; B) the secondary sources which are from the available published books both here in the U.S. and in China, in both Chinese and English languages, as well as a few unpublished manuscripts. The reason for doing this is to make sure the authenticity of its history. The Chinese books are rather limited, yet informative. Though these Chinese books have very different viewpoints, they certainly have academic value. I do not intend to make judgment, but I will analyze their views in this book.

In order to map out the author's intension, a brief introduction of researcher's methodology is necessary. Since archives contain the main sources of primary historical materials, "Archives are accumulations of documentary materials (papers, photos, letters, etc.) in private collections, museums, libraries or formal archives."[24] the researcher tried to locate all of the important places that had anything to do with Fu Ren University: (1) Beijing Normal University Archive, because this university took over the major part of Fu Ren University and because the original archive of Fu Ren was taken over by it. Many important documents should be there. While this researcher was doing research, I asked the archivist about other possible places where documents might also be available in Beijing. He told me to go to the Beijing City Archive. I did find some interesting documents there, especially resources concerning the political issues. The reason why the city of Beijing possesses Fu Ren materials is unknown. (2) Saint Vincent Archabbey in Latrobe, Pennsylvania, was the place where the Benedictine Fathers started to establish the university. Many important documents have been found there. (3) Saint John's Abbey in Collegeville, Minnesota was another place where monks were assigned to work in Beijing and where the abbot was rather active in fund-raising for Fu Ren University. In addition, the researcher went to examine the archive of the Sisters of Saint Benedict. This was the convent where the first six sisters were sent to Beijing to establish the Women's College at Fu Ren in1932. (4) The Divine Word Fathers in Chicago, Illinois who took over the university in 1933 at the request of Holy Father. Its archive certainly should have a great amount of documents. However, I did not find as many correspondence letters there as I found at Saint Vincent's and at Saint John's. I did find two very important English magazines *Fu Ren Magazine* published by the university in Beijing, and *Christian Family and Our Missions*, which was printed in Chicago. Some biographies of the Divine Word Fathers, as well as two catalogues of the university also were discovered. While the researcher was there, I coincidently met Paul Han SVD, a Divine Word member, who wrote a short biography on Father Fu, the dean of the disciplines at Fu Ren University. Father Fu kept some old materials on Fu Ren University that presently are in the hands of Paul Han. The materials were mostly about Saint Albert's College at Fu Ren. I was thrilled to have such additional information. Meanwhile, I also paid a visit to the Holy Spirit Sisters and researched their archive, for they succeeded the Benedictine Sisters in 1936 to run the Women's College.

Because of the distance and expense, the researcher was not able to travel to Germany and to Rome where more materials might be available. Germany should have materials archived because Fu Ren University had a German rector during the Sino-Japanese War period. He and other priests probably corresponded with people in Germany. In China and in the U.S., I have found a lack of materials from this German rector, Father Rudolph Rahmann, and from the university as well during these war years. I tried to contact available German archivists via e-mails and phone calls. Unfortunately after many attempts, no answers were received. Rome has always been the center of the Catholic Church and was very influential in the founding of Fu Ren University. The two religious orders: Benedictines Fathers and Divine Word Fathers have their Superior General in Rome, where additional documents might be stored. Due to the unavailability of the European resources, I decided to eliminate the possible extra materials from these two places. I kept focus on the materials that I have found in the available archives.

In summary, all these archives but one, which is the Beijing City Archive, had direct contact with Fu Ren University. All the important materials produced from these archives will constitute my primary source for this writing. The limitation is the unavailability of those two places: Rome and Germany.

(A) The primary sources all come from archives located both in China and in the U.S. These sources are crucial to prove the theme of Fu Ren University as both Western Catholic and Chinese. I will research all the firsthand documents, such as: personal letters, memos, newspapers, articles, as well books produced during that period of time from the available archives that had connections with Fu Ren University. Additional personal accounts include the individual writings about the missionary congregations: the Benedictine Fathers and Sisters and the Divine Word Fathers and the Holy Spirit Sisters who were there, who had seen the growth of the university and who experienced the political turmoil in Beijing and at the university. These personal writings are certainly crucial to this writing as well. Therefore, their views, observations and interactions with the university, the Warlord, the Nationalist government and the Communist government are certainly most reliable and therefore contribute much to this study. The existing records of the university have been carefully analyzed and organized in the effort of this writing. These primary sources certainly will offer additional proof and testimony of Fu Ren's authentic history.

Only three English publications could be found in the archives: *Fu Ren University Bulletin*,[25] *Fu Ren Magazine* and *Christian Family and Our Missions*. The remaining sources largely constitute the private correspondence of many kinds: letters from Rome to the Benedictine Fathers and vise-versa, and letters of all kinds from Fu Ren to the abbots, priests and sisters. Biographies of some priests who worked in China also are included. All of these will be used and analyzed with care in this writing.

(B) The secondary sources are the articles and books relevant to the writing that are available in the U.S. and in China. These sources will give readers a general sense of the university and of the political background at the time when Fu Ren was in operation. Meanwhile, it will help us understand how the Chinese understood Fu Ren University. Though many books have been published on Christian higher education and on the politics and wars in China, only a few authors specifically mentioned the Catholic Fu Ren University. Therefore, I use these secondary sources to serve the following two distinctive purposes:

First, the secondary sources will provide a picture about the complicated historical background of China during Fu Ren University's existence. Numerous books can be found which have been written on a variety of topics that happened in China during the early years of the twentieth century. Fu Ren University had involved itself with many of the political events. All of these, both directly and indirectly, had tremendous impact on the life of the university. I will summarize the relevant and important political issues connected to Fu Ren University in Chapter Seven.

Next, the secondary sources will provide information on the following important views: 1) Many thought that Fu Ren was completely under the Church's control and therefore they ignored the Chinese nature of university. There have been disputes on this issue. 2) Fu Ren was as an imperialistic tool of the Americans as well as of the Catholic Church in general. While this has some truth to some Christian universities in China, it was not true to Fu Ren's mission at all. These popular misunderstandings, by both Chinese intellectuals and the general population alike, sparked many anti-Christian and anti-Western movements. In fact, Lutz has a whole book *Christian Politics and Christian Missions* dedicated to these movements in the 1920's. It certainly developed and became more severe later. 3) Fu Ren was regarded as supportive to the Japanese through its continued presence in Beijing during the war years. In reality, Fu Ren constantly resisted the Japanese.

When the Communists took over China, the anti-Christian and anti-Western movements became fatal and all Christian-owned organizations such as schools, hospitals, and universities were taken out of the Church's hands. All churches were closed and all non-Chinese, mostly missionaries, were either expelled or imprisoned. In Fu Ren's case, the university was closed, the rector was put in prison and the remaining Divine Word missionaries were expelled. Many Chinese professors left the university and went to Taiwan. A well-developed Chinese Catholic University was finished, forced to stop its mission in China.

Roadmap to this Book

The rise and fall of Fu Ren University were driven by the different wars and politics of China, as well as the Church. Any scholar who tries to understand the complicated issues of Fu Ren University has to have objective views on any sort. It is therefore, Chapter Two provides the literature that is relevant to this dissertation, through which the readers can gain a clear picture of what have been done by the previous researchers: structural development of the university, the political activities and curriculum. An analysis of the existing materials is made so that the readers also can see the research problem this researcher is proposing. The research been done on the university is very limited thus far. The framework of this writing is established by reviewing the literature. Readers therefore, will come to realize that the uncovered history of Fu Ren University is rather rich and a lot of research work needs to be done. Such is the effort of this researcher's work.

Chapter Three discusses the establishment of the university and states the mission of the university and explains how the university came into existence. It took a long time to establish the university in Beijing. Since the initial petition from Vincent Ying and Ma Xiang-bo in 1912 until the 1925 when Fu Ren was officially opened, it took many people's efforts in trying to make it happen. The name and location of the university, as well the its nature will be discussed thoroughly in this chapter. In China, the name has always been important, the location of the institution, however, is important everywhere in the world. This chapter will also discuss in detail how the Vatican and the Benedictine Fathers worked out plans to establish the university in Beijing, which fulfilled the petition from the two Chinese Catholic scholars.

Chapter Four deals with the finance and development of the university. The Benedictine Fathers were ambitious to make the university a first-rate university in China. To be financially sound, Fu Ren had a lot of work to do. This chapter describes and analyzes how the finances troubled the Benedictine Fathers. The funding really affected the university growth and administration, as well as the development of the curriculum and physical growth. In the end, the university had to be transferred to the Divine Word Fathers. How the two religious communities financed the university will be discussed in detail. Despite the fact of wars and political turmoil, Fu Ren continued to be financed and developed through the years. Generally

Introduction 17

speaking, the tight budget and the various wars did not stop Fu Ren to develop. On the contrary, Fu Ren became well known in China.

Chapter Five discusses the growth of the university, mainly on curriculum, faculty and students. These three crucial aspects of the university will be discussed separately because of the complicatedness of these issues. Since they are all intrinsically related, I discussed them in a chronological way. How the curriculum developed throughout the years, how the numbers of professors increased and their qualities, and why the student enrollments increased rapidly throughout years will be discussed thoroughly. The statistics of the faculty members and their characteristics will be discussed in the appropriate section, as well as the statistics and characteristics of the students. Special attention will also be paid to the Women's College and to Saint Albert's College where priests were enrolled. The good qualities and achievements of the university will be analyzed respectively.

Chapter Six discusses the extra-curricular activities of the university. These extracurricular activities of Fu Ren University made the university not only known within the China, but also known worldwide, if not, at least throughout Asia. Sports at Fu Ren University earned the university the name "Notre Dame in Asia." Helping refugees and fund raising for the poor and the afflicted were signs of Fu Ren University's active social involvement during the Chinese wartime period. The whole university was involved in such services, including the president Chen Yuan, as well as the faculty members. Religious attendance and organizations were unique in all aspects in comparison with other Christian universities. They were all voluntary. The religious arts and paintings and secular paintings earned the admiration of many. The School of Christian Arts harmonized the Western and Chinese methods in their own productions. Details will be discussed fully.

Chapter Seven deals with the political issues that Fu Ren involved. For Fu Ren University, the political entanglements were almost like a life-long commitment. During its 27 years of history, Fu Ren went through four different governments: namely, Warlord, Nationalist, Japanese and Communists. All these governments had impact on the university. During the political turmoil and the wars, Fu Ren continued its growth without ceasing. Anti-Christian and anti-Western movements also impacted the university. Though the university had a non-political stance policy throughout the years, the students were still actively involved with politics. There are many issues that will be dealt with in this chapter. I will try to categorize different sub-themes into different sections so that each one can be discussed individually, such as, student activism, the relationship with each individual government and its impact on the university. All these political entanglements indeed showed how patriotic Fu Ren University was, especially during the Sino-Japanese War period.

Chapter Eight concludes the discussions and restates the theme of this book. An analysis of why the university developed this way will clarify some doubts that readers might have as to how Fu Ren University was both Catholic and Chinese. The contributions of Fu Ren University to the Catholic Church and to Chinese culture, as well as its contribution to Chinese higher education, will also be specified. Fu Ren preserved the tradition of its Liberal Arts nature during the Sino-Japanese War while others in the free land were all changed and reorganized in order to meet the national needs during the wartime. Fu Ren University, along with other Christian universities, disappeared in 1951 not because they were foreign, but because of the nature of the government. The new model that the Communist government adopted after 1951 was not a Chinese but a Soviet Union model. The main object of higher education was to train leaders for national service and reconstruction of the nation. Therefore, the Liberal Arts were neglected and religion was prohibited in China after 1951. The reorganization of the higher education institutions at that time changed the purpose of higher education.

Acknowledgment

This book is developed from my dissertation research. Inspired by the comment that was made by my dissertation director Doctor Philip G. Altbach, who is also the editor of this series, that this original research might benefit many scholars, I started to work on this book. I am deeply indebted to Dr. Altbach for his help and guidance, as well as *"RoutledgeFalmer Studies in Higher Education"* for showing interest in my work. The pastor of Sacred Heart Parish, North Quincy, Father John O'Brien, has always been a source of moral and spiritual support throughout the years. To God, I am forever grateful.

CHAPTER TWO

Critical Literature Review and View Points

Fu Ren University was established in 1925 and developed into a nationally known university during the warring years and political turmoil when the Sino-Japanese War started. As the only Catholic university in Beijing, Fu Ren could ride out the political tide, even when the Japanese tried to colonize China in the modern society. This university was the only one that survived in Beijing under its own autonomy throughout the Sino-Japanese War. Therefore, many historians and political scientists have had variety of interpretations as to why Fu Ren University could achieve its status quo, while other universities in Beijing suffered tremendously during the Second World War in China. When the Japanese were defeated and the Chinese Communists took over China, Fu Ren University came under the control of the Communist Party and soon disappeared along with many other private universities. This chapter establishes the framework of this book.

The interesting development of Fu Ren University certainly attracted my attention. Some researchers have done research on the university, and their works are not in depth or comprehensive. In order for readers to get a general sense of the university, this chapter is dedicated to describe in detail what has been written on Fu Ren University and what has not by reviewing and offering critiques on the existing works. Though my purpose is to discover materials that have not been mentioned previously by researchers, I also intend to dispute some views I disagree with and to offer some comments and reinterpretations so that the history of Fu Ren can be rectified.

Fu Ren University deserves an authentic and complete history of its own as any other universities do. Unfortunately because of different interests and political stands such as those of the pro-Nationalists or pro-Communists, part of Fu Ren's history has been interpreted differently. Most importantly, because of the unavailability of the certain materials, especially in China, only parts of Fu Ren University have been researched and written on. A rather complete history has not yet been written until now. In order to be true to the nature of Fu Ren University and also to see the significance of this university in the history of Chinese higher education, this chapter is constructed as the following: Part I: Overviews of educational systems in China prior to the founding of Fu Ren University, which provides readers a sense of how Chinese higher education came to be and how Catholic higher education looked like, (1) Overview of Chinese higher education in the modern China and its relationship with Christian higher education; (2) Overview of Catholic higher education in China. Part II: Discussion of the existing literature on Fu Ren University. In this section, the general structure and understanding of this university is laid out. Part III: Analysis of the available literature. In this section, the two important issues, namely, structural and political, will be identified and specified. In the meantime, I will make some comments and offer my professional interpretation based on the existing literature I have discovered from the archives. The limited available research, both collectively and individually on this Catholic university in Beijing simply cannot reveal the true nature and development of the university. I provide readers with an urgent sense of the need to make this book available in order to contribute to the existing knowledge of Catholic higher education in China, especially in regard to the history of Fu Ren University. The survival of the university in that environment was almost nearly impossible, yet it survived and developed into a well-known private university.

SECTION I: OVERVIEW OF CHINESE HIGHER EDUCATION

(1) Chinese Higher Education and Christian Higher Education

The turning point of Chinese higher education system was the year 1905 when the Qing (Manchu) government officially abolished the traditional Imperial Examination after thousands of years of practice. The "eight-legged essay"(*Ba Gu Wen*) was the type of Chinese public education which came from the old Confucian examination system for entering government offices. This long practiced system gave way to a modern educational system, of which Fairbank and Teng state that "to replace the old examinations the Chinese government adopted a new educational program based on Western and Japanese models."[1] As anyone can imagine, this change was extremely difficult. In order for readers to get a sense of the complicated educational system, I should review briefly the modern Chinese education system, as well as the Christian education that was parallel to it.

In his extensive study of Christian missions in China, Latourette mentioned in more detail all the ensuing changes and the qualities of such newly established schools. He pointed out that the most significant was in the intellectual life of the nation which under the "leadership of the radicals, some of the basic features of traditional Chinese civilization were discarded or altered."² The exploration of establishing a new Chinese higher education system was under way.

> 'In 1905 the old system of civil service examination was abolished and there passed into oblivion an institution which had been one of the strongest anchors to China's past. In the same year, a Ministry of Education was created and to it was entrusted the organizing of a new school system in which both Western and Chinese subjects were studied. Schools in China which had offered courses on Occidental learning suddenly became popular and hundreds of new ones, often with woefully low standards and poor equipment, sprang up almost overnight.'³

Ruth Hayhoe more clearly explained this new Chinese higher education system by categorizing it into four types in her article, "Towards the Forging of Chinese University Ethos: Zhendan and Fudan, 1903–1919" of which I discuss as the following.

The government tightly controlled the first type of school. By the turn of the century, Qing officials and some intellectuals finally awakened fully to the pressing need of absorbing as much Western learning as possible in order to revitalize the nation—a goal perceived as necessary for national salvation:

> 'The Qing government was proceeding cautiously with modern schools in which western languages, sciences and even social sciences were being taught within the framework of Chinese traditional philosophy, the superior essence of which was unquestioned and which was to shape western techniques for the service of China.'⁴

The second type of school was established and controlled by the Protestant Church. Hayhoe called this the alternative to the government-style higher education. This type is familiar to many as the American Liberal Arts College, which started as early as 1860,

> '...Although there was a sincere desire to serve China through the education provided in these colleges, little attempt was made in this early period to adapt either the administrative style or the curriculum to the Chinese situation.'⁵

These two types were rather confrontational in reality. The Chinese government was reluctant to recognize Christian higher education, even though it was established long before the Chinese model. On the other hand, these Christian higher education institutions did not have any intention to possess registrations with the Chinese government until the mid-1920s. Because of the unrecognized status of these higher education institutions, the degrees from these colleges, therefore, prevented the graduates from Christian institutions seeking official jobs within the government. At the beginning, when the student numbers were limited, the Christian churches could at first employ their graduates. It was therefore not necessary to have government recognition. When it was unlikely for the graduates to seek government's official jobs, the Christian higher education institutions decided to comply with the government's rules. The rest of the two types of institutions did not have troubles with the government. According to Hayhoe, the third type, which was revolutionary schools. Their emphasized on military training and was controlled by a form of representative students. The fourth type was the schools established by reform-minded gentries with the intention to preserve Chinese classical teaching and to show their nationalism in the meantime were recognized by the government.[6] Though these four types were co-existed, the first two were dominant. Indeed, the Chinese higher education system in the early part of the century was only at the beginning of its establishment.

Elsewhere, Hayhoe makes some specification of the different models of Chinese higher education. In her book *China's Universities 1895–1995: A Century of Cultural Conflict*, she writes,

> '...In the period before 1911, Japan was the most important model, both for imperial bureaucrats and for large numbers of young teachers, writers, artists and revolutionaries who went to study in Japan. In the period between 1911 to 1927, one can see first an attempt at conscious emulation of European models, particularly those of Germany and France, the considerable interest in the American model, culminating in the establishment of Qinghua University, as a national institution...'[7]

Unlike the American higher education system, Chinese higher education was still in the process of rebuilding and updating. Sometimes, the seeking process to reconstruct Chinese education became political. Even the scholars could not have a consensus of the best type for China's modernization. Zhang Zhi-dong, the scholar-bureaucrat who played an important role in drafting the legislation for a modern higher education system, proposed, "Chinese learning as the essence, Western learning for its usefulness" which guided the overall thinking behind of Chinese higher education legislation.[8]

In order to strengthen the Chinese higher education system, the government decided to send students abroad to study the different systems:

> '...Started to send students abroad in 1872, by which the Imperial government had arranged training either fully or partially for several carefully chosen groups of students in the US, France, England and Germany...the foreign trained students did not have access to political responsible positions but technical employment...'[9]

As Chinese higher education developed gradually by carefully adapting a variety of models: Japanese, Europe and American, the government still could not enforce Christian higher education to comply with its rules under the Treaties. However, the government was able to make the academic degrees issued from those non-registered universities unmarketable in the society. This indeed limited the opportunities for the graduates from these universities to develop and work in China. Because of this, Christian universities eventually had to comply with the Chinese governmental rules by registering. In fact, registering with the government was to make, first of all, the degrees issued from those institutions became marketable; secondly, the students from those institutions were eligible for transfer. Though the Ministry of Education became powerful, each individual higher education institution still had its own autonomy and special curriculum except the courses on religion that should not be required.

Wang Zhong-xin confirmed this in his book, *Ji Du Jiao yu Zhong Guo Xian Dai Jiao Yu*. He discussed how missionaries really influenced Chinese education by setting up private schools first, and later they became involved with the government to help it set up the system in the late 19th century.

> 'On October18, 1895, Timothy Richard became an important person in the government. At the suggestion of the tutor of Emperor *Guangxu*, Weng Tong-he, he wrote a proposal to the Emperor suggesting the changes of the educational system, one part of the proposal was to suggest to establish the Ministry of Education, and to establish elementary schools, middle schools and universities...'[10]

Some other scholars in China who did rather extensive research on Christian higher education, such as Professor Zhang Kai-yuan who is the editor of a series of books on Christianity and China[11] and Xu Yi-hua, all made references about the interactions between Christian higher education and Chinese higher education.

(2) Catholic Higher Education

Unlike Protestant higher education, Catholic higher education was not as influential in China simply because the Catholic missionaries approached education differently when they went to China. Fairbank concludes the following: "the Catholics emphasized work in the more rural areas, sought conversion of entire family or villages, attempted to build integrated local catholic communities, and tended to restrict their educational efforts to the children of converts only."[12] Catholic higher education was not a concern for many Catholic missionaries. Yet there were two major universities and many seminaries under the auspice of the Catholic missionaries before Fu Ren University was established. They were: Two Jesuit universities: Aurora University (Zhen Dan Da Xue) in Shanghai and Hautes Études (Jin Gu Da Xue) in Tianjing. These two universities were established and run by the French Jesuits. Numerous seminaries were owned by different religious orders to train priests. They were in many places in China and are discussed as the following.

Other Catholic Universities:

Aurora University, also called Zhen Dan Da Xue in Chinese, was founded by Ma Xiang-bo who invited the French Jesuits to be on the faculty. In the beginning, it was located in *Xu Jia Hui* which was the west end of the city of Shanghai. Ma Xiang-bo used a great proportion of his property as an endowment to establish the university with the intention of studying Chinese and Western philosophy and literature.

> 'The curriculum was organized by Ma into four sections which reflected both the emphases of his own French Jesuit education, and his desire to put western knowledge into a Chinese framework. The first category was language and literature, and Ma had a carefully worked out scheme for building up knowledge of Chinese classical literature, as well as an approach to European literature...'[13]

For this reason, he invited the French Jesuits to staff the university. Soon after, they could not agree on the mission of the university that involved "disagreement on curriculum, administrative style and the selection of students".[14] Ma Xiang-bo left the university decisively with many students to start another one which became Fu Dan Da Xue.[15] The French Jesuits were left alone to run the university. Later in 1908, the French Jesuits moved the university to a site in the French settlement.

The French Jesuits wished to provide education in China as they envisioned. Because of their understanding of their own mission and Chinese culture, they did what they could to provide both secondary and higher education to the young Chinese as Hayhoe described:

> 'Equivalent to what they would be able to get in Europe, so that Chinese students could have the benefits of a European education on native soil...in the light of these goals, there was no hesitation in setting up a curriculum modeled on the French one.' [16]

Anthony Li also concluded that Aurora University's curriculum was almost entirely modeled after the French pattern of education. This university received generous support from the government of France which made the university prosper. By the year of 1914, the university had the faculties of Arts, Law, Science and Civil Engineering, and Medicine.[17] Interestingly enough, by 1927, the professors on the faculties were mostly French Jesuits and only ten laymen were also French.[18] Latourette mentioned that the university was not as large, either in equipment, teaching staff, or student body, as were several of the institutions of higher grade maintained by Protestants.[19] In 1932, the university was finally registered with the Ministry of Education. Another School of Dentistry was added in 1933. This university eventually developed into a very prestigious university in Shanghai which greatly influenced the field of Chinese medicine. Latourette said, "Much of the instruction was in French, but as a necessary concession to the popular demand, English was also taught."[20] The School of Medicine required six years and the rest only four years. It was simply a French university in China.

The second Catholic run university was Hautes Études in French, and was known as Jin Gu Da Xue in Chinese. It was also called Tianjin College of Commerce and Industry in English. This college was established by another group of French Jesuits in the British settlement of the city of Tianjin. This four-year college was established for specific purposes because of the location of the city. Tianjin was the center of industrial and commercial city in northern China. Anthony Li described the university as: in the year 1925, the college department was formally opened with two faculties, industry and commerce with 11 Jesuits, 6 Chinese and 11 European lay teachers on the faculty. The curriculum was Engineering: consisted of departments: civil, mechanical and architectural engineering; Commerce: business administration, finance and accounting, and imports and exports: public works railway construction, hydraulics, building construction, and drafting topography.[21]

Seminaries

There were many seminaries where the priests were trained in China. Latourette described "every vicariate, indeed, seems to have had at least one seminary where a beginning of the preparation for the priesthood could be made, and there were a number of schools where the training could be completed."[22] Roman Catholics were far behind Protestants in their general educational achievements. But in scholastic standards set for the clergy, they were much advanced than the latter.[23] There were 64 seminaries already in China in 1906.[24] Surely, the course of study required of candidates for the priesthood was long and exacting. The priest candidates had to study many different subjects with specific purposes: to study Chinese classical scholarship to command the respect of the educated; to study the theology, history and liturgy for the performance of their religious duties.[25] Unfortunately, the result was not satisfying at all. These native clergy were trained to be "pious and moral" in cloistered seminaries which kept them away from normal society. As a result, "they were timid and inexperienced to work alone for the conversion of souls, and as a rule they were not physically robust."[26] These native priests were only the second-class citizens in the eyes of many missionaries which caused disrespect from Chinese educated intellectuals.

Overall, Catholic higher education institutions were mostly isolated from others in comparison with Protestants ones. Aurora University was simply a French university in China; Heutes Études hardly had any Chinese in the administration and the seminaries were all controlled by non-Chinese and isolated from the society. The poor judgments made by the Catholic missionaries in the modern history prepared the establishment of Fu Ren University.

SECTION II: EXISTING LITERATURE ON FU REN UNIVERSITY

Unlike other hot topics, the history of Fu Ren University has not attracted many researchers' attention thus far for variety of reasons. Only a few researchers have showed interests. Some of the research is rather extensive and in depth, and some is very general. Even with their combined efforts, the history of the university is still incomplete. It is therefore necessary to identify each one of them to see what else that needs to be done in this writing.

Researchers and Their General Contributions

Among the few researchers who have shown interests in Catholic higher education in China, I have found the following authors who showed their interests in Fu Ren University. Most of the works are available in English, and only one in Chinese. Anthony Li, in his book *The History of Privately Controlled Higher Education in the Republic of China*, has one chapter on Catholic higher education institutions[27] during the years from 1912 to 1936. Of which he only dedicates one section on Fu Ren University. He gives some general information on the establishment and development of the university during this period: the mission of the university, structural and curriculum development, as well as student enrollment. Wu Xiao-xin, in his dissertation "A Case Study of the Catholic University of Peking During Benedictine Period (1927–1933)",[28] gives a synthesized view of the university during this period. He points out that the university was a joint effort of the East and the West: how the Chinese scholar and Benedictine Fathers worked together, registration, curriculum and instruction, as well as some political involvement with anti-Japanese movement. Edward J. Malatesta, S.J. in his article, "Two Chinese Catholic Universities and A Major Chinese Catholic Thinker: Zhendan Duxue, Furen Daxu, and Ma Xianbo,"[29] gives a brief history of Fu Ren University and who Ma Xiang-bo was in relationship with the university. In this article, he basically points out the important role of Ma Xiang-bo in building up the university. Paul Varg in his book *Missionaries, Chinese, and Diplomats*, also provides a chronological development of the university from 1927 to 1938 in one chapter. He in fact provides more information than Wu does, though it is still very general. Sophia Lee, in her dissertation, "Education in Wartime Beijing: 1937–1945"[30] dedicates one section on Fu Ren University in chapter three in which she gives a comparative view of the political involvements of the university. Her miscued interpretation of the university deserves special discussion which will be dealt in the politics. He Jian-ming in his Essay "Fu Ren Guo Xue he Chen Yuan"[31] discusses how Fu Ren University emphasized Chinese culture under the leadership of the president, Chen Yuan. He points out the roles that the three scholars Vincent Ying, Ma Xiang-bo and Chen Yuan, played in promoting Chinese culture at Fu Ren.

Overall, these authors have discussed a variety of topics on Fu Ren University: working together of the East and West in the university, physical development of the university, and the political involvements of the university were all covered but incompletely. Together, most of the materials are rather repetitive. To be more specific about each authors' writing, I categorize them into different topics as following so that readers can see their common contributions and individual contributions. The literature will be generalized first and specified later in order to avoid their repeatedness.

Specific Elements of the University

A few specific elements of the university have been commonly mentioned and researched by these above-mentioned researchers. These elements are certain important to the existence of the university. The following two elements are certainly the important ones to the structure of the university. I will discuss them first before I analyze each of the individual author's work.

(1) The establishment of Fu Ren University. Three authors briefly mentioned this aspect: Anthony Li, Wu Xiao-xin and Edward Malatesta. They all presented the chronological development of Fu Ren University, no matter how briefly or extensively they were. We come to understand that the initiative of establishing the Catholic university came from China rather than from Rome. The Chinese scholars petitioned the Holy Father to establish a Catholic university in Beijing as early as in 1912. This university was eventually established and was first staffed by the American Benedictine Fathers with a certain number of famous Chinese professors in 1925. After two years of development, the university was registered with the Beijing government in 1927 under the warlord Zhang Zuo-lin. It was recognized as university status. In addition, Anthony Li explained the necessity of establishing such a Catholic university in Beijing because of the urgent needs of the Catholic Church to attract more Chinese intellectuals. The petition Letter to Pius the X which was written by Ying Liang-zhi and Ma Xiang-bo to the Holy Father has details.

(2) The Development of the university. This aspect has been discussed in detail by the authors in their writings. More or less, all the authors have written on the following: Fu Ren University started with only one preparatory school, *Fu Ren She,* which was also called *MacManus Academy.* Later, the university was reorganized and developed into a university with three schools in 1929, namely: School of Arts and Letters; School of Natural Sciences and School of Education with totally twelve departments. All these structural developments of the university have been commonly discussed. These authors give us a general description of what Fu Ren looked like during those few years of development. Within only four years after its establishment, Fu Ren University developed into a full-fledged university

with recognition from the Chinese government, which no other private university had achieved.

These two elements of the university are certainly significant from a developmental perspective. It is impressive to see a young university to develop from a school with three departments, rather a preparatory school, to a university with three schools within only 4 years. It would be interesting to know the efforts of the administration, the finance to meet the needs of expansion and the curriculum development during these years. The reasons of what really caused the university to expand and how the university achieved this expansion are certainly in readers' minds. Since the existing literature doesn't have details of these issues, I will certainly fill the vacuum in relevant chapters. Thus far, I have not specified each author's specific contributions in providing information about the university. These previous two aspects are very general and limited. Therefore, it is necessary to specify each author's contributions.

(3) Individual author's unique contributions. The works of these researchers need to be specified so that their contributions can be properly demonstrated. Because there are only a few of them and the limited areas they researched, it is relatively easy to specify each one of them in addition to the previously mentioned materials.

Anthony Li makes an effort to mention the further chronological growth of the university by providing some extra information on student growth, the addition of the postgraduate program, the university museum, finance in general, as well as pointing out a future center of Fu Ren to train Chinese clergy. He details how the university came to be and how the university developed to be a nationally known university by its reputation for its courses in literature and the sciences, as well as its School of Arts. Moreover, he mentions one very unique thing that made Fu Ren stood out in the Far East—its Institute of Microbiology.

In his dissertation, Wu Xiao-xin deals with only part of the history of Fu Ren University. His study on the Benedictine era of the university from 1925 to 1933 is indeed rather extensive yet far from complete. He tries to provide a synthesized view on the joint effort of the East and the West through the lens of Fu Ren University. He also tries to provide an integrated view of educational and cultural exchanges between Chinese scholars and the American Benedictines. His focus is mainly on the structural development of the university, from which we can understand the mission of the university and its interactions with the nationalist government and with the anti-Japanese movements. The students' involvement with the protests during that period was briefly described in his writing. He also mentions the specific mission and goals of the university which showed the efforts that the Benedictine Fathers and Chinese Catholics were making in the early years.

Paul Varg's time frame of the university goes beyond Wu's research limit. He provides additional information on the university after the year

1933, which was the year when Fu Ren was transferred to the care of the Divine Word Fathers. He states that from the year of 1933 onwards, Fu Ren was transformed: student enrollment and faculty membership increased rather rapidly. In 1937, St Albert's College (Chinese Clerical College) for the advanced training of Chinese priests in Chinese literature and sciences were added, and a school of Chinese Christian Arts was also established. An agricultural research program was initiated. Eventually a women's college was added to the university in 1938. The university had maintained a printing press, which published some well-known journals: *Fu Ren Sinological Journal* and *Monumenta Serica*. These were all research-oriented journals. All these information are indeed considered as the achievements of the university without much detail to show its development.

Sophia Lee takes a completely different approach in her research on the university. This approach is rather important in understanding the whole history of Fu Ren University. She focuses on the political involvements of Fu Ren University during the Sino-Japanese War period in comparison with other Christian universities. Though her view is rather disputable, her attention is centered on the survival of the university during wartime in China. She gives some statistics on the student enrollment to indicate the effects that the Sino-Japanese War had on the university. She also mentions one unique point that the Fu Ren students "devoted more time and energy to charity work in wartime Beijing than students from any other institution of higher education in the city who were engaged in similar work."[32] She provides a list of some specific charitable works that Fu Ren students were doing, such as operating a free medical clinic, opening a gruel kitchen especially during the winter months, and offering relief to the unemployed as well as those seeking refuge from war and natural disaster.[33] She thinks that the wartime history of Fu Ren affords an interesting lesson in historiography and concludes that the war years brought Fu Ren University unprecedented attention and popularity.

He Jian-ming, however, emphasizes the theme how Fu Ren University preserved the Chinese culture by discussing the relationship between the university and its president, Chen Yuan. In the early part of his essay, he stresses that the intention of the university's founders was to make the university Chinese. The mutual friendship between Chen Yuan and the founders encouraged him to change his profession from the medical field to historical research. Under his leadership as the president, Fu Ren achieved its mission to promote Chinese culture.

> 'As a non-Christian, Chen Yuan emphasized on religious freedom, as patriotic Chinese literati and educator, he led Fu Ren University to make Chinese studies as priority, to do research in order to exceed others countries in this field. Fu Ren achieved this and had tremendous influence in China.' [34]

He thinks that the history of Fu Ren and the person of Chen Yuan were inseparable: "if there had been no Fu Ren, Chen Yuan would be impossible to become the one we know now; in the same way, without Chen Yuan, Fu Ren would also be impossible became the one we know."[35] He indicates that under the influence of Chen Yuan, the patriotic person, Fu Ren achieved its mission to study and to develop Chinese culture. The reverse is true in He Jian-ming's conclusion.

> 'In the next 26 years after Chen Yuan joined Fu Ren in 1926, he did not betray Ma Xiang-bo and Vincent Yin's wishes. Facing the national and international political crisis, Chen demonstrated his patriotism and human dignity. His heroic spirit and great talents, excellent teaching methods and studious attitude led Fu Ren to become an more democratic, free and patriotic university...' [36]

Because of this, he adds that even the Archbishop Zanin, the Apostolic delegate, praised Chen Yuan. In 1930, the university hired many famous professors to be on the faculty and therefore made the university's faculty of Arts and Letters the best among all private universities. It was on the top of the list of all the universities, including public ones in China.[37]

SECTION III: ANALYSIS

Having discussed the existing materials on the history and development of Fu Ren University, it is time to make some analysis of these issues. By analyzing the specific issues, I will point out what is lacking and what needs to be developed or explored, as well as the areas that I think need to be reinterpreted. Due to the complicated political issues and to each author's research interest and political stance, some literature might not have done justice to the university. In fact, Sophie Lee and He Jian-ming are contradicting each other in their findings about Fu Ren University. Therefore, I think both structural and political aspects of the university should be analyzed so that readers might have a better understanding of Fu Ren University. It is to be noted that the political aspect will be analyzed carefully in light of Sophie Lee's writing because it is crucial when we try to understand the complicated situation in Beijing when Fu Ren was developing and expanding.

General Comments

Based on the existing materials, I make a summary of the existing literature on Fu Ren University: the basic ideas of the establishment of the university (1912–1925), the structural development of the university (1925–1938), as well as the political involvement of the university during the Sino-Japanese War period (1937–1942). It is hard for readers who are unfamiliar with China to piece together what the university was really like because these scattered pieces are neither coherently connected nor are able to provide a whole picture of this university. In order to know the history of Fu Ren University, the existing materials on the establishment and chronological development of the university are far from enough. Even the combined time frame was short from the real life span of Fu Ren University. The remaining years of its existence need to be discovered and analyzed in depth. More importantly, the political involvement with the government during the years from 1937to 1945 needs to be reinterpreted. Sophie Lee's view needs to be carefully scrutinized. The whole political stance of the university needs to be re-examined. Over all, the three authors which will be discussed later only focused on a certain specific periods of time of the university according the their own interests. These periods were certainly important in the development of Fu Ren University and deserved analysis. However, these particular periods don't tell the whole history of the university. Therefore, each individual author's view will be specified.

Comments on Individual Authors

Wu Xiao-xin offers us his view in his dissertation that Fu Ren University was a joint effort of Western and Eastern scholars during the Benedictine period. This view is well taken. His conclusion of Fu Ren University was actually a reflection of the social, historical and educational situations in China[38] is also justified. However, his simplified generalization of Fu Ren without further explanation falls short. Therefore, some points he has made in the conclusion are apparently different from what I have found. In fact, the readers cannot understand fully where exactly he is coming from. There are two things in specific I have to point out. First of all, he cuts short the history of the university during the Benedictine period by two years, whether intentionally or not. He has not treated the first two years of Fu Ren University from 1925 to 1927 as part of its history. Though Fu Ren University was not yet registered with the government, it was the continual part of the university run by the Benedictine Fathers. From a developmental point of view, this does not do justice to the university, nor to the American Cassinese Congregation of Benedictines. Many other readings have included those two years as part of the university. Secondly, later in his conclusion chapter, he makes three rather inaccurate research statements of which I specify: (1) the initial goal of the university. He inaccurately stated the early goal of the university was "As far as the American Benedictines were concerned, the initial goal for the establishment of the university carried a strong sense of evangelism and Christianization, which was characteristic for all Catholic missionaries then." [39] He over generalized the Catholic mission in China. The Benedictine Fathers did not intend to do that. (2) The religious activities. He described the religious activities on campus as such, "These activities were limited to the residential quarters of the missionaries, which were separated from the school campus."[40]

These two conclusions contradict what I have found the mission of the university was to provide education under the auspice of the Catholics with emphasis on Chinese culture, and the religious activities were completely optional for students on campus where services were available. Only those Catholic students who lived in a separate house with the missionaries were obliged to take turns to offer their services. Wu somehow over generalized the aspects of mission and religious life without taking the whole university into consideration. (3) The Women's College of Fu Ren. His implications for future studies indicated that Women's College was never recognized as college status.[41] This was true when the Benedictine sisters were there. Also, he was not clear about the time frame of the Benedictine period of the Fu Ren University. Women's College was a separate section of Fu Ren University that was first administered by the Benedictine Sisters and later was transferred to the care of the Sisters of the Holy Ghost in 1936. Eventually, the women could take the same courses from the men's section, which indicated that Women's College met the qualifications of the university. Overall, Wu did not treat the university as a whole in a developmental point view, even during the Benedictine period. His research might have led readers think that Women's College and Fu Ren University were two separate entities. This might also explain why the first two years of Fu Ren University were not treated as the Benedictine period in his writing. It is my understanding that he might have only focused on the government-recognized period of the university without making it known clearly. These issues will be clarified in this book. Moreover, from his work, we can also get a sense that even within this Benedictine Era that Wu discussed, there were still enormous political and academic issues left uncovered. Examples include how the university interacted with the governments and what the faculty and student enrollment looked like. The reasons that caused its expansion in 1929, when it was extremely difficult to raise funds for the university, are certainly in need of explanation.

Sophie Lee is the second author whose work I am obliged to offer some comments on. As previously mentioned, Lee offers a unique political view of the university in comparison with other researchers. Her study of the university during the Sino-Japanese War period is certainly important, but her views in general are rather disputable because my research has found quite contrary views to hers. In a comparative way, she studies two missionary universities in Beijing, one is Yan Jing University, which was controlled by the Protestant Church that I don't intend to study; the other is Fu Ren University, which was controlled by the Catholic Church, on which my research focuses. Her views on Fu Ren's politics are rather presumptive because my own archival research has found concrete evidence that is very different from her interpretations of Fu Ren's political history. I intend to specify the points in the following.

First of all, her statement in the beginning of the chapter sets her on the opposite side of the university:

> Missionary education has been credited with introducing to China beneficial cultural and social elements. It has also been roundly condemned as a facet of imperialism. Richly endowed and distinctly un-Chinese, many missionary schools in the Republic of China symbolized much that were diametrically opposed to the country's contemporary needs and nationalistic sentiment.[42]

Her indiscriminate political view of the missionary universities is a serious charge on Fu Ren University in her entire research. She does not treat Fu Ren as it was, but judge Fu Ren through her own nationalistic and patriotic lenses, which makes her writing to be too subjective. Fu Ren University was quite different from any other universities in Beijing from its very beginning. Ruth Hayhoe and He Jian-ming also have the different views from Sophie Lee. The details of the mission of the university and its gradual development will be discussed later to dispute her view.

Secondly, since Fu Ren University, along with Yan Jing University (American Protestants), were able to operate in Beijing before the Japanese attack on Pearl Harbor in 1941while the government institutions had moved to inland, Lee concludes that Fu Ren University was sponsored by the "Puppet Government."[43] After the Japanese attacked Pearl Harbor in 1941, the United States and Japan became enemies which caused many troubles for Americans and their institutions in China. Many American Protestant Church owned higher education institutions were forced to move inland, including Yan Jing University in Beijing. While most of the colleges and universities moved out of Beijing, Fu Ren University continued its operation in Beijing under the leadership of German missionaries. Once again, Lee accuses the university was cooperating with the Japanese by allowing the Japanese authorities to visit the campus and to conduct investigations, as well to carry out occasional arrests. This conclusion she draws is not base on archival materials but her own speculations. She has not produced any hard evidence herself in her work.[44] Though she realizes the variety of interpretations of the university's political stance, she is convinced Fu Ren was under the supervision of the Japanese. Her conventional wisdom[45] really does not support a researcher's effort to discover the hard evidence. More over, another statement of hers is also quite contrary to what I have found through my research. I quote,

> A semi-official history of Fu Ren University in Taiwan claims that the school had received secret instructions from the ministry of education of the nationalist government to remain open so as to be able to utilize its international connections to cultivate patriotic youth in occupied China and to continue national (presumably as opposed to slave) education. Moreover, according to this source, Fu Ren was advised to band together with other international educational organizations in Beijing-Tianjin area in observing three principles: (1) administrative independence, (2) academic freedom and (3) no display of the flag of the "puppet government."[46]

After careful examination of the archival materials, I doubt the validity of the so-called "semi-official" statement. In my extensive research, I have not come across such reference at all from all the archives. Those three principles were actually embedded in the institution since the very beginning of its establishment. Lee has some doubts of the above statement, but she eventually confirms this by speculating that the university in fact did function as this and chose to accommodate itself to the political authorities. I conclude that Fu Ren University tried to adapt to different political policies without compromising its principles of making the university a Catholic and Chinese university.

In general, Lee has not researched on Fu Ren University well. First of all, she has many facts wrong about the university and secondly, she makes speculations based on no hard evidence. She thinks the university was founded in 1927, when in fact, it was recognized as university status in this year. She thinks that the official language of the school was English. However, both English and Chinese were official languages[47] which were the same as many other universities in Beijing. She thinks the Sino-Japanese War really affected the student enrollment during those years, while in reality, it was growing in number and quality. The administration, the president's tenure and power, and the rector's power were mostly stated erroneously in her research during the Sino-Japanese War period. Sometimes she also contradicts herself when she talks about the university's resistance to the Japanese. It is impossible for her to reconcile her statement that the university was sponsored by the "puppet government"[48] on one hand, and "dissuade students from joining the Beijing government after graduation or engaging in profiteering ventures"[49] by the president of the university on the other.

Although Lee has done questionable research on Fu Ren University, she does touch upon one important political issue, which the university had been struggling with throughout the years. Political entanglements affected the life of Fu Ren University tremendously. From the beginning years of Fu Ren until its demise, politics were a major part of its life. Fu Ren was established during wartime in 1925 and demised in the midst of another political movement in 1952. Lee merely touches upon one short period in its entirety. Actually as I have indicated in chapter one, Fu Ren went through all these: the warlord period (1924–1928), the Nationalist period (1928–1937), The Japanese Government or 'Provisional (Puppet) Government' (1937–1945) then again the Nationalist period (1945–1948), and finally the Communist period (1949–1952). The transition from one government to another was never easy and affected the university. Therefore, all these periods are in need to be discussed systematically.

In addition, one more glimpse of the political environment that Fu Ren University was in should be mentioned. This was revealed by Father Rigney who was the last rector of the university. Unfortunately, he failed to discuss the details of the politics but his own experiences with the communists. In his memoirs *Fours Years in a Red Hell*, Father Rigney wrote about some of the terrible things he experienced when he was in prison, such as: persecutions of the Church, the government attempt to take over the university and force it to change its curriculum, etc. All these occurred during the last few years of Fu Ren University before the Communists dissolved the university. As the last rector of the university, he was also persecuted under the regime of the Communist Party.[50] He touched upon his own encounters with the Communists but did not mention much on the university itself.

Analysis of the Structural Aspect

As a researcher, I think that beside the inadequate literature on political aspects of the university, the literature on the chronological development and structural growth of the university reviewed previously is also inadequate. They both need to be reconstructed as well as enriched. In their current form, they are simply not efficient to tell the history of Fu Ren University. Additional aspects need to be identified and researched. All of these elements are crucial if a rather complete history of the university is required: Finance and curriculum development; Faculty and Student growth; Extracurricular, Student Activism, as well as the political entanglements the university had with the local governments. All of these elements where my research lays upon are important to the existence of the university. From these detailed elements, people can see and judge whether the university was prestigious or simply mediocre; whether it had its autonomy or simply was subjected to politics. All these elements should certainly also cover the whole life of Fu Ren University as much as possible rather than cover a specific period of time. The items in the table of contents will be fully discussed whereby the previous researchers either did not go into or simply ignored completely.

Obviously, even the combined efforts of the previously mentioned authors cannot provide a good history of Fu Ren University. The university was certainly not a separate entity but was in relationship with many others, both politically and economically. More specifically, it had connections with the local governments, Chinese culture and the Catholic Church in China, in the United States and Rome.

Analysis of the Political Aspect

Having reviewed the relevant literature, I have offered some comments on the authors' research. The existing literature has unveiled tremendous information about Fu Ren University, but their works have not yet covered the university in its entirety, especially in dealing with the latter part of the university from 1938–1952. The internal development and the outside connections are quite unexplored. Even dealing with political aspects, those who have studied Fu Ren University cannot provide us with a clear and systematic picture of Fu Ren's position.

The insertions of external political power into the university did make the university react and change. I have found that occasionally the university had to make certain adaptations without compromising its principles when the political pressure was pressed upon it. As a result, Fu Ren was very successful in overcoming all the external pressures and became better and stronger each time except when at last the Communist Party took over Beijing. Lee's conclusion that such adaptations would be under the sponsorship of the government is unsustainable because Fu Ren had always under the sponsorship of the Vatican.

Summary of the Background of Political Entanglement of the University

A brief summary of the political entanglements that Fu Ren had to deal with is appropriate at this time because it helps readers to see the complicated situation when Fu Ren was in operation. Thought I have analyzed the political aspect, the analysis does not situate Fu Ren in its real position and does not tell us what parties were really involved. In order to understand the political aspect of Fu Ren, the political environments in which Fu Ren was involved is necessary. None of the above researchers has really positioned the university well in a cultural and political environment. Since the university was not existed in a vacuum, the cultural and political movements had impacts on it. Therefore, I am obliged to describe this unique environment around Fu Ren University so that readers can have an objective view of the university. Unless we know the environment, we cannot understand fully the history of Fu Ren University.

Culturally and politically, China was anti-Christian and anti-Western when Fu Ren was about to be established. The rising of nationalism in the early 1920's really strengthened the anti-Christian and anti-Western movements. Jessie Lutz in his book *Chinese Politics and Christian Missions* has details of the conflicts that the Christian missionaries had with the Nationalist Government and the Communist Government of which I do not intent to repeat. These movements shaped many scholars' views on the purpose of higher education. As one professor stated:

> "Our goal is twofold: first to offset the pro-Western cultural propaganda of foreign mission schools in China by giving Chinese students a taste of Soviet culture; second, to teach the Chinese the lessons of our revolution..."[51]

Fu Ren University was already involved with politics even before its establishment simply because of its Catholicity and its location in Beijing. The Nationalist and Communist Parties who organized the United Front, who frequently designated separate representation for intellectuals and students to attack the missionary schools and to justify their own positions on the revolution. Lutz concludes that:

"The intellectuals served more than one purpose: the adherence of new youth provided cadre leadership and broadened support, while the prestige of scholars helped legitimize the revolutionary cause."[52]

Worst of all, the campaign leaders tried many tactics to eliminate Christian education as if the Christians were enemies. Some even suggested the destruction of the buildings and the forcible taking over of the schools. During the years 1924–1925 when Fu Ren was in the middle of erecting, some tried to persuade parents not to send their children to Christian schools. Others demanded immediate government registration of all educational institutions with closure of unregistered schools after a designated date.[53]

During the years between 1925 and 1952, China changed dramatically because of the Westernization and wars. In the mist of the continuation of anti-Christianity and anti-Western movements, Fu Ren University was established and developed into a nationally known university. Paul Varg has the following description:

> July 1 (1927), Jiang Jieshi proclaimed the establishment of a nationalist government. He tried to reunite the nation split into five major areas by warlords. Nationalist and Communist Parties propagandists preaching a heady gospel of anti-warlordism, anti-foreignism, and anti-Christianism. Many fled, and died...under the leadership of the Roman Catholic Church, decided to keep its missionaries in China and to discourage them from seeking reparations for damages suffered at the hands of the Chinese.[54]

Fu Ren University continued and developed despite all of the hostilities. The Nationalist Government promulgated some regulations even before China was unified. These regulations were harsh to any private school and indicated that the Nationalist Government was also anti-Christian and anti-foreign. According to Lutz and Latourette, the following points of the government's regulations were enforced. In order for Christian universities to meet the requirement for registration, the schools had to: (1) require no religious instruction or activities; (2) acknowledge the primacy of education rather than religious goals; (3) practice equality in the treatment of Chinese and Western faculty members; (4) provide a majority of Chinese in the administration; (5) insure that the president or vice-president was Chinese; (6) have government supervision.[55] It is obvious that the existing universities had to make great changes in order to survive; Fu Ren was no exception when the needs to survive became imminent.

Fu Ren University was just founded when these governmental regulations were enforced. The university did everything according to the requirements from the National government because the founders intended to comply with the requirements in order to make the university a Chinese one. It certainly would be interesting to see how the Catholic university adapted and developed the policy, and in what way could it be Catholic and Chinese. This actually is the theme that this book intends to discuss. Starting from the very beginning, Fu Ren began to get involved with the politics. Politics constantly shaped the development of the university. The university acted and reacted for its survival and development while external forces kept changing, and sometimes attacking the university. It was impossible for the university to be immune in the anti-Christian environment. It was also impossible for the university to survive if it had not complied with certain rules of the governments. It was also impossible for its survival if the university had not been Chinese at all. Unfortunately those authors who have shown their interests in this particular university, to a great extent, ignored the above-mentioned elements.

After spending eight years under Japanese vigorous attacks, Fu Ren University was not survived, but developed into a rather prestigious university nationwide. Besides the increased quality of student enrollment and faculty, the graduated programs were instituted. While Fu Ren was ready to compete with all the universities when they moved back to Beijing, the civil war threw China into deep financial trouble. Eventually, Fu Ren could not survive the Communist's control when the government took it over in 1950. In 1952 Fu Ren University disappeared under the Communist regime, along with all other private universities. Therefore, the interesting question that needs to be answered is such: How could the Communist government manage to take control of all the universities? Within three short years after the Communists took over Beijing and two years after taking over Fu Ren, the fully- developed and a well-known university in China disappeared. This certainly showed the power of the Communist government.

Conclusion

Fu Ren University simply has not had a real thorough written history which it deserves. Speculations can certainly be made in dealing with this subject. One well-known scholar and historian Zhang Kai-yuan confirmed my suspicions that there were not enough archival materials to write on Catholic universities in China.[56] My own research efforts have proved this to be true. There are not many files available in Beijing where I have researched two archives. I am more convinced that it is not that scholars did not *want* to write on the subject of the Catholic higher education, but that they were *unable* to do so. The summary of the background of political entanglements of the university serves the purpose of putting readers in the frame of mind that the environment in China was terrible when Fu Ren was established and developed. In the midst of all the troubles, Fu Ren developed and became one of the best universities in China. Therefore, Fu Ren University certainly deserves its own telling. From the analysis I provided, readers can easily understand that in order for Fu Ren to survive, the university had to deal with all kinds of political issues. Adaptations of some governmental rules were unavoidable. Even though the environment was extremely hostile to the university throughout the years, Fu Ren University did become a nationally known university within a short period of time. It is certainly surprising to everyone in the field of higher education that Fu Ren could achieve its status within short 27 years. This book will certainly clarify many scholars' curiosities about the reasons of its rapid development and its increased reputation. This book will certainly provide future writers to look deep into the Catholic Church, Chinese culture and politics.

Arthur Miller says it well, "in China, if you try to nail things down, you are hammering on the surface of the ocean. We must make an effort to understand the culture, history, and the goals of the Chinese."[57] This is especially true as I try to write the history of the Fu Ren University. There are many issues need to be discussed objectively. In an effort to nail things down so that a rather complete and authentic history of the university will be done, I will first to take a step to explore the establishment process of the university, which was from 1912 to 1925 in the following chapter. From which, readers can see the interactions within the Church and the purpose of the establishing university as both Chinese and Western. The university was intended to be among the elite universities in China and for China. The establishing process was strenuous. It took the Catholic Church thirteen years to make the proposal come true. My discussion will go as far as back to the year 1912 when the Emperor was just thrown off his throne and the Republic of China was just founded. This was the year when the proposal was made. In the meantime, the Catholic Church's missionary work was in a difficult time, the Vatican did not have its' autonomy over it until early 1920s. The control of France and Italy over the missionary work prevented Rome from doing anything in China. The establishment of Fu Ren University in Beijing indeed helped the Vatican to reclaim its power over the Church and resume its' leadership role of the missions in the Church.

CHAPTER THREE

Establishment of Fu Ren University

The establishment of Fu Ren University did not come true easily. The petition proposal to the Holy Father to consider erecting the Catholic University in Beijing was made in 1912, and this did not become reality until 1924. Many things both within the Catholic Church and in China had happened during those 12 years. The first two chapters have illustrated some events, such as church politics, wars, unstable politics and anti-Christian movements that certainly made things difficult for the Catholic Church to work in China. This long-delayed project was certainly understandable because of the crises both in China and within the Catholic Church.

Because of complicated entanglements between China and the Catholic Church, this chapter simply deals with the internal politics of the Catholic Church and how the university came into existence. The purpose of doing this is to make materials manageable and to explore the nature of Fu Ren University as both Western Catholic and Chinese from its beginning. The different topics that are discussed in this chapter will help readers understand how the university came to be, and steps that Church and her Chinese counter-part had to take also shaped the development of the university. Because of the actions and reactions from both sides, the university became a unique Catholic university in Beijing and in all of China when it finally was established.

In reality, the establishment of the university took many years of discussions, debates and collaborations within the Catholic Church. The Pope and the Propagation of the Faith eventually had to decide which religious community would be a good candidate to take the responsibility and in the meantime, not offending the French government and French Church. Even when Doctor O'Toole visited the Rome in 1920 as I discuss later, it still took Rome another four years to come to a final decision to establish the Catholic University in Beijing in 1924. In China, it also took years of patience and perseverance that required from Vincent Ying Lian-zhi and Ma Xiang-bo, who were expecting a response from Rome. During the period of waiting, Vincent Ying took an proactive approach to establish a small academy called *Fu Ren She* with a purpose to develop a group of Catholic young men who would be as cultured and well-educated as any other classes or circles in China and whose conversation would redound to the glory of Holy Mother Church to the good of their native country:

> 'In the face of this sad state of affairs, I early felt it my duty as a Catholic to perform my part, however insignificant, towards bringing about the regeneration of China. And, with this in view, I established, as far back as the year 1913, in Hsiang Shan, a locality not far from Peking, an academy of Chinese letters under the name of *Fu Ren She*.'[1]

In 1912, the year after the fall of Chinese Emperor, Vincent Ying and Ma Xiang-bo had already made the petition to Rome called *Letter to Pope Pius X* to establish a Catholic university in Beijing[2]. In 1913, *Fu Ren She* was immediately established and financed by Vincent Ying. In fact, he used all his own means to support the students at this academy to the acquisition of literary proficiency. Vincent Ying achieved a lot through this academy, in his own humble words, "though they did not come up to my most sanguine expectations, proved, nevertheless, a source of considerable satisfaction and earned many expressions of praise and congratulations. The literary composition and research-work of the students appeared frequently in Chinese newspapers and periodicals, with the result that no little admiration was aroused at the proficiency of these youthful Catholics in the field of literature."[3] Realizing his own limited resources, he continued to call upon the attentions from the Church hierarchy. To reinforce the earnest ideas of founding the university in Beijing, Vincent Ying wrote another famous letter-article *Exhortation to Study*[4], a letter that was mainly distributed to all the bishops in China to remind them of the urgent need to educate the Chinese youth and to raise the quality of the Catholic clergy. This letter-article was well accepted in China and was sent to Pope Benedict XV in 1917. Nothing could be done until the Pope reclaimed his power in the Church and the proposal became reality in 1924 when the American Benedictine Fathers eventually came to Beijing to erect the university. Surprisingly, it took the Catholic Church hierarchy twelve years to pass the proposal, but only took the Benedictine Fathers one year in Beijing to do the necessary preparations before the official opening of the university on October 1, 1925.

The Vatican's delay needs to be discussed at this point. Two major factors really affected Rome's decision, which caused the delay. First, the outbreak of the European war brought grave problems to the Catholic Church. Latourette mentioned, "many missionaries, especially French and Belgian, were called to the colors."[5] Second, France became the protector of Roman Catholic missions, which prevented Rome from doing anything

Establishment of Fu Ren University

about missionary work.[6] By the year of 1914, there were about 1500 Catholic missionaries in China. France alone had 850 there, among whom there were between two and three hundred bishops.[7] Although the Congregation of the Propagation of Faith was the major actor in the world missions, it simply could not bypass the French government. In 1918, the French government even protested vigorously when the Chinese government proposed to establish direct relations with the Vatican. As a result of this, the implementation had to be postponed.[8]

In 1920, when Doctor O'Toole made a trip to Rome after he visited China, the Church was evidently ready to take up the challenges of France since the officials in Rome decided to show their interest in this China-initiated project. A variety of topics are discussed here: first, the earnest petition from China, and then the reactions of the Catholic Church, which have two parts: Rome's and the American Benedictines' reactions. Later, the establishment of the university is discussed, the location of the university and the meaning of the name of the university are illustrated and finally, a conclusion is drawn for the chapter.

Earnest Petition from China

In July of 1912, the year after the establishment of the Republic of China, Mr. Vincent Ying Lian-zhi and Ma Xiang-bo saw the opportunity for the Catholic Church to develop and made a joint petition to His Holiness Pope Pius X to petition for the establishment of a Catholic university in Beijing. These two well-known Chinese scholars were the only Catholic ones among the many elite scholars, who cared for the Catholic Church and Catholic missionaries' activities in China. The missionaries in China at the time did not appreciate Chinese culture and ignored the effective way to convert the Chinese by utilizing Chinese culture and trying to make friends with the intellectuals. Unlike the early Catholic missionaries who intended to bring a Chinese Catholic faith to China, the new missionaries after the Opium War (1840) considered Chinese culture to be uncivilized and therefore needing to be changed. The early Jesuits, such as Matteo Ricci and his fellow companions, Father Schall and Father Veribest were the models of Catholic mission in China. They became the friends of Chinese intellectuals because they respected and learned Chinese culture. As a result, they influenced the Chinese Emperors and their family. Some Jesuits even held high positions in the imperial court. They tried to find the similarities between Catholic teaching and Chinese culture rather than trying to change Chinese culture.

After the great Jesuits missionaries, Matteo Ricci, Schall, and Veribest, who had visions for the Catholic Church in China, no other missionaries had such understanding of evangelization in China. Their presence, in many ways, offended the Chinese intellectuals. Knowing the success of the early Jesuits in China and the native culture, as well as the hostilities the missionaries received, Vincent Ying and Ma Xiang-bo, the only two Catholic scholars among hundreds of Chinese intellectuals, decided to take an initiative to promote Chinese culture in order for the Church to survive. They were probably the only two who really understood the compatibility between the Church and Chinese culture after the early Jesuits. They tried to rekindle the Jesuit missionary spirit in China and eventually succeeded.

Vincent Ying[9] was an educator, journalist and reformer. He studied all religions in China before he studied Catholicism. He converted to Catholicism as an adult because of the works of Giulio Aleni, and Saint Thomas's *Summa Theologica*. On June 17, 1902, he gathered talents and subscribers and founded *L'Impartial*, later to be widely known as *Da Gong Bao* (the Imperial), which was in *Pai Hua* (colloquial). He was the editor-in-chief from 1902 to 1912. Under his control and management, the newspaper enjoyed a reputation of being a fearless critic from its very beginning. The voice of the newspaper was strong, vibrant, and compelling. All issues, no matter whether national or international affairs, were discussed.[10] Ma Xiang-bo[11] was an ex-Jesuit, theologian and philosopher. He founded two universities[12] in Shanghai and once was the president of Beijing University. Because of their concerns for the Catholic Church in China the well-being of the Chinese clergy and educated laity, they were unhappy with the missionaries. Driven by their vision for the Catholic Church in China, these two scholars petitioned the Pope to establish a Catholic university in Beijing, the old capital and cultural center of China. The purpose of the petition was self-evident: to make the university a center of Chinese studies and Western sciences, to promote Catholic higher education in China, to discover faith in Chinese culture and to make known the Catholic Church among Chinese intellectuals. They knew this was the effective and influential way for the Catholic Church to grow in China.

In their petition letter to the Pope, they stated their purpose clearly after a brief narrative of the Catholic Church in China. I paraphrase the history in the following three points which caused their greatest concerns: (1) the dearth of priests continued for more than two centuries from Yuan Dynasty; (2) China resembled the paralytic of the Gospel, deprived of the use of his members in Ming and Qing (Manchu) Dynasties; (3) Science proved to be an excellent means of attracting Chinese to the truth of the Gospel which the Jesuits manifested. These two great Chinese Catholic literati knew exactly the background of the Church mission and what the Church needed to do:

> 'But what do we see to-day? While the Protestants of England, Germany and America are building schools and universities, we note with sorrow that the Catholic Missions alone remain indifferent to the educational movement. In this capital of China, the Catholics have no university; no secondary schools, not even primary schools. The sole exception being a Franco-Chinese school at which the board is so expensive that pagans are

the only ones able to attend it; besides the students who graduate from it can only enter the service of Frenchmen.'[13]

More importantly, they felt the pains caused by the intellectual incapability of the Catholics in China. Catholic missionaries were busy saving souls by trying to convert the poorly educated farmers by providing them food and daily needs. They ignored the association with well educated the elite group who enjoyed great reputation in China. Though these Catholic missionaries had good education, they were either incapable of teaching or reluctant to teach. They simply wanted to be missionaries who would be directly associated with the local people in the countryside or faraway places. Their counterparts, the Protestant Church missionaries, were doing just the opposite which was the right thing to do in China. They tried to be in the cities and in the costal areas in order to associate with the more educated Chinese. They were actively involved with education, mostly higher education. They had attracted many Chinese intellectuals and relatively wealthy people. In comparison, the Catholic Church put itself in an inferior position in China because the farmers and poor people were not educated:

> 'During the last years of the Qing Dynasty, the government had under consideration of idea of giving the direction of the National University to the Catholic mission. The Catholics however, were unable to accept, and the institution fell into the hands of the Protestants, who have succeeded in insinuating themselves into all branches of government administration. They have not failed to make rapid progress in the race from which we Catholics have voluntarily eliminated ourselves without having been excluded...
>
> 'Our missionaries of our day confine their instruction to those emanating from the lowest ranks of society...New China does not see any Catholics capable of sitting in Parliament, or in provincial and departmental assemblies.'[14]

This inferiority of the Catholic Church did not seem register in the missionaries' minds, but certainly realized by the Chinese scholars who respected education rather than providing food for exchange of religion. They needed conviction. Vincent Ying and Ma Xiang-bo were great Catholic laymen had earned their respect from the elite group in China. They both worked for the Chinese government for many years in various capacities. Each had a promising career and both had great influence among Chinese intellectuals. Presently, they tried to use their influence to help the Catholic Church regain its respect from the intellectuals. They visualized an effective way for Catholic missionaries to do in the China was to establish a university in Beijing:

> 'A Catholic University here (in Beijing) would see large numbers of students, both Christian and pagan, flocking to its doors; it would constitute

a strong bond of union between Catholicity and the nation at large, whereby advantages immeasurably superior to those, which mere treaties of protection pretend to guarantee, would be secured for the Church—this University...

> 'Send us learned men, meek and humble of heart, that they may become our leaders; men of divers nationalities, that Catholicity may be spared the reproach of being the religion of any particular nationality; men of different religious orders, in order to do away with all exclusiveness, all jealousy, all party spirit.'[15]

By stating the current conditions in China, they tried to reinforce their vision for the Church in China and pronounced their earnest petition to the Pope: "the disorders in administration, illiteracy, incompetence and insincerity prevalent in every quarter and the nation tried to react to against these. And only the educated classes realized that religion alone could maintain the prosperity and morals of the people."[16]

Vincent Ying was not only a man of ideas but also a man of action. He did not waste any time after sending the petition letter to Rome. In 1912, he established *Fu Ren She* at *Xiangshan Park* using his own money as an endowment to train Catholic youth. This was later to be revived by the Catholic University of Beijing as the *MacManus Academy of Chinese Studies* or *Fu Ren She*, which was its original name. Eventually the university took this name as the official one when it was registered with the government as Fu Ren University. Moreover, in 1917, he wrote another letter to all the bishops in China to urge them to pay attention to education, as well as to the Holy Father for further persuasion. This letter was called *Exhortation to Study*. In it, Vincent Ying stressed once again the urgent needs in China that the Catholic Church had to meet. In this letter, he eloquently argued the importance for the Church to utilize the rich Chinese culture in church missions rather than disregard it. He boldly charged the Pope for these wrong doings,

> 'Many of our young native priests are, unable so much as correctly to compose a simple letter: their embarrassed and awkward style would be unworthy of an ordinary clerk in commerce...
>
> 'Useless to insist on other points: the forgetfulness of the Holy See is the cause of great harm to the reputation and dignity of the Catholic Church in our country.'[17]

Rome's Reaction

The initiative from Chinese Catholic scholars should have motivated the Catholic Church to rethink its failed mission in China, unfortunately this earnest petition to establish a Catholic university could not be put into practice during the reign of the Pope Pius X because of some internal power struggles in the Catholic Church. Italy and France were strongly against Rome's initiative toward China. They did not want the Pope to bypass them, simply because they, especially French government, wanted to be the protector of the Catholic Church and wanted to have China as its own mission. Since it is not my intension to get into this, I conclude that the politics within the Church delayed all of the actions that Rome intended to do for China. According to Eric Hanson, two occasions were blocked when Rome attempted to establish a formal relationship with China. The first time was in 1886 and the second time was in 1918:

> 'As the Catholic missionary effort in China grew, the Vatican attempted to bypass French government control. In 1886 the Holy See initiated a negotiation to establish direct contact with the Chinese government, but France threatened to recall its ambassador from Rome. The French government further hinted that it might repudiate its concordat with the Vatican, which protected religious orders and congregations against French anticlericalism. Rome dropped its China initiated, but warned that this action did not constitute recognition of the French protectorate....
>
> 'The Chinese government made the second attempt at establishing direct relations. In July 1918 it issued a presidential mandate appointing a Chinese minister to the Vatican. Rome responded by appointing a nuncio to Beijing. France and Italy protested vigorously. Late in August the Chinese government announced that, due to certain inconveniences, negotiations with the Vatican would not be resumed until after the war.'[18]

Facing the threats from the two powerful countries of France and Italy, Rome did not stop trying to help the Catholic Church in China in any way possible. Rome cared for China mission deeply. The petitions from China indeed produced a profound impression at Rome.

> 'The Holy Father, Pope Benedict XV, appointed Msgr. De. Guibriant Apostolic Visitor to China, and the report ultimately made by the latter was in substantial agreement with the representations of Mr. Ying, especially, with reference to the imperative need of a Catholic University in Northern China. The Holy See, accordingly, was very anxious to have such an institution established in the capital of the Chinese Republic.'[19]

In fact, Vincent Ying's *Exhortation to Study* had a tremendous impact on Pope Benedict's Encyclical *Maximum illud*. According to Praragon's article *Ying Lien-chih (1866–1929) and the Rise of Fu Jen, the Catholic University of Peking*, many of the doctrinal points and practical guidance which Vincent Ying had raised, urged, or suggested in his exhortation to study, were contained in this encyclical when the Pope tried to address missionary work in non-Christian countries.[20]

In 1920, while the Apostolic Visitor was still in China, Dr. Barry O'Toole, a seminary professor and Oblate of the Archabbey of St. Vincent, was traveling in the Far East. He went to China to explore the educational situation. He arrived at Beijing on October 18, 1920 where he made the acquaintance of Mr. Vincent Ying. After days of inquiry with Mr. Ying and some others in Beijing, he was convinced that a solution to the problem must follow the lines proposed by these two eminent Chinese laymen. On his way back to the United States, O'Toole went to Rome to pay a special visit. While staying there he found that Holy Father Benedict XV was intensely interested in the problems of Catholic education in China. The Holy Father showed much interest in inquiring about the conditions prevalent in China. As a result, the Holy Father was looking for a dependable consignee, to whom the long-contemplated project of founding a Catholic university at Beijing might be most advantageously entrusted.[21] The Benedictine order became the candidate to take the responsibility after O'Toole's visit in Rome. Other religious groups were excluded from partaking in this project.

Unfortunately, Pope Benedict XV did not accomplish the project before his death. On February 6, 1922, Pope Pius XI was elected as the next Pope. He also showed great interest in the China mission. The newly elected pontiff Pope Pius XI continued what Benedict XV had started in requesting that the Benedictine Fathers should take on the responsibilities for establishing a university in Beijing. He became intensely interested in this proposed Benedictine foundation in Beijing to erect the university. To encourage them and the realization of this task, he first directed a sum of 100,000 lire ($5,000) to be set aside as his personal contribution, and promised to have all Vatican publications sent to the library of the new institution.

The Sacred Congregation of the Propaganda was very instrumental, during the course of these years, in encouraging the American Benedictine Fathers to take on the responsibility of erecting the university in Beijing. In 1921, the secretary of the Sacred Congregation of the Propaganda, the Most Rev. Fumasoni Biondi suggested the Archabbey of St. Vincent as possible consignee for the task of founding the university in Beijing. Later in a letter to the President Abbot Aurelius Stehle in1922, Cardinal William Van Rossum, the prefect of the Sacred Congregation of the Propaganda, urged the entire American Cassinese Congregation of the Benedictines to undertake the foresaid work:

> 'Conditions peculiar to the Church in China demand that no human means of furthering the propagation of the Faith among the cultured and educated classes should be neglected...'

> 'Now among means of this sort none is more important than a superior school or college, in which Chinese studies of an advanced type will be cultivated. From some years past, a Catholic University has been contemplated for the city of Beijing, but hitherto nothing has been done to put this project into execution...'

> 'In any case, I shall appreciate it very much, if you will take pains to make known to them all that it is the most intense desire of this Sacred Congre-

gation of the Propaganda, that the Order of St. Benedict, which during the Middle ages saved Latin and Greek literature from certain destruction, should found an institute of higher Chinese studies in the city of Beijing, as the most apt means of fostering a more vigorous growth of our Holy Religion in the vast territory of China.'[22]

Such were the concerns from Rome. In general, Pope Pius X had interest in the China mission but was unable to bypass France and Italy.[23] The other two Popes, Benedict XV and Pius XI, as well as the Congregation of the Propaganda were all interested in establishing a Catholic university in Beijing and acted upon it carefully. Unfortunately, the untimely death of Benedict XV only left his successor to continue the work. The new Pope Pius XI and the Congregation of the Faith indeed took the initiatives to choose a responsible and dependable consignee—the Benedictines, to whom the long-contemplated project of founding a Catholic university in Beijing was bestowed. They chose the American Benedictine Fathers and encouraged them in any possible way to erect a university in Beijing.

The American Benedictine's Reaction

Overall, the reactions of the American Benedictines to the invitation from Rome to establish the Catholic University in Beijing were mixed. It took them a rather long time and went through some complicated processes to make a final agreement with the Holy See to take on this task. Although a few within the community were quite positive and active on this matter, the community as a whole had to measure up their abilities to achieve this grand proposal. This Congregation of Benedictines required a community's effort rather than any individual's when major decisions had to be made.

In 1920, when Dr. O'Toole was in Rome meeting the Pope, the Benedictines already became the ideal candidate in the Pope's mind to be responsible for the future university because of their contributions to the Church in the Middles Ages and their spirituality.[24] Meanwhile, O'Toole also met with the Primate of the Benedictine Order, the Most Rev. Fidelis Stotzingen, to whom he recounted his Chinese experiences. The primate showed his interest in this project as well. These common interests from the influential figures of the Church also prepared for the Benedictines' future readiness for the project in China. Later, when O'Toole returned to the United States, he lobbied for this mission to establish a Catholic university in Beijing,

'On his return to the United States, Dr. O'Toole was at pains to bring his findings to the attention of the Rt. Rev. Aurelius Sthele, O.S.B., Archabbot of St. Vincent, the Rt. Rev. Ernest Helmstetter, O.S.B., Presiding Abbot of the American-Cassinese congregation, and several other eminent American Abbots. All of them, however, were of opinion that, whatever might be said in favor of such a step, an enterprise like a university was too large an undertaking to be compassed by the resources of a single abbey.'[25]

When the official request from Rome finally came in 1921 to ask the American Benedictines to establish the university in Beijing, the Archabbot of St. Vincent declined the invitation to take upon the task. He did not feel that one abbey could afford taking this project. In his letter to the Primate of the Congregation of the Benedictines in Rome dated on April 23, 1922, he reaffirmed his belief that the task was too much for a single monastery, "I wish to state," he said, "that it will scarcely be possible for one abbey to undertake so great a work."[26] He pleaded for cooperation from all other monasteries. In another letter to the abbots of all the monasteries, he reaffirmed his position by referring it to the General Chapter for cooperation. He made such a reference,

> 'Some two years ago a letter of inquiry came from the Cardinal Prefect of the Propaganda. This letter urged that desirability of founding a Benedictine institute of higher studies at Peking, China. We did not feel, however, at the time, that St. Vincent Archabbey should undertake so large a venture without the co-operation of the other Abbeys of our Congregation."[27]

In August 1923, the abbots and the delegates of the twelve monasteries of the American Cassinese Congregation gathered at Saint Procopius Abbey, Lisle, Illinois, for the Congregation's twenty-first general chapter. Jerome Oetgen wrote,

> 'In the fifth session they took up the question of whether to accept the mission to China. The American Benedictine leaders were reluctant to take on such a monumental challenge, but to decline a mission specifically requested by the Holy See was not considered a viable option for the American abbots.'[28]

Though they reluctantly accepted the undertaking initially, the Benedictine abbots pointed out that their constitution did not allow for enterprises to be continued by all the communities of the congregation, only a specified monastery could take the lead. Therefore, they entrusted the project to Saint Vincent Archabbey "with the promise of support, both moral and physical, on the part of all other abbeys of the congregation."[29] After two sessions, the General Chapter carefully considered this matter and decided to take upon the responsibility by allowing Saint Vincent Archabbey to be the prime party for this project in China.[30]

Having decided that Saint Vincent Archabbey should take the responsibility of establishing a Catholic University in Beijing, this Archabbey acted upon it rather quickly to do the necessary preparation such as choosing the personnel and funds for the university. On May 14, 1924, the rector of Saint Vincent Seminary, Father Amnorose Kohlbeck was sent to Rome by Archabbot Aurelius to consult with the Congregation of the Propagation of Faith in working out a satisfactory program for the future university in

China. On June 10, 1924, the actions had already taken place. Two monks from Saint Vincent were sent at once to Beijing to start the work. Father Ildephonse Brandstetter, former prior of Saint Vincent and Father Placidus Rattenburger left for China to make preliminary plans and seek locations for the university. They arrived in Beijing on July 4, 1924. Vincent Ying and Archbishop Celso Constantini welcomed them there and the Archbishop invited them to stay in his residence.

Establishment Process

After sending two of his own monks to China to be ready for the foundation of the Catholic university, the archabbot Aurelius was once again empowered by Rome. He received an issued letter from the Holy See dated June 27, 1924. The Holy See authorized the Archabbot of Saint Vincent with full powers to appoint professors and to regulate the academic programs of this Catholic University of Beijing as a pontifical university.[31] The establishment process officially started at that appointment.

Unexpectedly, this apostolic mission also encountered some obstacles from within the Church in China. The Benedictine Fathers met some challenges from the very beginning when those two monks arrived in Beijing. The bishop of Beijing, Stanislaus F. Jarlin, C.M. who was French, and also the vicar apostolic of northern China, did not agree with the plan that the two Benedictines proposed. Bishop Jarlin was not unfamiliar with this great project, since both Saint Vincent and Rome informed him about it sometime ago. Archabbot Aurelius wrote to Jarlin in 1922, inquiring about the situation of China and seeking his collaboration. "Some steps should be taken to meet this educational problems, and its solution would be greatly hastened, if the Benedictines could be persuaded to undertake the establishment of a university or college at the capital of China."[32] Cardinal Van Rossum also wrote him in 1923 to plead for his cooperation with the Benedictines:

> 'I am sure that Your Lordship will receive the two religious in question with great charity, and that you will be towards them profuse of advice and assistance...
>
> 'Your Lordship may be assured that you will give to the Holy Father the greatest consolation by cooperating in all manners to the good success of the work.'

Naturally, it is unnecessary for me to speculate on this bishop's intention because it is not possible to do so. There is no evidence in the archives to mention this matter. Certainly, Rome could not do much to him because he was a Frenchman. These two monks simply had mixed feelings about things from the very beginning when they first arrived. On one hand, they received encouragement from Archbishop Costantini. On the other hand, the local bishop discouraged their plan by insisting on a "Gymnasium

Major Course." At the end, they agreed with Rome's proposal rather than the Bishop's. They continued what they had planned to establish a university not a "Gymnasium" in Beijing. Having determined to do so, the most challenging issue became urgent which was to purchase the ground for the university, of which, they also pleaded for an immediate action:

> 'The bishop refers to the word "University" as mentioned in our document most emphatically. He expresses himself positively against the establishment of a college as such, but is willing to concede a two years preparatory course for the university. This preparatory course he calls a 'Gymnasium Major Course". His reasons for opposing the rection (creation?) of merely a college are as follows: 1. There are already colleges in Peking. 2. A mere college will not attract the Chinese Students. 3. The document from Rome demands the erection of a University...
>
> 'All sources giving advise agree that ground should be purchased as soon as the erection of a university has been decided upon...would it be wrong to suggest, that as the undertaking has progressed so far, a meeting of all the abbots of our congregation be called to see what could be done at once.'[34]

Bishop Jarlin's refusal of a gradual development of the university actually helped the Benedictines to focus on the effort of building a true university. His insistence on the immediate establishment of an institution of higher learning set the establishment process on the right track. After spending many years in Beijing, Jarlin certainly knew the situation in Beijing, as well as in the whole country of China, yet, the cooperative spirit between them did not prevail.

In the meantime, Archabbot Aurelius received another letter from Father Francis X. Clougherty[35] who was encouraging him to build up a university in Beijing. Clougherty also thought that a Catholic university in Beijing was necessary for the Catholic Church to have. Clougherty told him to consider his high school in Kaifeng as "a feeder to the University."[36] By promising this, the future candidates for the university were certainly secured. This certainly had a positive impact on Aurelius' decision making.

Archabbot Aurelius decided to seek as many assistants as possible from all other abbots of the American Benedictine abbeys. On October 5, 1924, he sent a letter "call to arms" to all the abbots in the United States to urge them to assist this project. Meanwhile, he laid out his plans for the foundation in Beijing,

> 'We draw inspiration and confidence from the glorious past of Benedictinism, but we may not rest upon the laurels earned by the sweat of those, who have preceded us. Rome admonishes us that a "might task", one that is "assuredly difficult" lies before us, and has, in consideration of this fact, authorized us to appeal for aid not alone to our Benedictine confreres, but likewise to all the Bishops and all the faithful of America. The task, which confronts us, is one that will tax every resource available to

Establishment of Fu Ren University

us, and we cannot, therefore, afford to neglect any legitimate source of revenue. Our non-Catholic competitors in China have richly-endowed universities, with learned faculties and splendid equipment. To vie with them, we must muster all the resources at our command.'[37]

Within this letter he laid out two very specific plans which will be discussed in the next chapter: fund raising and personnel recruiting. The most striking thing is the devotion and zeal of this Benedictine abbot from Saint Vincent in making the future university to be the best in China. To establish the university in the heart of old Beijing, the cultural citadel, the Catholic university should "stand out in the midst of other mighty Protestant and government-protected institutions as a symbol of Catholic enlightenment and altruism."[38] The competitive nature of the future Catholic university prevailed.

Because of the demands for the establishment of the university in China, the Archabbot decided to pay a visit in January 1925 in order to work out the necessary plans for the foundation. Meanwhile on January 15, he appointed Dr. Barry O'Toole as the rector of the future university. They sailed together to Beijing in order to complete the work for the establishment of the university.

In Beijing, the immediate problem to be solved was to secure property suitable as the location, extent, and improvements for the university. Their eyes were laid on the palace of Prince Dai Tao (Tao Pei Le), uncle of the deposed Emperor of China. Through the kindness of Dr. J.H. Ingram, a Protestant missionary doctor of Beijing, who was a warm friend of the Benedictines and who acted as physician to the Trappists in north China, aided in negotiations with Prince Dao Tao to purchase his palace. In fact, Doctor Ingram also was a friend of Prince Dai Tao, and acted as the interpreter in the negotiations between the latter and the archbishop. His presence was a great help to the Church because the Benedictines saved a lot of money when they bought this palace, which will be discussed later in this chapter.

On March 20, 1925, the archabbot signed a preliminary contract with Prince Dai Tao and left for the States. On March 26, a final contract for a perpetual lease of the Tao Pei-le (Dual Palace and grounds of Prince Tsai T'ao). It was signed in the American Legation at Peking. The American Treaty with China prescribes a "perpetual lease" instead of purchase. Meanwhile, the Fathers received the right to reside in the "flower garden" of the palace during the interim of the prince's occupancy. On July 26, the prince turned over the complete possession of the premise to the Benedictine Fathers.[39]

The property consisted of eleven acres, located in the so-called "Tartar City" of Peking. The buildings thereon comprised about 500 rooms. There were beautiful walks and gardens. It was huge enough to be a good-sized university at the beginning, and had room to expand if necessary. The property was valued at more than $500,000. Through the negotiations, the Benedictine Fathers only paid the purchase price of $85,000.00 in gold in the end. The Benedictines certainly had a great deal in buying the property. Unstable political situation caused the Prince to make the decision to sell at so low a figure, because he simply feared a possible confiscation of his property by the military authorities.[40] This political situation in China caused everyone feel insecure, especially the imperial officials who were the enemies of new China.

Immediately after taking over the palace in the end of July, the Benedictine Fathers began to renovate the buildings, install steam heat, modern plumbing, and electric wiring, and to convert the "Western Library"(*Xi Shu Fang*) of the palace into a school fit to house the long contemplated *Fu Ren She* or the Academy of Chinese Studies.[41] During the process of renovation, Chinese artists were engaged to restore the various structures to their original splendor. The result had exceeded expectations.[42] These were all done at the directions of the rector, Dr. O'Toole and of Vincent Ying, who was appointed dean of the Academy of Chinese Studies. Meanwhile, the academy took on another name *MacManus Academy of Chinese Studies* because of the financial support of Mr. Theodore MacManus who endowed $100,000 to secure the best professors for this school. The curriculum was designed and the faculty was secured with four prominent professors. These will be discussed in detail in chapter five. The school was officially opened to the public on October 1, 1925 with some students.

The Name of the University

Two names, Gong Jiao and Fu Ren, were used for this Catholic university. Gong Jiao was used in the sixteen century by the first group of Jesuits. Fu Ren, however, has rich meaning in the Chinese culture as I have explained in the first endnote in chapter one. A name itself in the traditional Chinese culture is very important. A particular chosen name contains rich and deep meanings. Traditionally thought, a name could bring good fortune and bad fortune as well. A name also could symbolize or predict a person's or an institution's future. The Chinese people had this thought before, and it is still exists in people's minds presently. It happened in the same way to the founders when the Catholic university was about to be established. It also took a while for them to select a good and authentic name to symbolize the future and the nature of the university. It took two different stages to finalize the name Fu Ren and to make this name known in China and in the Catholic world. Fu Ren actually brought tradition and cultures together. The tradition was the Jesuits' mission in China and the cultures were the cultures of the West and the East.

Tradition is continued in the process of selecting the name for this Catholic university in Beijing. The Jesuits' mission in China was revisited. This new foundation at Beijing by the Benedictines was precious in their

Establishment of Fu Ren University

hearts, and especially held dear by the chancellor, Archabbot Aurelius. He tried to select an adequate name for the new university. He was influenced by two considerations:

> The first of these was that, in referring to the Benedictine institute of studies at Peking, the documents of the Holy See invariably used this expression. The second was that this name embodies the ideal of universal brotherhood in contrast to nationalism, separatism, or particularism of any sort.[43]

In fact, this was what Rome desired that it should be the keynote of the whole undertaking. Cardinal Rossum expressed this clearly, "the Benedictine Fathers from America to the inhabitants of China, it will once more be made manifest that the Catholic Church knows no territorial or national limits, and is universal not only in name but in very truth."[44] Therefore the Benedictines determined not only associate themselves with the Europeans but also with members of secular priests and of other religious orders, as well as prominent Chinese littérateurs and scholars so that the university would be true to its name as an universal entity.

After inquiring Mr. Vincent Ying, the great Chinese littérateur and the dean of the MacManus Academy, the first Chinese name *Gong Jiao Da Xue* was chosen for the university. It could first convey as precisely as possible the meaning of the Catholic University and also contained the meanings of non-nationalistic, non-separation of any sort. In fact, the name *Gong Jiao* (Universal Religion) was first used by the Jesuits in the Ming Dynasty when they first came to China successfully and was widely accepted by the emperor and Chinese intellectuals.[45] It was also a continuation of the manifestation of the enculturation of the great Jesuit missionaries in China who were respected by the Chinese intellectuals. After many centuries in which the Catholic Church stayed away from the intellectuals, Vincent Ying brought back the tradition of the Church in China to be associated with intellectuals as well. Secondly, this name was acceptable in Beijing because all the colleges and universities took only two Chinese characters as their names. Since this name connotes the religious aspect that caused the university to take another name when the political environment changed in Beijing. This name was Fu Ren which was used for the *academy for Chinese studies* when it came for official registration with the government in 1927.

Cultures of the Western Catholic and Chinese met when the university instituted its first school, the Academy of Chinese studies. Eventually however, when the Catholic university was registered with the government in 1927, its official name became Fu Ren University, which began its official competition with others. The government did not want the university's name to indicate any religion of any kind. Therefore, the name *Gong Jiao* had to be removed. Logically, Fu Ren was most acceptable by all.

Fu Ren was carefully chosen and used many years ago in 1913 when Vincent Ying set up his own school for Catholic youth in Beijing. This name became more significant in 1927. It connected every aspect of the university. Because of the steady deterioration of the intellectual and moral life of the nation, Vincent Ying wrote this:

> 'In the fact of this sad state of affairs, I early felt it my duty as a Catholic to perform my part, however insignificant, towards bringing about the regeneration of China...
>
> '...to develop a group of Catholic young men, who would be as cultured and well-educated as any other class or circle in China and whose conversation would redound to the glory of Holy Mother Church and to the good of their native country.'[46]

A cultural environment and the intention that Vincent Ying had to train the younger generation to revive Chinese culture had been shown in the founding of this Academy of the new Catholic university. In a Western Benedictine-run university, Chinese culture became the primary object. This certainly could prove the American Cassinese Benedictines' effort of making this university as Chinese as possible.

More importantly, the name *Fu Ren* was taken from the Chinese philosopher *Zeng Zi*'s writing. The true meaning of Fu Ren is 'Through literary studies the man of noble parts enters into communion with his friends and through their friendship his righteousness is safeguarded (*Jun Zi Yi Wen Hui You, Yi You Fu Ren*).'[47] Within this one simply phrase, all the elements of a good human life and human relationships are portrayed. The achievement of human life to be righteous is accomplished as well. The Catholic Church, who cared much about all the aspects of human life and dignity, certainly coincided with the traditional Chinese culture here in the founding of the first school of the Catholic University. The name *Fu Ren* itself bore the nature of the Catholic University in Beijing as a center for Chinese and Western Catholic cultural studies.

Location of the University

Location has always been an important factor for any institution in any place and at any time. Mr. Vincent Ying and Mr. Ma Xiang-bo simply knew this well when they suggested that Beijing should be the location for the future Catholic university. They knew well that Beijing was the best place for the university to be effective and influential. The importance of the Catholic university in Beijing could not be overestimated. Beijing was not only the center of Chinese emperors and the new Republic, but also a center for students in China. The following description was reported in April 1921 *Peking News*:

> 'Peking is the national student center; two-thirds of the national government higher institutions are in Peking...a large number of the most impor-

Establishment of Fu Ren University

tant educational institutions in China are in Peking. The National University, the National Customs College, the Higher Normal Colleges, the Colleges for training officers of the Army..."[48]

By the year of 1925, there were already many universities and colleges in Beijing, among which there were six privately controlled ones besides the government-controlled ones.[49] There were totally about thirteen higher education institutions in Beijing. All of them were well endowed and operated. The competition and challenges that the future Catholic university had to face were certainly self-evident.

The Catholic university indeed took the best location in Beijing in comparing with all other institutions. For those who know the setup of the old capital, Beijing, know that the city was circular and divided by ranks in the Imperial Court. The center was the famous Forbidden City for the Emperor and his family; the next was the Imperial City, for the high-ranking officials. The third was the Tartar City where Catholic Fu Ren University located. Dom Callistus Sthele's description of this city was rather detailed:

> 'Its walls more than thirteen miles in length, are the pride of Peking. It was the home first of Tartar, then of the Manchu; the Chinese were excluded—though this exclusion lasted but a short time. Here they engaged in trade and prospered: they are far better merchants than Mongol, Tartar, or Manchu, and the Chinese city is still the great marked-place. Designed to house races of successive conquerors, contains most of the important places of historic interest in Peking.'[50]

Fu Ren, located almost in the center of the Tartar City, was close to the most important places of interests. Everything was within walking distance from the university. This location became very attractive to students when the university opened to the public because all other institutions were located on the outskirts of Beijing. The commute was certainly very convenient for Fu Ren students and for the faculty as well. Moreover, the concept that a beautiful traditional Chinese style palace of the prince could become the Catholic university campus was certainly a plus to the development of the university. The Benedictine Fathers certainly preserved, renovated and developed the university within the original characteristics of the palace. Future development also followed the original style. This great location also helped to make the university known later during the political movements when other university students had to go to the front of the Forbidden City to demonstrate. They had to go by the front of Fu Ren University.

Purpose or Mission of the University

Just as that every institution has its mission statement, the Catholic University in Beijing was no exception. Its mission became clear long before it was established because the petition letter from the two Chinese Catholic scholars expressed very clearly and precisely. Its university magazine *Bulletin* reported this rather explicitly in an article entitled *A General Prospect of the Institution*. Of which I also mentioned previously in Chapter One of which is worthwhile to demonstrate again:

> 'The aim of the founders of the Catholic University (Peiking Kung Jiao Da Xue) is to supply the demand of a large group of the younger Chinese for higher education under Christian auspices. The university, as planned, is not intended to be primarily a professional school, but rather is intended to lay special emphasis on general culture and learning, which seems to be most needed in China at the present time.'[51]

This mission statement opened the horizons of the Catholic university. It made clear the nature of the Catholic university to be Western and Chinese. The university would not only educate the Catholic youth, but would also educate all those who wanted to be educated under the Catholic auspices. More importantly, the mission statement pointed out the signs of time and cultural development. The Catholic university intended to provide what China needed the most as time went on: the revitalization of the culture and scientific knowledge.

The purpose of establishing the Catholic university was once again emphasized in the Vincent Ying's Exhortation to Study, which was widely circulated among the bishops in China and the Pope in Rome. In that letter, he became more specific on the issues that he really concerned about the Catholic Church in China. As a Catholic and a Chinese scholar, he cared very much about the future of the Church in China, somehow exceeded most of the missionaries. He attacked the obscurantism of some of the Catholic missionaries and urged the Chinese native clergy to study their own language and literature more in order to make the Catholic respected and well-rooted in China.

> 'Although the means of propagating religion are various, in order to convince its followers, in sure its existence, and reach the far corners of the earth, literature is the most important factor involved. During the last several decades in order to combat the evil practices which are still propagated by our country's churches I have urged repeatedly that we give serious thought to the reading of books and the promotion of learning until my voice was broken.'[52]

His enthusiasm for the promotion of learning for the Chinese youth and his concern for the Catholic Church, coincide with the petition letter to the Pope in 1912. He insisted and emphasized the tradition of the Catholic Church and cultures of both West and East that was exemplified in the life of Fu Ren University. Though Vincent Ying could not live long to see the growth of the university because he died at the beginning of 1926, the university developed in light of that mission. Its faculty and curriculum development, as well as the students enrollment at the university demonstrated this mission well throughout its 27 years of existence.

Conclusion

The joint petition *Letter to Pope Pius X* from Vincent Ying and Ma Xiang-bo in 1912 and the *Exhortation to Studies* of Vincent Ying in 1917 attracted the attention and interest of Rome and the American Cassinese-Benedictine Fathers. These two Chinese scholars rekindled the Catholic Church's apostolic zeal in China. The Church reacted eventually at the requests from China by taking interest in the future project of establishing a Catholic university in Beijing. The Popes of the Catholic Church were interested; the Congregation of the Propaganda of Faith was enthusiastic; the American Benedictines were excited, yet concerned; the two Chinese Catholic laymen were patient and looking forward to the coming of the good news. It became reality when Fu Ren University was established in 1925.

Those twelve years of waiting and discussing were actually a time of thinking, exploring and maturing the ideas of establishing such a university in China. Those years were not wasted. The Congregation of the American Benedictines understood more clearly what really laid ahead of them if they had accepted the task. These years strengthened their commitments as a religious community to the Church and to the cultures of different countries where they served. They came to understand their responsibilities in China. Rome, however, became more realistic with China.

First of all, the effort should have been made to "preserve and Christianize Chinese literature, art, and philosophy. This means that we must place before the eyes of the Chinese people an ideal exemplar of truly Christian civilization."[53]

Secondly, there were many reasons for starting with this school in Beijing. It sufficed, however, that the Sacred Congregation of the Propaganda looked upon the foundation of such a school of Chinese Studies as the most important phase of the work which it requested them to undertake in China—"t is the most intense desire of this Sacred Congregation that the Order of St. Benedict, which during the Middle Ages saved Latin and Greek literature...should found an institute of higher Chinese studies in the city of Peking."[54]

Thirdly, the severe competition in Beijing needed to be faced. "The educational competition at Peking is very keen. Not to speak of the greater institutions such as the National University, the Peking Union Medical College, the Yen Ching (Yanjing) or Methodist University, and the Tsing Hua (Qinghua) College, there are at least ten other universities and colleges in the city of Peking whose annual income is not less than $100,000 per annum. In the face of such competitions, it would be better not to enter the field at all than to put up an inferior institution incapable of upholding the prestige of the church."[55]

The American Benedictine Fathers measured almost everything whether in China or in the Church. They committed themselves to make the university a first-rate university in China. They understood well their abilities to achieve, and what China needed the most at that time. In fact, the university had been given a national Chinese character through the establishment of the school of Chinese Studies.[56] The Preparatory Academy of this school was already in operation by 1925.

More importantly, the reason why the American Benedictines were chosen, rather than any other religious orders, by the Holy See to take upon the responsibility was because of the nature of their stability as monks and their wisdom as intellectuals and scholars. They have been known for their ability to preserve and revitalize traditions and cultures. Since early 20th century China was like the Church in the Middle Ages, the culture needed to be revitalized and the tradition needed to be preserved. Because of modern influences, many youth thought the traditional Confucian culture, which had dominated China for centuries, should come to an end. Therefore many New Culture Movements were destroying Chinese culture. Rector O'Toole had details:

> 'To-day a similar danger confronts the ancient culture and civilization of china. Since the fall of the Chinese empire in 1911, there is no conservative force at work to preserve the artistic and literary treasures, which have been accumulating down through those forty centuries of china's interminable past. The day of the scholar is over. The imperial examinations are o more. The weeds are sprouting amid the yellow tiles of the Winter Palace and in the crevices between the marble slabs that pave the vast court of the temple of heaven. China is disrupted by the strife of military governors, victimized by the propaganda of Russian Bolshevism, and exploited by the selfishness of Japan and European powers.'[57]

In reality, we have to understand the efforts the Benedictine Fathers and the university administration had to make when the university was officially opened to the public. Though the destruction of Chinese culture was the work of a few scholars in a short period of time, the process of healing and reconstruction of that same culture could take a long time. It could only be accomplished by patient labor by many scholars over many years. Some new reformers and foreign powers such as the Japanese and the Europeans tainted traditional Chinese culture. As a result, many educated younger generation in the early 20th century decided to abandon and to destroy the culture rather than to rebuild it. The Catholic Church and the Chinese Catholic lay scholars understood the situation in the divided China that military forces from other various countries were working for disintegration in China. However the Catholic Church, especially the Benedictines, could rescue this unfortunate nation from the rapacity of its exploiters and the fanaticism of its reformers. Without her saving influence, Chinese arts and letters are doomed to perish and, with them, the soul, as it were of that mighty and ancient people.[58]

Establishment of Fu Ren University 61

This new Catholic University in Beijing had officially started in 1925 under the name *Gong Jiao Da Xue* while China was still in political turmoil. However its location, its campus, its first school and its administration demonstrated its unique characteristic as both Chinese and Catholic. This good start promised the university a great future and soon it was officially recognized as university status in 1927, which will be discussed in the next chapter. The long establishment process welcomed a great beginning of Fu Ren University and a prosperous future.

CHAPTER FOUR

Finance and Structural Development of the University

Finance and development are closely related in academic institutions. Although Fu Ren University appeared to have had a promising beginning because of the ambitions of the Benedictines and Rome as well, it is necessary to provide a sketch of the university's history so that readers may understand how Fu Ren developed and was financed, as well it's true need to have sufficient flow of money throughout the years.

Though the American Benedictine Fathers were ambitious to make this university in Beijing a first-rate university in China, the economy, political movements and wars made it difficult for the university to develop. The Benedictines gathered enough funds to buy the property in Beijing and to finance the newly established university, which was a good start. Unfortunately, this good start did not guarantee a smooth future development. When unexpected incidents happened in 1929 that were beyond the Church's control, namely the Great Depression in the United States and the Nationalist Government's threat that Fu Ren was going to lose its university status in Beijing because it did not meet the government's requirement, Fu Ren also began to experience the financial difficulties required by the physical expansion and administration reorganization. As a result, the Benedictine Fathers were unable to finance the university any longer, and Fu Ren University had to be transferred to the hands of the Divine Word Fathers at the order of the Holy Father Pius XI in 1933.

Fu Ren University was in deep debt after the Benedictine Fathers finished building the first university building to meet the requirement of the government by adding two more colleges. Finance suddenly became a crucial problem in the life of Fu Ren University. It simply could not fund the expanse of the university. In order to compete with other universities, especially the well-endowed Protestant universities, Fu Ren could not afford to remain in debt for too long. On the contrary, it needed constant flow of cash and a good sized endowment. The Great Depression of 1929 indeed threw the American Benedictines on the edge of merely surviving which affected Fu Ren. Saint Vincent Archabbey could not spare but to borrow money from various places to finance the university. The financial crisis of the Benedictines could paralyze the development of the university if other ways of funding were not sought. Throughout those years prior to his death, Archabbot Aurelius single-handedly worked to raise funds in the United States to finance the university. However his untimely death in February of 1930 actually threw Fu Ren into limbo. No particular Benedictine abbot had the courage to take the responsibility upon himself, though the abbot from Saint John's Abbey tried unsuccessfully. Apparently, the Benedictine ambition of making Fu Ren a first-rate university became financially impossible. In order to keep the university to stay alive, transfer of the administration became inevitable.

This chapter will discuss and analyze the details of how the finances of the university affected the whole life of Fu Ren University, including both the administration and the structural development. The secured property which was the first purchased palace and the endowment from MacManus in 1925 certainly gave the university a good place of habitation and a potential to achieve the original purpose of establishing the university. Right after the establishment and opening of the university, it developed rather quickly. The university was registered with the government two years later in 1927 and became the first private university in the city of Beijing with a recognized university status.[1] Later in 1929 it developed into a university with three schools, according to the government's requirements for higher education institutions.

In 1933, Fu Ren University was transferred to the hands of the Divine Word Fathers because of the financial difficulties the Benedictine Fathers had been experiencing. This new administration was rather successful in developing and expanding the university though the budget was somehow still tight. They managed to erect more buildings and bought more properties to add onto the university until when the Communists took it over in 1950. At this time, Fu Ren University had become a university with six colleges in total: College of Arts and Letters, College of Natural Sciences, College of Education, Women's College, College of Agriculture and Saint Albert College. In addition, there were two middle schools and a primary school with a kindergarten. This development certainly needed the flow of money. The Divine Word Fathers eventually transformed the university into a first-rate university which was highly regarded by Chinese intellectuals.

The university in fact stopped developing when the Communists were about to take over Beijing in the early 1949. When the principle of the Catholic Church could not be followed and the autonomy of institution was threatened at the demands of the Beijing Communist Government, the rector of Fu Ren University refused to finance the university. He was arrested and thrown into prison for four years before his early release. Fu Ren became the first private university to be taken over by the Communist

Finance and Structural Development of the University 65

government in 1951. The university was eventually dissolved in 1952 when the government reorganized the universities nationwide.

Evidently, only with good finances, could the university develop well, yet, it is a difficult issue to discuss. Because of the complexity of the issues that this chapter deals, I first provide an overview of the steady income of the university throughout the years, namely tuition, fees, the interest of first endowment and the subsidy from Rome. Then I discuss in detail other necessary finances and the two administrations: the Benedictine Fathers and the Divine Word Fathers. They will be discussed separately: A) Benedictine Fathers' Era: how they raised money for the university and what they achieved. B) Divine Word Fathers' Era: how they raised money and what they achieved. Finally, a conclusion will be drawn about the nature of this development and about the third era of Fu Ren University, which was the Communist's era.

Overview of Steady Income

In the beginning, it was the general understanding that the congregation of the American-Cassinese Benedictines would finance the university in Beijing. They agreed to establish and to finance the Catholic university in Beijing at the request of the Holy Father who would provide a certain amount of money to subsidize the university annually. During the twenty-first General Chapter of their congregation in 1923, all of the abbots of this congregation agreed with the proposal to select Saint Vincent Archabbey to assume the principle role in carrying out the wishes of the Holy Father. The other abbeys would provide the moral and physical support, which I have discussed in the previous chapter. Therefore, the money for the university in general came from all the abbeys of the American-Cassinese Congregation and from the Holy Father, as well as from the students' low tuitions and fees.

When Fu Ren was first established, there were only two dozen students and a handful of professors. The university had enough money to cover all of the expenses then. It was financially sound. According to Mr. Vincent Ying, dean of the school, the students' tuition, board, and lodging should be free of charge, except a nominal charge of $7.00 per year.[2] This indeed lasted for a while. Later, the situation in China changed which caused the university to reassess the situation. The wars caused increases in the price to purchase things and other expenses of all sorts. Things became more expensive to buy and to maintain, especially after the Japanese surrendered in 1945. Inflation was extremely high in the nation (I will discuss later). Therefore, the university decided to increase the monetary charges in accordance with other private schools. The list of all the items were as following: Tuition: $35.00 per year; Miscellaneous needs: $6.00; Lodging: $20.00 per semester.[3] The total income from each student was only $81.00 per year. This rate was constant almost until the end when the university was taken out of the control of the Divine Word Fathers. No archival material have I found to mention the total amount of the student tuitions and fees in general. It is not my interest to speculate whether the student tuitions and fees would be adequate to cover certain expanses of the university. One attempt was made to raise the student fees by the university administration but failed because of some political movement in Beijing, which caused Fu Ren students to protest. It was in the late 1940s, when the inflation got too high, the university decided to raise fees for heating in the winter, the student organized a strike on campus to protest. More details will be discussed in chapter seven when I discuss the politics. As a result of the student strike, that decision had to be reversed. During the course of the development of the university, of course, the laboratory fees were added on accordingly.

The specific yearly budget for the university was difficult to find but one available record in the Benedictine era during the fiscal year 1929–1930 which will be specified. The expenditures of the university certainly could be met except for the new building that cost Benedictines dearly for the immediate expansion of the university. There were only a few professors in the beginning, and their salaries were not high at all. In 1935, however, the Divine Word Fathers provided a specific budget for the fiscal year 1935–36. In a way, it also provided some information on student tuition. From here, we can make some inference about the previous years. Father Joseph Murphy, who was the second rector of the university, reported the budget of 1935:

> 'In a time of such startling need we wonder whence the neat sum of $100,000 gold can be raised to cover the annual current expenses. That is what the Catholic University needs over and above student tuition which, according to American standard. A student in China pays one tenth of what his American brother must pay for a college education, and there are institutions where his training may be just as thorough, and at but one-fiftieth of cost.'[4]

During the Benedictine era, the sources of the regular annual income were: the Holy See provided the amount of $15,000.00[5]; the interest that the MacManus Funds generated was probably around $10,000.00[6] annually. All the rest was variable from time to time and depended on the needs of the university and fundraisers from those two sponsoring orders, of which cannot be generalized in one or two sentences. I will specify each one of them accordingly.

When the Society of Divine Word took over the university, the Benedictine Fathers withdrew their financial support for the university while the Holy See continued to contribute $15,000.00 annually. The rest of the budget depended on the Society of Divine Word Fathers to take care of. Tuition was increased. Yet it was still minimal in comparison with the cost. It did not appear that the Divine Word Fathers had much difficulty in raising money for the university.

Nowhere in the archives could I find any references on the financial supports from China, therefore, it is impossible to know how the Catholic Church in China supported the university. Most of the financial statements mentioned the major resources from Rome and the United States. Fu Ren University was located in Beijing to educate the Chinese students mostly, but no record had been kept that the Catholic Church in China or any other places in China that helped to finance the university. The conclusion could be that the university never sought money from within China.

A. Benedictine Era 1925–1933

Overview of This Period

The Benedictine Fathers established and financed the university for only eight years (1925–1933). Though this administration did not stay very long with the university they helped to establish and to finance, the achievements the Benedictine Fathers made were tremendous. From the beginning in 1925 to the end in 1933, they made the small preparatory school become a qualified and accredited university with three colleges. They bought the palace of Prince Dai Tao, established the Catholic university in 1925 and registered it in 1927 as a university. They also built a new hall in a Chinese style for the university in meeting the requirement from the government to expand. They developed the university into a full-fledged university with three schools for men in 1929 and had one school for women, which was also called Women's College in 1932. This women's college started as a middle school, which became a college in 1936. The fast growth of the university certainly cost the Benedictine Fathers tremendously while the Great Depression in 1929 greatly affected the Benedictine monasteries in the United States. Some of the Benedictine communities even faced bankruptcy. Therefore, the Benedictine Fathers themselves had a hard time maintaining survival. The university needed a steady stream of income from the Benedictine Fathers to keep it in operation. The Benedictines simply could not raise sufficient funds to maintain the university in Beijing after the death of Archabbot Stehle. As a result, the administration of the university had to be transferred to the care of the Divine Word Fathers in 1933 by order of the Holy Father. The following are the details of their efforts.

Benedictine Fathers' Era 1925–1928

As of 1924 when the Benedictine Fathers came to China, they were financially sound. The first purchase was the Ducal Palace and grounds of Prince Dai Tao, who was the uncle of *Xuang Tong*, the deposed living Emperor of China. The property comprised 65 mu (11 acres). The Palace with its garden structures comprised in all 650 Jian (One Jian is a roofed space enclosed by four pillars). It was the creation of the famous architect who built the *Wan Shou Shan Summer Palace* for the late Empress Dowager of China, and was valued, according the conservative estimates, at more than $500,000.00. With the help of a Protestant as I mentioned previously, the Benedictine Fathers only paid $85,000.00 to purchase it. They saved a lot of money in this first purchase.

The usual Chinese walls surrounded the whole palace. It was like a compound with three street gates. The main gate faced south with two others facing East and West. *Fu Ren University Bulletin* has a detailed description of it.[7] Immediately after they took over the property, the Benedictine Fathers started a complete renovation. They converted different parts of the Palace to accommodate the monastery, classrooms, offices and library according to their design of the new Catholic university campus. "Chinese artists were engaged to restore the various structures to their original splendor. The result has exceeded expectations."[8] Though the amount of the expenditure for this renovation was not provided, it is easy to guess that the price was certainly costly because of the beautiful art and the size of the palace which was not kept up well. Since the design of the palace was modeled after the Summer Palace of Beijing, the newly renovated university gave visitors an impression of "never-to-be-forgotten" of the artistic genius of the Chinese people.[9] To have this kind of result, the cost for the renovation was undoubtedly expensive.

With the opening of the first school *Fu Ren She* or *MacManus Academy of Chinese Studies,* the university secured an endowment of $100,000 from Mr. MacManus to hire the best professors for this school in 1925. Prior to this, Saint Vincent Archabbey already had started the process in 1924 to raise money for the university, immediately after two of their monks were sent to China. In a letter addressed to all American Benedictine abbots dated on October 5, 1924, Aurelius Stehle addressed this point clearly, and asked all the monasteries to help build up the university. He had a vision and a proposal for the future Catholic university. In terms of raising funds, he made the following three points,

(1) 'Regarding collections: they can use their influence with the local ordinaries and the local clergies to secure a welcome in the various parishes for such of our representatives as will be sent to preach collections in said parishes, and this will be especially feasible in the case of Benedictine parishes. In fact, one document from the Holy See makes particular mention of the advisability of an appeal to parishes presided over by Benedictine pastors. Nevertheless a general appeal to all dioceses and parishes is authorized, as the enclosed document indicates.

Finance and Structural Development of the University

(2) 'Regarding mission-societies: in parishes, colleges, schools, etc. under Benedictine auspices and otherwise, there are generally mission-societies, whose contributions could not be better utilized than in supporting a project so dear to the heart of the Holy Father as that of the Catholic University at Peking.'

(3) 'Regarding donations: one often meets with individuals both of the laity and of religious communities, who have the desire as well as the means, to do something for the Foreign missions. A timely suggestion given to such persons would induce them to espouse the important cause of furthering the success of the aforesaid university.'[10]

In all efforts to make the Catholic university in Beijing a first-class university, it had to be financially sound. Archabbot Aurelius Stehle knew well the challenging situation in Beijing. In another letter to all the abbots dated on February 22,1926, a year after the founding of the Catholic university, Aurelius Stehle made such references about the challenges they were facing. There were many well-to-do universities in the Beijing area such as "the National University (which is also called Beida), the Peking Union Medical College (called Xiehe), the Yen Ching or Methodist University (which was called Yanda) and the Tsing Hua College (was founded by the American Boxer Indemnity in 1907), there are at least ten other university and colleges in Peking whose annual income is not less than $100,000.00 per year."[11] Obviously, that was not a small amount of money. The chancellor aimed to have such an amount of income for the new university yearly, which would allow the university to compete.

Meanwhile, Aurelius made a report on the financial status of the Catholic university at the moment. This report was a strong encouragement for all who were involved with this missionary work in China. It provided them a great hope of competing with other universities. They had all the reasons to feel that way because they had a successful start. The figures could speak for themselves. He addressed all abbots of the Benedictines about the first year's income of the university,

The Holy Father contributed	$5,000.00
Cash collected	$60,000.00
Contribution of St. Vincent Archabbey	$25,000.00
Annual income from the MacManus Fund	$10,000.00
Pledged for the immediate future	$10,000.00
	Total 110,000.00 Dollars.[12]

This list of income sources is in need of explanation to all parties' credit. The first one was the amount that the Holy Father pledged to the university. The second one, "Cash collected," came from the parishes that the Benedictines Fathers served and the mission parishes that liked to contribute. The last one "pledged for the immediate future" came mostly from the other monasteries and some bishops who were mission-oriented. Certainly the remaining two accounts are obvious and need no explanation.

For a startup university as small as this one was, this amount of money was more than sufficient. In fact, this amount of money could put the university right on top of the money list in Beijing. This amount of money surpassed all other universities at the moment in terms of their sizes of students and faculty. In addition, two more sources had not been included in the list: the annual contribution $15,000.00 from the Holy Father and the endowment from Mr. MacManus. Yet, no matter how much money was there for the university, it would never be enough to run and expand the university, especially in the city of Beijing where there were many great universities. The archabbot continued to plead for financial assistance. "It was more than sufficient to cover the purchase-price of the property. Our expenses, however, for improvements, equipment, etc., etc. have been rather heavy. Hence we shall be very glad to receive any financial aid which the other abbeys of the American-Cassinese Congregation may find it possible to give."[13]

The university was established and prominent professors were hired to be on the faculty of the Catholic University. The university developed and student enrollment increased in the following two years.

In 1927, after two years of development, the Catholic university preparatory school *Fu Ren She* or the *MacManus Academy of Chinese Studies* was officially recognized and registered with the Beijing Government as *Gong Jiao*[14] *Da Xue* (Catholic University). This registration with the government made this Catholic university the first registered private university in the city of Beijing (Yan Jing was in the outskirt of the city). The Chinese government also recognized degrees from this Catholic university, making it marketable and as valuable as the degrees granted from all other national universities. The result of this registration with the government was fruitful in a long run, especially when the Second World War broke out in China. Father Ildephonse Brandsetter wrote that with the official government recognition, applications for admission were "pouring in" rather lively, and over 250 applications had now been received...[15]

Being able to be recognized by the government certainly boosted the university. For the future development, the administration wanted to expand by securing more property. Their eyes lay on another palace, *Gong Wang Fu*, which was just next to the university property. Though they did not succeed in purchasing the property because of political problems,[16] they were certainly ready for the expansion and they had enough money to do that then.

On December 10th, 1927, Abbot Aurelius showed his enthusiasm in his letter to his fellow abbots and to the Benedictine communities,

> 'You will be gratified to learn that we have acquired the excellent property adjoining our original holdings. It is the famous Kung Wang Fu, contain-

ing sixteen acres with buildings suitable for our educational purposes. The purchase of the entire property was rendered possible by the generosity of the Missionary Association of Catholic Women, Milwaukee, Wis., whose president, the most reverend Sebastian Messmer, is a member of our advisory board of the Catholic University of Peking. The missionary association of Catholic women has agreed to raise one hundred thousand ($100,000.00) dollars to establish an American Catholic women's Memorial for the Catholic University of Peking.'[17]

Benedictine Fathers' Era 1929–1933

Unfortunately, the external economic and political reasons caused the sound university finance came short. The Benedictine Fathers began to experience financial troubles when the university was required to reorganize by the Nationalist Government and the Great Depression (which caused disasters in the U.S.) came together. According to the budget record from the archive in Beijing, the university had the following savings during the 1929–1930 academic year, itemized as:

Savings:	92,665.51 Yuan
Interest from MacManus funds	14,857 Yuan
Holy Fathers' subsidy	3,9212.52 Yuan
Benedictine Fathers	138,001.91 Yuan
Total:	284,746.94 Yuan[18]

The budget of the university for the academic year was 102,886.52 Yuan. Even without any income that year, the university could still have 181,860.38 Yuan in the bank, which would sustain the university. At this point, Fu Ren was still financially viable.

In order to build the new building to meet the expansion required by the government, they did not want to touch funds that were already at Fu Ren, but to raise them from the States. Archabbot Aurelius decisively approved the proposal for the building. They began to borrow money in the States, despite the fact of the Great Depression. This was the period when the Benedictine Fathers had to meet the challenges and frustrations caused by the finances. The building was completed in 1930, but the debt was deep for the Benedictines which beyond their ability to pay off. Eventually, for the sake of the university, they had to give up their administration, as well as the property they purchased and built. They could not overcome the financial hurtle that was put before them in 1933. Their mission in China came to an end.

In reality, the great ambitions of the Benedictine administrators faced two enormous challenges in the year 1929 and another one in 1930. The first challenge was from the Chinese Nanjing Government, which threatened the university by canceling its official registration if the university had not complied with the new educational policy. The government required all universities to have at least three schools, otherwise, those so-called universities would be demoted to colleges or independent schools. Such demotion was considered as less prestigious. In order to keep its status, Fu Ren University had to expand either through building or buying properties. Two more colleges had to be added before the university lost its status as a university. The second challenge was that the Great Depression in the United States paralyzed almost the whole country and affected the rest of the world. This especially affected the Catholic university in China because the money to maintain and to develop the university came from the United States. In 1930, the sudden death of Aurelius Stehle, the archabbot and chancellor of the university, brought more troubles to the university. He was the one who tried to raise sufficient money single-handedly for the Catholic University in Beijing. Some private letters speculated that his death was because of the tireless work for Fu Ren. Financing the university since then became a tremendous burden for the American Benedictine Fathers.

This policy from the Nanjing Nationalist Government had already issued in 1928. It was not immediately enforced in Beijing simply because that Beijing was still under the Warlord Zhang Zuo-lin. He was still powerful enough that the nationalist policy could not be implemented there. When this warlord left Beijing and died in June of 1928, it was then Beijing officially came under the control of the Nationalist Government and its policy began to take effect in Beijing.

On January 16, 1929, the Educational Administration Bureau of the Beijing University District transmitted to Fu Ren University a general order from the newly established Ministry of Education at Nanjing insisting upon the compliance. Two articles from government requirements for universities needed to be discussed here because these two threatened the status of Fu Ren University and caused the rapid expansion of it.

> Article (4): A university (tahsüeh or Da Xue) shall be divided into colleges (yüan),v.g. College of Arts, College of Science, College of Law, College of Medicine, College of Pharmacy....

> Article (5): Only those institutions that have a college of Arts and a college of Science, together with a third College, may be called university. Those institutions that comprise but one school, or even if more than two, schools not in conformity with the programs outlined in article (4), must be called colleges...[19]

Without complying with these articles, Fu Ren University would be demoted to a college, because it had only one school. In order to keep their status, the university had to expand. Therefore, the administration reacted quickly to work out the details for improvement, including quickly adding two more schools. A Benedictine priest, Father Dom Adelbert Gresnigt had already put in place a design for the New Hall[20] in March of 1929. Although the university officials did intend to expand, even before the order from the government came, the university was not prepared to adapt to the new requirement because it came suddenly and at a bad time. On the other hand, the sudden order from the Ministry only sped up the expansion process despite the terrible time for the Benedictines.

On July 2, 1929, the rector of Fu Ren University, Dr. O'Toole and the university authorities held a conference to budget the amount required for erection of the New Hall. Chancellor Archabbot Aurelius Stehle approved this proposal to build this New Hall for the expansion of the new schools' classrooms, laboratories, expanding library, etc. The faculty also reacted rather quickly to work out its new curriculum, which will be discussed in chapter five and therefore, persuaded the ministry not to demote the university at the present time. The hard work by the administration helped to keep the status of the university so that the following semester would not be affected at all. When the university opened in the fall semester of 1929, the preparatory school was eliminated and changed to a middle school (Junior and Senior) and a full-fledged university as required by the government.

When the new blueprint was approved by the university administration, a general contract with a construction company had been signed in August under the supervision of Dom Adelbert Gresnigt, the designer. His Excellency, Archbishop Celso Costantini on November 13, 1929, solemnly laid the corner stone. The construction of the whole building only took one year to complete. By November 1, 1930, the work of the New Hall had completed and the contractor on that date formally turned over the completed building to the university authorities. Though cost of this building was not reported, the debt the Benedictines had to pay later could tell us something. The Divine Word Fathers refused to inherit the heavy debt and the Benedictine Fathers did not want to pay either because of the transfer. After Rome's intervention, eventually, by the year1940, the Benedictines, along with the help from others, finally paid the debt of the amount $304,956 in total which did not include Archbishop Spellman's payment. They worked out the deal to pay for it. I specify as the following:

> Archbishop Strich from Mueller Germany paid $150,000; Propagation of Faith paid $100,000; Archbishop Spellman from New York paid the rest (the total unknown). All the Benedictine Abbeys contributed as following: Saint John's $15,000; Saint Bede's $4,000; Assumption Abbey $2,500; Saint Mary's $5,000; Saint Benedict's $9,500; Saint Gregory $2,700; Saint Procopius $6,600; Saint Bernard's $5,000; Saint Martin $4,156.62; Saint Andrew's $500. [21]

After completing this project to expand the university, the Benedictine Fathers never had an easy time of raising funds for the university. They were heavily in debt, yet, they managed to develop the university in the meantime. In 1931, the University Press Department became the most modern one in Beijing by installing a "three linotypes, handset facilities, huge Miehle press and other equipments." It was the only commercial printing house that used linotypes as well as handset processes In China[22]. Also through the help of the Benedictine Sisters, they established the Women's College in 1932. The untimely death of the chancellor in 1930 was also a factor for the future debt and transfer of the administration of the university. Colman Barry, another Benedictine wrote,

> Archabbot Aurelius, Dr. O'Toole, and the Chancellor, Father Francis Clougherty, O.S.B., exhausted every energy in the cause, and Archabbot Aurelius proceeded to borrow money to preserve the institution. His untimely death on 12 Feb. 1930 brought the whole issue to a head. For in his enthusiasm Stehle had been carrying the whole issue to a head. For in his enthusiasm Stehle had been carrying the burden of the university almost alone among American Benedictines.[23]

The tremendous work Aurelius had done to the university really showed itself after his death. His really dedicated himself to finance the university so that it would be financially sound. Hugh Wilt summarized the whole situation in 1966,

> "In July of 1929 the Chinese government again took the lead by forcing the fuller development of the university. Under a threat of canceling its official registration Fu Ren had to expand rapidly to three fully developed colleges with all the necessary faculty and equipment. This threw a sudden burden on Archabbot Aurelius who had to obtain an expanded force of men and immediate funds to build. In the process of obtaining the needed support and financial assistance abbot Aurelius died rather suddenly on Feb. 12, 1930. His untimely death, coupled with the Great Depression years in the United States, made the early 1930's very difficult for the university but the growth and fuller development of the Fu Ren University did not suffer."[24]

Another Benedictine Father who worked in China had similar words:

"Naturally, the immediate effect of the Great Depression was felt keenly in China. The Program of studies and the expansion of facilities was not stopped nor seriously curtailed. In the field of planning fro the future, however, the effects were immediately felt. The sustaining body of the project—the American Cassinese Benedictines could not give the Holy See at the time a written guarantee of an annual sum deemed necessary for the maintenance of the undertaking."[25]

The university was in terrible need of money. One monk, Columban, expressed his feelings in a letter, 'we here are most anxious that our chancellor should be a man with only the world of chancellor. Edmund, we really need millions and need them now. China needs the Catholic University, needs it badly.'[26] Later, in another letter, another monk mentioned the desperate need of funds, "The government requested that we establish a department of athletics and physical hygiene but we are unable to do so at present. The department of pharmacology was also requested by Nanjing but we are unable to do so for lack of funds."[27] Another monk felt even helpless in knowing the situation, he said this in one letter, "I must confess that after reading your letters, viewing the pictures, and listening to Sylvester's Lecture, I was completely carried away. I was almost tempted to go out and rob a bank in order to secure funds with which to take care of some of your expenses."[28]

The United States was basically the only source of income for Fu Ren University. And Archabbot Aurelius Stehle was the only person in the United States who managed to get them money. The 1929 Great Depression caused most of the American Catholics to tie up their pockets. They, as well as the Benedictines, lost almost all their investments. Many abbeys were either in danger of closing or thinking to file bankruptcy. As a community at this point, they were trying to help each other to survive. The most important point was that Archabbot Aurelius did not ask other Benedictines to work together to form a committee for Fu Ren University. Fu Ren became his personal cause rather than the congregations'. After his death, his successor did not want to continue and all of the abbots had tried a little but could not do it.

The Holy Father did not want the university to be closed after only a short few years of operation. Therefore, he declared on 28 July 1932 that the support of the university should be an all-American Benedictine affair of both the Swiss American and American Cassinese Congregations. Barry said that the Swiss abbeys maintained that they had never been approached directly or officially by Rome and the other abbeys could not afford to add another burden during the hard times of the 1930s.[29]

Rome realized the financial crisis of the United States, as well as the Benedictine Fathers' troubles during those years. The Holy See commissioned Cardinal Rossum, the head of the Propagation of the Faith tried to encourage the American hierarchy and the Benedictine Fathers to cooperate under that economic crisis and even pointed out the direction for them to work. In the letter to the American hierarchy in 1931, Cardinal Van Rossum said,

> 'The work that the Benedictine Fathers do in China is a work of capital importance for all the missions in China; unfortunately, however, the University is passing through a grave crisis at the present time, due to the lack of adequate funds...
>
> 'Two particular ways in which the members of the American Hierarchy may co-operate in furthering this great and important undertaking:
>
> 1. By favoring as far as possible the efforts of the Benedictine Fathers to collect funds for the University and to form and association of the friends and benefactors of the institution.
>
> 2. By taking into consideration when contributions for the missions are at their disposal, the grave needs of the Catholic University which is very

close to the heart of the Holy Father and which must be saved and maintained at any cost.'30

Another letter from Rome to the abbots in 1932 explained more about the Benedictines' responsibility as the sponsoring congregation for the university,

'... True it is that the economic crisis which prevails everywhere makes the collecting of funds somewhat difficult and at times even arduous, but at the same time brings it about that this collection is really necessary and indispensable, for the very existence of the University depends upon it.

'...Now, if the whole responsibility for the University, which the American-Cassinese Congregation has generously assumed, appear to be rather great when considered in itself, yet it should be light if each one of the fourteen Benedictine Abbeys should annually contribute at least four thousand dollars to the university. No one should consider this sum an excessive burden.'31

According to the figure Rome provided, the sum of money potentially collected from all of the Benedictine abbeys would have been quite large. The Benedictines could contribute at least $56,000 annually, which would have helped the university to remain under their administration. In reality, this sum, plus the Holy Father's subsidy and the interest from the endowment could have put the university in a good financial position. Further, in the same letter, Rome made a suggestion for the Benedictine Fathers to follow:

1) That a special promoter of the University, a man suitable for that kind of work, be appointed in each Abbey; one who would be free from all other duties and charged and thus able to devote himself exclusively to the promotion of this enterprise.

2) There should be a special organization of the students of both primary and secondary schools in charge of the Benedictine Fathers.

3) There should be an association of Friends of the University and additional membership for it should be solicited.

4) The above enterprises will derive special support from the foundation of periodical magazines, either of a popular or scientific character.

5) The circumstances of place and person will suggest to each Abbot other means suitable for the attainment of the purpose intended.32

Though Rome had tried, and still had expectations of the American Benedictines, the abbots really could not live up to it. All the Benedictine abbeys' were basically paralyzed by the great Crash of 1929. The Benedictine Fathers who worked in Beijing knew the situation in the States and were frustrated and almost exhausted everything due to the lack of funds. They could not do anything in China but to plead for help from the U.S. Father Basil begged his own abbot from Saint John's Abbey,

"...Already the Fu Ren enjoys a nation-wide reputation and students from every province, but two, are attending here during this school year.

...We need money very urgently, because already over a month ago the community, at the advice of the Apostolic Delegate, borrowed money to meet the current obligations. It was a question of life and death..."[33]

Abbot Alicus from Saint John's Abbey, Minnesota was rather enthusiastic about this project, even though many of the Benedictines were ready to give up the mission in China. He still had a little hope for this great missionary work in China. He called for another General Chapter meeting to plead for helping Fu Ren financially,

'I have therefore summoned this chapter, to get the sentiment of this community. If the sentiment of the chapter is in favor of our congregation's retaining the university, I shall do all in my power to induce the other abbeys to take the same stand and to set up an organization to raise funds. If the majority of our houses, especially the larger ones are opposed to the project and want it dropped, I suppose we shall, of necessity, to be compelled to join in a petition to the Holy See to relieve us of the task...

'But this development has brought us face to face with a most serious problem—that of financing its maintenance, not to speak of further development.'[34]

Efforts had been made on all parts: Rome, the U.S. hierarchy and the Benedictine abbots, as well as the Fu Ren University rector. They simply could not raise funds to maintain the university. O'Toole, the rector of the university, described the effort as "the work of collecting money has been exacting and tedious. Some of the dioceses had to be visited repeatedly, either because one of the bishops was absent at the first visit or because he had to be reminded of his unpaid pledge. In the process of collection, too, I had to write nearly a thousand personal letters and visited many dioceses."[35] Moreover, there was something subtle happening. Many of Benedictine abbots and monks simply did not want to continue this project anymore. According to the Divine Word Fathers, the monks from Saint Vincent Archabbey did not like the way Aurelius Stehle handled the project from the beginning. Therefore, they elected the new abbot whom they thought would not be like Archabbot Aurelius Stehle. The new abbot in fact, did not disappoint the monks. He became very instrumental in persuading the Divine Word Fathers to take over the university.[36] As a result, for the sake of the survival of Fu Ren University, the Holy Father ordered the Benedictine Fathers to transfer it to the care of the Society of the Divine Word at the end of the academic year of 1933.

More importantly, it is also necessary to mention other changes that the university had to make. First, in 1927, when the university was registering with the Beijing government, one of the requirements was to have a Chinese as university president. Second one was the change of the university name, which should not contain religious meaning. This requirement was for all the privately controlled universities that desired government recognition. He Jian-ming described that when Fu Ren was going to seek the government's recognition, the Education Ministry just issued a decree on private education institutions requiring all private universities to have a certain number of Chinese to be on either faculty or in administration:

> "Up to the year of 1925, none of the Christian universities had a Chinese president. Except the department of Chinese Literature, all other departments had westerners. As the anti-Christian movements and Shou Hui Jiao Yu Quan (Restoration of Educational Rights) progress, the Christian universities should adapt the Chinese style to appoint Chinese as presidents. Except Saint John's University in Shanghai and Beijing Yan Jing University (because of special reasons), can have foreigners as presidents, all others should have Chinese presidents by 1927."[37]

Chen Yun, the dean became a natural candidate at that time because the founder Vincent Ying, who at his deathbed, requested Mr. Chen Yuan to succeed him as the dean. Therefore Yuan was chosen to be the president of the university.[38] In 1929 when the Nanjing Nationalist Government issued the mandate to all the private universities, Fu Ren was not exception. Chen Yuan was officially registered as the president of the reorganized Fu Ren University. As required by the government, the Board of Trustees was also reorganized. Archabbot Aurelius was the Chancellor and Mr. Zhang Huai was selected as the chairman of the board. This board was comprised of prominent scholars and officers of the government. Two positions need to be specified here. One is the Vice-Chancellor and Rector. His duties were: he represented the chancellor in his absence, to the extent of his delegated authority. Besides, he enjoyed all the powers that the constitution assigns to the rector. The other is the president. He looked after the Chinese interests of the university. His function, determined by legislation of the Chinese government, was mostly collateral to those of the rector (the rector's office had no place in the requirements for a Chinese university at the time).[39] In the mind of the government, having a Chinese president was to secure the Chinese nature of the university. Somehow, Fu Ren University made a giant step forward which none of other Christian universities had made in appointing a non-Catholic as its' president. History eventually proved that choosing Chen Yuan as the president was the right decision.

B. Divine Word Fathers' Era 1933–1950

Overview of This Period

In February 1933, Rome invited the Society of the Divine Word to take over Fu Ren University in Beijing. In obedience to the Holy Father, this religious society answered the invitation and began the process of taking

Finance and Structural Development of the University

over the university by the end of the school year. Though the "superiors and treasurers in Techny, Illinois were not exactly enthusiastic over this new responsibility"[40], they continued the project by appointing Father Joseph Murphy as the new rector of the university. Meanwhile, Father Ralph Thyken opened a special university office in Chicago to collect the necessary funds. The new administration of the Divine Word Fathers was rather successful despite the difficult situation in Beijing. They did not only maintain the university, but also developed it into a rather prestigious university, which enjoyed a national reputation in China. The university continued to expand throughout the years with limited, but sufficient funds. Father Murphy, the first Divine Word rector of the university had a new vision for the university:

> 'In the difficulties that brought about the change of the past year, many activities were discontinued for lack of funds. From the moment that the new society took over the charge it decided to do its best to give these activities the attention they were clamoring for. Of these activities the biggest is "Buying". It is the one that hurts most. But a University must buy every year. The library is a glutton that never says "Enough", and the Chemists, physicists, etc., must be up-to-date. Another activity is "Selling". This time we speak of "selling the University" to the public. Or of advertising it.'[41]

In fact, this was the action Fu Ren took during the Divine Word Father's Era and they kept doing it until the end of the university's time. Later, though the Sino-Japanese War (1937–1945) and the Civil War (1945–1949) affected the university tremendously, its development continued. The Divine Word Fathers had to adapt to unstable political situations in order to keep the university in operation without too many interruptions.

Finance

Finance of the university basically rested upon the shoulders of Father Ralph. Just as Rome suggested to the Benedictine Fathers years earlier, the Divine Word Fathers tried to fund the university as a whole community in choosing of one particular person or committee to be in charge of the fund raising. They chose Father Ralph as the chief fund-raiser. Overall, Father Ralph spent nearly 50 years engaged in fund raising enterprises and financial problems of the Divine Word Father institutions throughout the Orient and in the United States.

> 'In 1933, he became the national director of finance for the Catholic University of Peking to Divine Word Father. Pope Pius XI requested the missionary congregation to assume direction of the university and that same year Father Ralph was given the responsibility as treasurer for rapidly expanding school in the Far East.'[42]

Father Ralph worked tirelessly for Fu Ren University of Peking until the Communists took it over in 1950. The progress of Fu Ren University was the success of his fund raising ability. He had a variety of ways to raise money that helped university development. I list three of them in the following:

First, he formed scores of local mission clubs in the Chicago metropolitan area. Many parishes in Chicago and other American cities sponsored the mission apostolate by holding mission exhibits and related fund raising parties to support the educational interests of Society of the Divine Word at universities as the international fund raiser for the foreign missions.[43]

Secondly, he edited *Christian Family and Our Missions* Magazine that was sent to all of the benefactors to solicit money. This magazine informed the readers of the events happening in Fu Ren University and at the same time, asked them for financial support for specific projects and buildings.

Thirdly, he and the university adapted the *Friends of the University*, which the Benedictine Fathers had used to raise funds. They kept informing and asking those benefactors of Fu Ren University who were considered as friends:

What can your dollars do? If you give: [44]

$1 you will be enrolled in an entire year's membership of the Dollar-a-year Club...or you will support a missionary teaching at the Catholic University for one day...

$3 you will contribute an ideal amount towards the annual tuition fees of one native student at Fu Ren...or you will buy his textbooks for one year in one course...

$5 you will pay for one preparation of vaccine against the dreaded "spotted typhus" evil, the plague of mission work in the Far East. Five Dollars will save one life!

$10 you will support an entire refugee family (father, mother and child) for one month.

$50 you will pay for a greatly needed piece of new equipment in the physics Laboratory.

$100 you will pay for one of the altars, to be erected in the Chinese Clerical College, where native priests will daily celebrate the Supreme Sacrifice.

$1000 you will endow a Chair, to be erected in your name for an educational purpose to be specified by you, after consultation with us.

All these employed techniques to raise fund for Fu Ren University were successful throughout the years and therefore, enabled the administration in Beijing to maintain and to develop the university so that the Catholic Church would compete with other institutions.

Structural Development

With sufficient money coming from the U.S., the expansion of the university became possible and the ability to compete with others increased. In 1934, Fu Ren University added another new dormitory for the increased student population. It was named Murphy hall, which was after the first Divine Word rector Father Murphy. In 1935, the university expanded by adding more classrooms for the Chemistry and Physics Departments. In 1937, just before the Sino-Japanese War started, Fu Ren completed the Benedictine Fathers' wish to purchase *Gong Wang Fu* (Gong Wang Palace). This sixteen-acre palace enabled the university to do great things. The president of the university was very proud of this and his reactions were described in a year review address,

> 'Fittingly enough, the President Honorable Chen Yuan, in the initial discourse, summoned up the manifold progress of the past academic year, emphasizing the expansive possibilities gained by the university in the purchase of an adjoining estate (*Gong Wang Fu*). Thru this, Fu Ren is gaining a new Microbiology institute, more dormitory space for students, at the same time enlarging its campus and garden. Finally, and what is most important, this tract is making possible the Postgraduate Course approved by the Government which enables the University to bestow the Master's Degree in Physics and History on its students.'[45]

More specifically regarding the expansion of the university, it is worthwhile to explore how the Divine Word Fathers were able to "buy" and to "sell" the university as Rector Murphy proposed in 1933 when he first took office. (1) This Palace provided an opportunity to establish another college: the *Collegium Sinicum Ecclesiasticum*, which was also called St. Albert College. In 1940, the university built another magnificent three-story building for this college, all equipped with well-ventilated and well-lighted classrooms, living rooms and laboratories.[46] The purpose of establishing this college was to fulfill another mission of the university to train the native clergy. This special college was established as an annex of Fu Ren University. The object of this foundation was to provide specialized training to Chinese priests who were chosen for teaching work either in schools or seminaries. (2) The grounds of Gong Wang Fu, especially the newly requisitioned northern or garden division of the palace estate, have helped materially in solving the problem of space. The artists of the Department of Fine Arts had been the most fortunate of all here, for they found a beautiful atelier almost ready-made for them on the beautiful grounds.[47] (3) In the year 1941, a fine, modern, two-story science hall was put up, adjoining the university to accommodate laboratory workers on Quantitative and Qualitative Analysis. More storerooms and research rooms were also gained thereby. The new laboratories also have been provided for the Micro-Biological Institute where typhus vaccines are prepared. The students of Biochemistry and higher Quantitative Analysis are also receiving new laboratories, created during the vacation interval.⁴⁸ (4) A great deal of additional dormitory space was also found in the so-called "Pavilion for Observing the Clouds," which was perhaps Peking's longest house. In addition, a fine auditorium for the Women's College was created from the former Shaman Temple on the palace grounds.⁴⁹

In addition to the construction projects in *Gong Wang Fu*, the university had built another additional dormitory in 1940 to meet the increase of the student population, which was 1950 in total. *Christian Family Magazine* described this as such, "The Murphy Hall which was built in 1935 grow two wings". Dormitory service for Fu Ren students had always been an acute problem throughout the years. In the year 1940 especially, this question had become articulate. Every available room was put to use because of the expansion of the university. Therefore, for the reasons of the space, two wings extending to the east would be added and quarters for 192 more students.⁵⁰ Out of necessity and also to make Fu Ren University a complete educational entity, the university added one primary school and a kindergarten in 1943. By now, Fu Ren became the only complete school in Beijing that had graduate schools, undergraduate schools, middles school, primary schools, as well as kindergarten.

Over all, the physical expansion of the university officially ended in the year of 1946 when the university added another school to it, which was the School of Agriculture.⁵¹ Meanwhile, the university purchased a piece of land outside of the city of Beijing, which was called Agronomic Field Stations for the school of Agriculture. Experiments were continually being made, in effort to modernize China's agricultural methods.⁵² Meanwhile, it should not be ignored that besides all the regular schools in the Men's section at Fu Ren, there were some other special institutes need to be mentioned: Microbiology Institute was established in 1937; Geo-Biological Institute was formally opened in Beijing in the university.⁵³ Later in 1947, Saint Thomas Institute was established for Chinese seminarians. Though these additions did not require much structural development, they certainly required necessary instruments and additional faculties members. The administration had to expand because of the needs.

Conclusion

During the years from 1925 to 1946, Fu Ren University developed rather quickly as a whole. Finance was of course, the major factor to its development. It also caused the university to change administrations a couple of times, from the Benedictine Fathers to the Divine Word Fathers and then from the Divine Word Fathers to the Communists' control of the university.

When the Communists began to have influence on the university in late 1948, many professors left the university and went to Taiwan or other countries. The government appointed five professors in the summer of

1950 to be on the faculty to teach Marxist philosophy and Communist theory. They asked the university to pay these professors salaries. The rector, Father Rigney refused such request from the government. Because of interference with the faculty administration, Father Rigney threatened to stop funding the university by October 1, 1950. It was at this time that the president Chen Yuan and some progressive professors decided to ask Beijing government to finance it. On October 1, 1950, the Minister of Education Bureau of Beijing decided to fund the university. Soon after, Fu Ren was taken out of the hands of Divine Word Fathers on October 12, 1950. [54] In May 1951, the president of Fu Ren, Chen Yuan led a group of 500 teachers and all kinds of people to go to the southwest of China to participate in the Land Reform. Fu Ren became almost empty because most of the students from the third and fourth year left the university to participate in the Land Reform movement in the west in March of 1951.[55] The development of Fu Ren was not on the agenda during those years.

Overall, Fu Ren University went through three distinctive administrations in its short twenty-seven years' history: Benedictines, Divine Word and Communist. Every time when the university changed hands, the university had to make some changes. Though the university had to struggle with limited funds and even changing administrations over the years, it did develop into one of the largest universities in Beijing. The student population was the second largest, just behind of Beijing University in the year of 1947.[56] In fact, the actual structure of the Catholic University of Beijing had been modeled on Chinese lines as I discussed above and in previous chapters. *Fu Ren Magazine* confirmed this by saying, "The entire building—just as its entire educational program is intended to be-fits without effort into the background. It is not something alien and aloof. It is a most natural part of the Chinese scene to the students studying there."[57] This was the intention that the founding fathers had when they established this university. This was the effort they had made throughout the years to achieve this. Unfortunately, when the Communists took over the university in 1950, they saw the university completely differently. The government thought the university was a place of American imperialism. They forced the university administration to comply with governmental policies to change its curriculum, together with its administration, and financially supporting the university at the same time. The rector of the university certainly refused to comply because of the uncompromised principles of the Catholic Church against Communism. His resistance led to his arrested in 1951 and was sentenced to 10 years in prison. His early release in 1955 was because of the international pressures imposed on the Chinese government. He returned to the U.S. immediately. In 1951, finance once again showed its importance, which influenced the university administration. The finance from communist government led the university to its closure. During the years from 1950 to the disappearance of the university in 1952, Fu Ren University was basically paralyzed and downsized until other universities divided it. There were not many activities going on but political activities on campus in those two years. This physical structural development leads to the next discussion: the university's inner development: curriculum, faculty and students.

CHAPTER FIVE

Development
Curriculum, Faculty and Student Growth

This chapter is a continuation of chapter four in discussing the development of the Fu Ren University. In the previous chapter, I discussed finance and structural growth of the university throughout the years until the government dissolved the whole university. I have emphasized that the physical developments were in line with the traditional Chinese style: two magnificent and large royal palaces became the property and campus of Fu Ren University, and many additional buildings were erected to meet the needs of the developing university. In this chapter I discuss another crucial aspect of the university, which is, the inner life of the university: the issues concerning who the faculties were and their qualities throughout the years; how the curriculum developed; and the relevant elements about the growth of the students during those years when Fu Ren University was in operation. The faculty was composed of many different members: missionaries, priests and lay professors from different countries. Chinese professors were the majority and were educated in different countries. The curriculum developed from the original pure Western style to a well accepted Chinese one, yet it still looked like a Western one because of the American influence on education in China. These combined issues, in fact, were the core of the university that could explain well the true nature of it as both Western Catholic and Chinese.

Elliot Eisner, professor of education and art at Stanford says well: "Clearly, there are few issues that are more central to the experience that students have in schools than the content of the curriculum and the ways in which it is mediated."[1] This one sentence contains all of the important items I intend to discuss. Due to the complicated issues of the history of Fu Ren University and the relationship between the curriculum and the faculty, it is difficult to state clearly the nature of the university as both Western Catholic and Chinese. Unlike the obvious physical structure of the Fu Ren campus, the curriculum and faculty were subtle. They needed to be compared and contrasted so that the nature of the university could prevail. The development of curriculum was indeed out of the needs of China. The Faculty had many Chinese professors who were educated in the United States or in Europe. The students were coming from all over China. Because of the unique political environment of China, they became more patriotic and nationalistic as time went on. These three aspects are hard to combine, therefore, I discuss them separately and extensively. It is to be noted that the curriculum and faculty, as well as the students as a whole that could make the university. Only together, they can reveal the nature of Fu Ren University. Student growth depended on the vitality of the curriculum and the quality of the professors of the university. I made clear earlier the competitive environment in Beijing when Fu Ren University was established. There were as many as thirteen universities both private and public in Beijing, and all of them were well established and endowed. Without a qualified faculty and a vital curriculum, it was certainly difficult for a university to survive, not even to mention its development.

This chapter is divided into three sections. Section one is on curriculum: how the curriculum was planned and developed throughout years. Its' development certainly revealed its Chinese nature. Some specific years' curriculum will be chosen to compare and contrast in order to see its nature of design and development. Section two is on the faculty: who they were and what they had done in their fields will be discussed sequentially. From these professors' works and contributions, readers will have a sense of the responsibilities they bore upon themselves in an effort to achieve the university's mission. The purpose of doing this is to show an example of their doings for the university. Two specific years will be pointed out at the end of this section to indicate the dramatic changes in the university. Section three discusses the enrollment of the students: who they were and where they were from. Finally, a conclusion is drawn from the discussions from these sections that Fu Ren University developed into a very competitive Chinese Catholic university in the field of higher education.

SECTION I: CURRICULUM

Overview

Curriculum development was a constant changing process during the years that indeed made Fu Ren University both Western Catholic and Chinese. It is good to keep in mind that the curriculum in China was modeled after American and European curricula. Therefore, being Chinese was simply based on the emphasis of the studies. I have discussed that American Protestant colleges and universities influenced Chinese higher education tremendously at the turn of the 20th century. To see the nature of the curriculum development at Fu Ren, we need to look at it from a developmental point of view. Throughout its 27 years history, the university developed from one academy at the beginning, to a university with four colleges[2] with many departments and even graduate studies. Before its demise, Fu Ren had six departments that offered graduate studies. Curriculum development was also an adaptation of urgent needs in China. Its original curriculum was like any Catholic university curriculum in the United States with some emphasis on Chinese studies. When the university was established in 1925, because of its size and faculty, only one academy for Chinese studies was possible. This was from the original proposal of Vincent Ying that the university was to revitalize Chinese culture and to increase the quality of Catholics. Eventually the development and expansion of the curriculum in 1929, as well as the later ones along with this line, were to vitalize the Chinese culture and to introduce western science for the well being of the Chinese youth.

Fu Ren University became known throughout China shortly after its' establishment for a variety of reasons, such as its unique nature to promote Catholic and Chinese cultures, prominent faculty members and the strict discipline on its non-political stance. Only from this developmental point of view to see the designs of the curriculum at different times, can readers easily discover that the curriculum was tailored to the needs of China and the promotion of Chinese culture. As curriculum developed, the faculty expanded as well with a high percentage of Chinese professors that any other private university did not have. The increase of student numbers was more obvious because of its nature as Chinese, their excellence, and the students' eagerness to learn. The three distinctive aspects that are discussed will certainly prove the truthfulness of the nature of the university as both Western Catholic and Chinese.

Original Planned Curriculum

The Benedictine Fathers already had a plan when they decided to answer the call from Rome to establish the Catholic university in Beijing. The plan was rather ambitious and original: The ambition was shown from the Benedictine Fathers' plan to have five schools for the future university. When they first designed this curriculum, they did not know much about the cultural and political situation in China because they were not there physically despite the fact that they intended to establish a Chinese university. The school and curriculum they envisioned were just like any typical Catholic university or any Christian university in the West, with the inclusion of a school of theology. The original design of the curriculum was certainly a starting force behind the efforts the Benedictine Fathers were making. School of Chinese Studies was included in the ambitious curriculum. It is as the following:

Original Planned Curriculum

School of Theology
    Department of Dogmatic Theology
    Department of Moral Theology
    Department of Sacred Scripture
    Department of Church History
    Department of Canon Law
    Department of Liturgy
    Department of Homiletics

School of Philosophy
    Department of Philosophy
    Department of Psychology
    Department of History
    Department of Social Sciences
    Department of Education
    Department of Jurisprudence

School of Chinese Studies
    Department of Chinese Philosophy
    Department of Chinese History
    Department of Chinese Literature
    Department of Chinese Journalism
    Department of Chinese Archaeology

School of Arts and Letters
    Department of Latin
    Department of Greek
    Department of English
    Department of French
    Department of Spanish
    Department of German
    Department of Philology

School of Sciences
    Department of Physics
    Department of Chemistry
    Department of Botany
    Department of Zoology
    Department of Astronomy
    Department of Geology
    Department of Drawing
    Department of Architecture
    Department of Engineering

The Benedictine Fathers in Latrobe, Pennsylvania had a seminary and college of their own. As educators, they knew and had the experience of the educational system in the United States. Their design of the curriculum for the future university in Beijing might well have been influenced by both their previous schools. Besides these five planned schools, the Benedictine Fathers also envisioned having two preparatory schools in addition to the university: (a) the Chinese preparatory school. It was intended for those who wished to enter the School of Chinese Studies, and (b) the general preparatory school. It was intended for those who entered departments outside the school of Chinese studies.[3]

This curriculum resembles the curriculum that the Catholic universities in the United States except for the School of Chinese Studies. The Benedictine Fathers were also limited in their understanding of the right curriculum for China. When the university was first established in 1925 as a small academy, the Benedictine Fathers were indeed ready because they prepared for it. Vincent Ying, the new dean of the academy, designed the new curriculum for it instead of the Benedictine Fathers.

Curriculum of 1925–1926

When the university was officially opened on October 1, 1925, it did not open with five schools at once as planned. Rather, it was only a preparatory school: *Fu Ren She* or *MacManus Academy of Chinese Studies*. Its official name was Catholic University at Beijing, (*Gong Jiao Da Xue*). This school was planned for students to take two years of Chinese studies before they started the college curriculum. These two years should be dedicated totally to Chinese studies. This was a good start for the university and the Church. This plan helped the university in a long run because of the political instability. The subjects of studies in the academy were:

1. Etymological study of Chinese Characters
2. Outline of Chinese Literature
3. Written and oral study of Confucian classics
4. Selected prose works by classical authors
5. Selected poetical works by classical authors
6. General survey of the different schools of philosophy and letters in history together with their representative works
7. General survey of the classical historical works and the method of investigation thereof
8. Historical geography
9. Science of chronology and computation of ancient calendars
10. Science of indexing and classifying Chinese books[4]

No one has cast doubt on the good intentions the Benedictine Fathers had in their efforts to build up this academy for the purpose of revitalizing Chinese classical culture. These subjects also helped the university to register with the government in 1927. One important issue of concern was the politics of the time that could easily target the university. The anti-Christian and anti-Western movements were constantly occurring. Chapter Seven will deal with these political issues specifically.

Curriculum of 1927–1928

This university was inaugurated in 1925 as a preparatory school and developed in size and in quality. It was officially registered with the government as Fu Ren University (Fu Ren Da Xue) in 1927 with only one school, which later became *School of Arts and Letters* with the following departments:

> Department of Preparatory Studies
> Department of Chinese Letters
> Department of History
> Department of English[5]

In the documents that were submitted to Ministry of Education in Beijing, the school officials stated that the above departments were actually functioning, while the others were in process of formation. The Department of Philosophy was planned to open and indeed was added on to the university in the year of 1928.[6] In fact, the first university curriculum earned the praises from government officials when they came to the university to inspect it. The Minister of Education encouraged Fu Ren students and addressed them at a meeting. Meanwhile, he confirmed the efforts the Benedictine Fathers were making to form the university into a real Chinese university with respect with culture and tradition.

> "I urge you all to remember constantly that the students of to-day will be the leaders of tomorrow. Great is your future and great is your responsibility; for the day will come when the salvation and regeneration of China will rest largely with you. Spare no effort to become worthy of your great vocation and to come up to the high expectations of your elders."[7]

Curriculum of 1929–1930

Fu Ren University made many dramatic changes in 1929. When the Nationalist Government established its capital in Nanjing in 1927, they established another Ministry of Education, which required all the universities, no matter private or public, to have at least three colleges in order to keep their universities' status. Chapter four discussed that Fu Ren University in Beijing was still under the governance of the Warlord, Zhang Zuo-lin, who was still powerful in the northern part of China. Therefore, the university was not affected by the order from Nanjing. In fact, the order could not reach Beijing until 1929. After the death of the Warlord, the Nationalist Government could take over the control of Beijing and the mandate from the Education Ministry was soon transmitted to Fu Ren University via Beijing University[8]. On June 24, 1929, Fu Ren finally received Mandate No. 796 from the Education Ministry. As a result, Fu Ren University had to comply with its policy in order to keep its university status. To fulfill the requirements, Fu Ren decided to expand by adding two more schools. The university redesigned its curriculum according to the current situation of China rather than the original one.

When the mandate from the Education Ministry took effect in Beijing, the target was not specifically at Fu Ren University. It appeared to be that way because the other registered universities in Beijing had already had at least three schools and Fu Ren only had one College of Arts and Letters. According to Anthony Li's study of the privately controlled universities, many of these private universities in Beijing met the requirements of the Education Ministry. In this respect, Fu Ren University was rather late to meet the standard, though they had intention of adding more schools eventually.

The mandate to require all the universities to have at least three schools in order to be worthy of a university status was across the board rather than giving troubles to the Catholic university. Fu Ren had to add at least two schools to meet this requirement. Because of the limited time to expand, the rector tried to persuade the Education Ministry not to demote Fu Ren to a college status while they were trying to comply with the policy.[9] He was successful because the university was granted provisional registration during the expanding process. The Nanjing government's regulation on the Constitution of Universities, comprised of a number of articles, stipulated one is particular for Fu Ren to follow. Article 4 reads, "Universities shall be divided into colleges of Arts, Science, Law, Education, Agriculture, Industry, Commerce, and Medicine." Two required schools for all universities in China: School of Arts and Letters and School of Sciences. Since Fu Ren had already had the first school, therefore the second one had to be added along with a third one. It took the university authorities some time to decide on the third school that was appropriate for Fu Ren to have in order to meet the needs in China:

> 'The University authorities had contemplated establishment as the third college (in addition to the existing College of Arts and a proposed College of Science) a School of Social Sciences. The foregoing regulation, however, does not mention such a school among those approved as component colleges of a university... A substituted college was advised. The University authorities decided to chose a College of Education.'[10]

Though there was no reason to have College of Education added to the university, the need to have teachers in China was certainly one of the main reasons. During the first meeting, the rector and the faculty members had decided to add those two more new schools, to revise the existing curriculum and to create a new curriculum for them. In the meantime, they had to find ways to secure scientific equipment for the School of Natural Sciences. Temporary laboratories for chemistry, physics, and biology were made available. More classrooms were added as well. The cost was certainly enormous. The work of drafting the new curriculum, covering hour by hour for the four years of the complete university was proceeding with almost feverish rapidity.[11] The curriculum they drafted was[12]:

School of Arts and Letters
 Department of Chinese Letters
 Department of History
 Department of English
 Department of Philosophy
 Department of Social Sciences

School of Natural Sciences
 Department of Mathematics
 Department of Physics
 Department of Chemistry
 Department of Biology
 Department of Pharmacy

School of Education
 Department of Pedagogy
 Department of Psychology

Based on this carefully designed new curriculum, the Ministry of Education approved Fu Ren University's university status. Eventually, some minor alterations were made to the designed curriculum when the university submitted the final proposal for registration in 1931. In addition, the mandate from the Ministry of Education in 1929 ordered the university to change its preparatory schools to middle schools, to which the university complied when the university expanded. In 1930, both the junior and senior middle schools were opened with appropriate faculty. Many students were enrolled.

Because of the complicated educational situation in China of the time, the Ministry told the university to make some changes to the curriculum in order to meet the government's standard for higher education institutions. When the formal petition was submitted in 1931, the department of pharmacy was dropped from the curriculum. During these two years, progress had already been made. The university added the Department of Fine Arts as an annex to the School of Education.[13] This caught the government's attention. By 1931, the Ministry of Education was very much concerned that the university should foster this branch of study. Later, this department became independent with three years of courses and became famous both in the Church and in the nation. Many of most famous Christian paintings in the Chinese native style came from this department, which will be discussed separately. Its original object of this department was the training of skilled teachers of the Fine Arts for the secondary schools. Eventually, it achieve beyond what planned. In a special way, Chinese Arts received special attention and was incorporated into Christian paintings. Fu Ren was the only private school that had a Fine Arts department in China out of three in total.[14] This was the only one in China that tried to incorporate Western style paintings into Chinese paintings. A three-year course was offered in this institute that embraced four subjects in the beginning:

1. Chinese Calligraphy—which treats of the various Chinese scripts or types of writing.
2. Chinese painting—which includes the Gong Bi or "Palace Brush" style, characterized by bright coloring and fine delineaments, somewhat similar to the English pre-Raphaelite School, and the Cao Bi or "Grass Brush" style, characterized by bold swift strokes, and bearing a comparison with the Impressionist school in France.
3. Principles and elements of Western Arts.
4. The Making of Chinese Seals.[15]

Before the university was turned over to the Divine Word Fathers in 1933, the curriculum was modified and developed. The department of Social Sciences was modified with two sections: Sociology and Economics. The department of Biology was modified with two sections as well: Zoology and Botany. Meanwhile, the department of Pharmacology was dropped, according to government regulations. The departments of Mathematics and Physics were combined into one department. The department of Psychology was expanded with four sections: General Psychology, Educational Psychology, Experimental Psychology and Child Psychology.[16]

The university curriculum at Fu Ren kept expanding in the following years during the Divine Word Fathers' administration. Though the core curriculum did not change much, more departments were added to the curriculum and graduate divisions were opened. The Graduate Division was opened in 1937. First was History, and later, Physics in 1938. Chemistry and Biology were opened in 1942, as well as Ethnology and Economics.

A university that could have a graduate program had a long history before Fu Ren had inaugurated its programs: a symbol of prestige and quality of the university. As early as 1928, the Nationalist Government started to establish the research departments which was only limited to the national universities. In 1929, the government established two research institutes: Central Government Research Institute and Beijing Research Institute. They were the symbols of prestige because only those universities that met the government's requirements were granted the power to grant master's degrees:[17]

(1) The institutions whose annual income exceeds 1,000,000.00 Yuan [18]
(2) Library has great amount of books, laboratories are well-equipped
(3) The professors who are experts in certain fields and certain expertise
(4) The students' qualities have to be well.

In 1930, some universities had started their work to promote research. By 1935, the Nanjing government passed the law to allow the universities to grant masters degrees. In Beijing alone, Beijing University, Qing Hua University, Yan Jing University were all qualified to grant master's degrees in 1935.[19]

Fu Ren president, Chen Yuan also stressed this aspect in 1935 when the university was planning for the next ten years. He said:

'Since I was appointed to succeed him (Vincent Ying) upon his untimely demise, I have endeavored to the best of my competence to promote the realization of his ideals. As a Catholic Institution for higher studies, this University, in my humble opinion, should strive after the following three objects as its immediate and practical tasks: (1) to Systemize the Chinese historical materials by applying in thereto the latest Western methodology. (2) To facilitate the research works of both Chinese and foreign scholars by compiling and translating reference works. (3) To promote international academic cooperation by publishing and circulating abroad the results of the latest finds and discoveries in the field of Sinological studies.'[20]

For the sake of prestige and the capacity to compete with other universities, as well as the intended dissemination of the knowledge, Fu Ren submitted a proposal in 1936 to inquire the establishment of a research institute, which was granted by the Education Ministry in Nanjing in early of 1937. Under the direction of the president Chen Yuan, the history department became the first one at Fu Ren to grant a master's degree at Fu Ren. In terms of the graduate program, Fu Ren was not too far behind of others.

Starting in 1938, students from the Women's College were able to take the same courses as the students from the men's section. It is necessary to make some clarifications at this point because of some confusing information from other researchers. Fu Ren University was not a co-ed institution prior to the Communist takeover in 1950. Men and women had different campus and took courses separately at the university. The Women's College was first established by the Benedictine Sisters in 1932 and was taken over by the Holy Spirit Sisters in 1936. It was a separate section of Fu Ren

University. The reason for this establishment was not specified in the archival materials. However, the situation in Beijing at the time did challenge the university to have such a college. The competing protestant university in Beijing, Yan Jing University had already had Women's College, and the university that established by the Nationalist government also had one women's college. This was far from enough to educate the women in China. In order to meet the needs of China to bring women to a higher level of education and out of their concern for women, probably in competition as well, the Benedictine Fathers decided to invite their own Sisters to educate Chinese women who were ignored for centuries in China. It has been a long tradition in China that women should not be educated. In order to help women, especially those from the well-to-do families in Beijing area to have education, the Benedictine Fathers decided to establish this school. This Women's College certainly had influence on the upper class Chinese who were well educated. Because of the limited space at Fu Ren, the Women's College could not accept too many applicants. No specific numbers of students in the freshman year were provided at the beginning. As the student statistics show later by the year of 1938, there were already 306 women students at the college. They had their own separate special curriculum in addition to the necessary ones from the men's section. Professors from the men's section came to their campus to teach them courses instead of them going out to take courses with men. The reason for this was for financial reasons.

It is worthwhile to mention that the department of Home Economics in School of Education. This was a special department for the Women's College when they were all allowed to take university courses in the men's section in 1939 with the enrollment of only 22 students. All of those women students "came mostly from wealthy homes, since other women hardly attain to a college education, but for the well-to-do Chinese women in the past, and that still hold good for the majority of modern young daughters."[21] These women students had to be treated quite differently because "manual work, especially ordinary house work, is not considered honorable. The 'better class' Chinese lady is neither asked nor allowed to do anything of this sort of work."[22] With these issues in mind, the Sisters designed a special curriculum for this department. It was first installed as a section of the Department of Sociology and Economics. Later in the academic year 1941–42, it became an independent department within the School of Education for the purpose of proper degree. Their senior year courses were the same as for the sociology students, but with their own special ones as following:

Freshman year:
Chinese composition, English, ethics, athletic training as general courses, and general introduction to social and economic origins, world history, hygiene and sanitation, home nursing as special courses.

Sophomore year:
English, logic, general psychology, food selection and preparation, elements of sociology, accounting, general education, bacteriology, and household chemistry.

Junior Year:
Sewing, textile, household technology, home management, art appreciation, interior decoration, and childcare and training. All these courses included practical work. Besides these, there were other subjects as well: educational psychology, secondary education, and philosophy of life.

The reason that the senior year's curriculum of the first woman group was the same as the men's section was "to preserve the necessary unity in the aims and studies, it was considered best to define as the chief purpose of the department the training of teachers of home economics for middle schools granting the Bachelor of Education with the major in home economics."[23]

Saint Albert's College was established in 1938 and was designed for Chinese priests for further studies in various subjects in Chinese literature and sciences. Originally it was started as summer school, and eventually developed and organized as a complete unit that was independent of Fu Ren University. This college had its own location within the *Gong Wan Fu* with a newly erect three-story building. In 1943, however, all priest students were registered as regular students of the university to cut down the cost of the university. They had their own special formational work of their own as a special group, but without their own unique curriculum. They attended lectures at the university[24] with the other students.

In 1946, the College of Agriculture[25] was established with only one department. The university bought a piece of land outside of the city of Beijing for experiments. The students collected data from all over China: South, North, West and East to study the fields. Interestingly enough, these three colleges: Women's College, Saint Albert's College and College of Agriculture were independent and had their own deans. They shared some of other three schools' curriculum, depending on the students' majors. The reason for this was to save the budget. The university could not afford to hire professors for these particular schools.

Curriculum in 1948–1949[26]

Fu Ren University continued to develop during the years, student enrollment continued to increase in number and quality because of the well-developed curriculum at the University. The following curriculum will certainly speak for itself:

College of Arts and Letters
    Department of Chinese Language and Literature
    Department of Western Languages and Literature
    Department of History
    Department of Sociology
    Department of Economics

College of Natural Sciences
    Department of Mathematics
    Department of Physics
    Department of Chemistry
    Department of Biology
    Department of Premedical Training

College of Education
    Department of Education
    Department of Philosophy
    Department of Psychology
    Department of Fine Arts
    Department of Home Economics

College of Agriculture
    Department of Agriculture

Graduate Division
    Department of Ethnology
    Department of History
    Department of Physics
    Department of Chemistry
    Department of Biology
    Department of Economics.

In addition:

Women's College
Saint Albert College

This curriculum developed along the line required by the Nationalist Government in 1929 when Fu Ren had to reorganize. Every single college within Fu Ren University was mentioned in the mandate from the Chinese Education Ministry. In other words, Fu Ren met all the requirements from the government. There was nothing imposed onto Fu Ren university from the US. The missionaries at Fu Ren were to serve China's needs.

Summary

It seems that the curriculum development was quite successful. The last available curriculum shows a typical Chinese curriculum as any other national university had. Of course, the Chinese universities were modeled after the American higher education system and they certainly resembled each other. However, if we compare and contrast the original curriculum before 1925 with the last available one of 1948, the difference is rather noticeable. The previous one is quite Western Catholic in style and the last one is very Chinese in practice. If these two were analyzed in detail, we can see not only the similarities but also the differences. The departments within the School of Arts and Letters changed from all languages to different subjects in Chinese and English. The original School of Arts was modified into one department within the school offering six[27] different languages: Chinese, English, German, French, Japanese, and Italian. The School of Theology was never established because the Chinese government did not allow religion as a mandatory course on the university campuses. However, the plan was eventually fulfilled when Saint Albert College for Chinese priests was established and later, Saint Thomas Institute for Chinese seminarians to study philosophy that was established under the Department of Philosophy. The School of Arts and Letters was definitely well established from the beginning. Those prominent professors, many of whom were recognized in their respective fields solidly staffed the School of Sciences and the School of Education. Besides all of the core courses within the three schools, the university also offered some special electives: Harmony, Musical Composition, Journalism, Sinological Research, Pharmacy, Political Science, History (colonial, geographical, diplomatic), Industrial and Commercial Management.[28]

The various departments' standards ran high as time went on. By the year 1939, the department of Physics became "the most modern kind and the even ranks the best that the average German university can produce."[29] The Department of Economics, along with the Department of Sociology became the most popular ones at the university because of the high enrollment of students and Economics department became one of best in China by 1943.[30] The Department of History became well known in China as well. According to He Jian-ming, many well-known historians in China who were the chairs of the history departments at many famous universities were the graduates of this department at Fu Ren.[31]

The Catholic university was flourishing in China before its demise. The student enrollment over the years kept increasing and the faculty kept expanding in order to meet the expansion of the university. Fu Ren achieved many goals in order to meet the needs in China. Unfortunately, this growth and expansion of the university was forced to stop by the Fall of 1948 when the Chinese Communists came to Beijing. A plan for the proposed College of Medicine (including a hospital), and the College of Engineering was formed but never fulfilled. "The establishment of these two colleges is in agreement with the wishes of the civil and ecclesiastical authorities in China, who recognize the vital necessity of having such colleges part of Catholic University in North China."[32] Evidently, the future of the development of the Fu Ren was still unending on part of the university administration.

SECTION II: FACULTY

Overview

The curriculum development certainly demanded the increased number of faculty members. Fu Ren's development attracted many professors. The outstanding and research-oriented faculty members made Fu Ren become one of the best in China. The characteristics of the faculty represented Fu Ren University well as a Pontifical and a Chinese university.

"Send us learned men, meek and humble of heart, that they may become our leaders; men of diverse nationalities, that Catholicity may be spared the reproach of being the religion of any particular nationality; men of different religious order, in order to do away with all exclusiveness, all jealousy, all party spirit."[33] Vincent Ying and Ma Xiang-bo suggested the Pope do so. It was self-evident, as the nature of the Catholicity revealed, the missionaries who were on the faculties demonstrated the university's character as cosmopolitan and its good qualities.

Since Fu Ren was a Chinese university, the Chinese professors were in the majority on the faculties, and they came from variety of backgrounds. The university hired many prominent professors in China. Most of them were educated in the United States or in Europe. Though the full time professors had always been a minority at the university, its number already had been increasing constantly. This section, therefore, deals with the characteristics, qualities and the statistics of the professors. Since it is hard to discuss the qualities of the all the professors and neither possible to name all of them, I simply specify the first group of professors who were hired by the university to demonstrate the high academic standard of Fu Ren University. The university did not lower its standard but increased as it developed. In the meantime, I highlight some special professors randomly with the purpose of representing the qualities of the faculty.

Characteristics of the Faculty

The characteristics of the faculties can be seen from two distinctive aspects: diversity and cosmopolitan. Diversity was one important characteristic of the faculty throughout the years. The professors at the university were made of a combination of Chinese and non-Chinese: Americans, Europeans, Japanese; a combination of priests and lay people; as well as the

Benedictine Sisters and Holy Spirit Sisters who were in the Women's College. More importantly, on the faculty, there were many non-Catholic members. Some of them eventually held positions either as department chairs or the deans, such as, Luke Chen who was not a Catholic when he became the dean of the School of Christian Arts. Specially to mention the president of Fu Ren University, Chen Yuan, he was also the dean and the history department chair at the beginning. He was not a Catholic when he became the president of the Catholic university. In fact, he never became a Catholic. For political reasons, he eventually joined the Communist Party when he was in his 80s.

Because of his knowledge, Chen Yuan became the dean at the request of Vincent Ying at his own deathbed. Later he became the president of the university in 1929. One simple reason was that Chen Yuan acquainted with Vincent Ying and Ma Xiang-bo. These two scholars praised him for his scholarly work and research on Catholic Church.[34] It is unthinkable even now that a Catholic Pontifical University would have had a non-Catholic president. More unbelievable was that Pope Pius XI honored him with the highest honor of the Church for a lay person: the Commander of the Order of Saint Gregory the Great (with badge).[35] There was no explanation in the archives to state why Chen Yuan was honored by the Pope as a non-Catholic.

Cosmopolitan was another characteristic of the faculty. In the year of 1931, this characteristic had already been prominent during the Benedictine administration. "The cosmopolitan character of the Faculties of the Catholic University of Beijing may be gleaned from the fact that its membership includes sixteen Americans, six Europeans, and forty-Seven Chinese."[36] Later in 1933, after the Divine Word Fathers took over the university, this characteristic became more prominent because of the international characteristic of this society. As an international religious order, the Divine Word Fathers attracted professors from all over the world. At one time in 1948, the faculty members represented ten different nationalities.[37]

Some of the foremost scholars of modern China were on the faculty as professors. Most of these Chinese professors were educated in different countries and were teaching variety of subjects. *Fu Ren University Bulletin* claimed, "In the Chinese department the very best teaching talent that could be found was enlisted to form the staff."[38] A number of them also held academic degrees from well-known universities and colleges in Europe and in the United States,[39] such as, University of Louvain, University of Berlin, University of Munich; John Hopkins, Harvard, Wisconsin, Northwestern, and Michigan. They scholars brought different educational methods to Fu Ren. Surely, some professors graduated from Chinese universities, such as Beijing University and Normal University.

Development: Curriculum, Faculty and Student Growth

Qualifications of the Faculty

The qualifications of the faculty members cannot be discussed individually because, first of all, it is not necessary to do so; secondly, it is impossible to do so because of the large numbers. From the very beginning, Fu Ren was trying to secure the best professors in China to be on the faculty. The first dean, Vincent Ying, wanted this to happen and the president, Chen Yuan continued to do this. Catholic missionaries who came to Fu Ren University to teach were well qualified. Therefore, the best way to discuss the qualities of Fu Ren professors is to divide members into two categories. Though this categorization is not completely accurate for measurement, it is a good way and manageable way to discuss the quality aspect: A) the first faculty of the university and the Chinese faculty members in 1937, as well as the faculty in general. B) Non-Chinese faculty members in general who were on the university throughout the years.

First Faculty and the Chinese Professors in general

The first faculty of Fu Ren University, generally speaking was selected with great care by the dean of the university. These faculty members were well known in China. Their qualifications and their reputations were outstanding which earned the university much respect in the world of Chinese intellectuals. Mr. MacManus' endowment was used simply to secure the good scholars for Fu Ren. These members and their qualifications of the first school of Fu Ren University: *Fu Ren She* or *MacManus Academy for Chinese Studies* are discussed as the following. All these were done according to an archival letter from Saint Vincent Archabbey in Latrobe.[40] They were:

(1) Dean of the Chinese Faculty: Mr. Vincent Ying Lianzhi, a native of Beijing, Essayist, Poet, Calligraphist. He held several minor offices in the government before 1901, when, at the request of the intellectuals of Tianjin, he founded the first Chinese newspaper in North China. Of this paper, which was known as "The Imperial". He became the director and editor-in-chief. The paper won wide popularity by reason of its fearless criticism of the decadent imperial court and the corrupt officials of the day. He inaugurated many movements and reforms. He introduced the use of *Pai Hua*, or the Spoken Language, as a vehicle of literary expression. He established the first modern school for girls and wrote a book against the practice of foot-binding. The first president of the Chinese Republic, Yuan Shih K'ai, offered him a seat in the State Council, but Mr. Ying refused to accept it. He established another free school for poor girls, and *Fu Ren She*, an Academy of Chinese Letters. In 1924, he was offered the post of the Director of Education for the Metropolitan Province, but he declined the offer. He wrote many books, essays and poems. He and Ma Xiang-bo are considered the two foremost Catholic scholars of China.

(2) Extraordinary Lecturer: Mr. Chen Yuan, who later became the dean of the Academy, and eventually, the president of the university. He was a native of Canton, and a specialist in historical research. A member of the Chamber of Deputies, he held various positions in the Ministry of Education and served on practically all of the educational and literary commissions of the government since the foundation of the Republic. For a brief period in 1921, he was the Minister of Education. Recently, when the government confiscated the deposed Emperor's property, Mr. Chen was appointed Director of the Imperial Library. He is also Extraordinary Lecturer at the National University. His historical works are universally acknowledged to be the most valuable contribution to the national histories of China. He succeeded in solving many vexing historical problems that had baffled Chinese historians for many years. Mr. Chen was considered by all to be China's foremost scholar in historical research.

(3) Professor of Chinese Geography: Mr. Chang Wei Xi, a native of Jiang Su province, geographer and archaeologist. He was for many years president of the Girls' High School of Tianjin. He was the founder of the Chinese "Geographical Society" and editor-in-chief of the Geographical Magazine. He discovered the tomb of the great Tartar Warrior and ruler, Jenghiz Khan, in Mongolia. He teaches, at present, in the national university. He was the author of "The Science of Geography", the Tomb of Jenghiz Khan, and numerous articles in the "Geographical Magazine.

(4) Professor of Chinese Literature and Philosophy: Doctor Kuo Chia Sheng, native of Beijing. He studied under the old system and passed the various provincial examinations successfully. He obtained *Ju Ren* or MA degree in 1893 and *Jin Shi* or Doctor of Literature degree in 1903. He joined the College of Doctors and graduated in the Law Department in 1906. He served in the capacity of Senior Scribe in various ministries and became the head of the "Department of Encouragement of Agriculture" in the Ministry of Agriculture and Industry. After the establishment of the Republic, he confined himself to educational work and was responsible for foundation of many schools. He authored many books.

(5) Professor of History: Mr. Li Tai Fen, a native of Chihli province and historian. He graduated from the Beijing Normal University having specialized in Chinese history, and then went to Germany where he specialized in European history. He is at present Professor of History in the national university, and gives lectures at two other universities. He is the author of a *Compendium of Chinese History* and of the *Outlines of European History*.

(6) Instructor and Secretary to the Dean: Mr. Lu Pen Chen, a graduate of national University. Mr. Ying regards him as one of the best-read young men in Beijing, and as full of promise.

Overall, not much archival material can be found to describe the Chinese faculty members except for the first group of faculty. This first group of professors first held other professorships in other prominent universities while Fu Ren hired them. Those universities where they were teaching included: Beijing University, Normal University and Yan Jing University. Eventually, they abandoned their professorships at other universities and stayed on at Fu Ren. Chen Yuan, for instance, was teaching at Yan Jing University for a while before he came to Fu Ren. Throughout the years, the Chinese professors mainly occupied the chairs of the departments of Chinese, history, and pedagogy, as well as department of Fine Arts. When the School of Natural sciences and School of Education were established, the religious priests mostly occupied the chairs of those departments. Only a few Chinese professors were teaching in those departments in comparison with the non-Chinese in the early years.

Fu Ren University's status quo really began to change when the Sino-Japanese War broke out in 1937. In order to escape the Japanese control, many universities moved out of the metropolitan area of Beijing. Fu Ren and Yan Jing became the only two universities remained in operation until 1942 when Yan Jing had to move out of Beijing because of war between the United States and Japan. During these years, Fu Ren University became an ideal place for many famous professors in China. According to *Beijing Shifan daxue Xiaoshi 1902–1982* (History of Beijing Normal University), I list the names here of the famous professors from other universities who joined Fu Ren faculty which increased the quality of the faculty tremendously: Zhang Zi-gao, Yuan Han-qing, Zeng Shao-lun, Sa Ben-tie, Sa Ben-dong, Li qi-ye, Chu Cheng-lin, Xu Xian-yu etc. Many well-known lecturers also joined Fu Ren, mostly in the School of Arts and Letters: Department of Chinese Language and Literature had more than 21 professors and lectures: Gao Bu-ying, Shen Jian-shi, Guo Jia-sheng, Yu Jia-Xi, etc.; Department of History had more than 6: Chen Yuan, the president, Zhang Xing-liang, Lu Fen-de, etc.; Western Language and Literature department had many more Chinese professors: Li Qi- ye, Yang shang-kui, Zhang en-yu, etc.; Department of Education: Xu Jing quan, Zhang Hui, Yang Chen-zhang, Sun Xi etc.; Department of Philosophy: Shen Nai-zhang. Sociology and economics department had seven more. Fine Arts institute had six more well know painters: Fu Xin, Fu Quan, Wang Rong, etc. Moreover, the School of Natural Sciences also accepted more than 11 well-known lecturers besides the professors: Zhang Zi-gao, Yuan Han-qing, Zen shao-lun, Sa Ben-tie, Sa Ben-dong, Chu Shen-lin, Xu Xian-yu, the lecturers were Chen Guan Xi, Wu Zhao-fa, etc.[41]

These were the years when Fu Ren University became very prestigious in the nation. In fact, no other university then would have such a strong and qualified faculty in China at the time.[42] There were many subjects to study, core curriculum was expanded and elective courses were added. This was the reason that also caused the increase of student enrollment during those years, and which will be discussed later.

According to the Fu Ren Catalogue of 1947–48, there were only 27 priests on the faculty, with the majority being Chinese. As I mentioned previously, most of the Chinese faculty members had degrees from the prominent universities in America and in Europe. The official teaching languages in the university were both English and Chinese, according the catalogue. Surely English was mostly used in science teaching classes as all other universities in China did, due to a lack of Chinese scientific terminology in translation.

Non-Chinese Professors on the Faculty

Though there were lay professors and secular priests from other countries on the faculty, the archives did not keep their biographies. I simply mention their existence because there is no way for me to find out why and how they came to the university. Out of many reasons I might be able to speculate one, which was the missionary zeal. As secular priests and lay Catholics, many were inspired by the Protestant Church to go to China to work for the Church.

Throughout the years at Fu Ren University, the Catholic missionaries, such as the Benedictine Fathers and the Divine Word Fathers were definitely the minority on the faculty in comparison with the number of Chinese professors. However these missionaries occupied most of the departments' chairs. They certainly had good qualifications to do so. I chose the year 1931 as a typical year for the Benedictine era because this year was the year when the university was granted permanent registration from the government, and the Benedictine Fathers made a great effort to build up the university. Also, records were available for this year. In this year, there were 70 professors and lecturers on the Faculty. Among whom there were only ten Benedictines on the faculty out of 27 non-Chinese professors on the Faculty. Those ten Benedictines occupied the following chairs of departments: English, Philosophy, Physics, Chemistry, Biology and Psychology. Most of these Benedictine Fathers had master's degrees in their respective fields. Comparing their academic degrees with the degrees the Divine Word Fathers who were on the faculty, the Benedictine Fathers were kind of inferior. Most of the Divine Word Fathers had doctorates. According to *Fu Ren University Bulletin* of 1931, only two chairs at the departments of Biology and Psychology were holding doctorate degrees.[43] The Divine Word Fathers were academically stronger than the Benedictine Fathers. Most of them earned their doctorates in their respective fields before they took positions at Fu Ren University. According to the available catalogue of the university of 1939-40, there were 189 professors and lecturers on the faculty. All sixteen faculty members in the graduate division (only two sections were listed here: history and physics) held Ph.D.'s except only three with master's degrees, one of which was a Divine Word Father. In the undergraduate level, most of 17 priests had Ph.D.s in their respective fields with only a few chairs occupied by them.

A worthy discussion is that many priests were well-known scientists in their own fields. Their achievements also indicated the quality of the fac-

Development: Curriculum, Faculty and Student Growth

ulty as experts in different fields. In general, the priests who were on the faculty at Fu Ren University were indeed "learned men, meek and humble" as the Chinese founders requested the Holy Father. One shortcoming that the non-Chinese faculty members had and was criticized by the priests from other Catholic Universities was that they did not speak Chinese. This was not unique for Fu Ren, all other universities were the same in this aspect. The Science courses were mostly in English because the Chinese language was lacking of the translations of the scientific words.[44]

To be more specific about some of the non-Chinese professors: Dom Adelbert Gresnigt, architect who studied European architecture and Chinese design as well. He was well known in his own field worldwide. Father. Schmidt was a scientist in the field of Ethnology who "spent forty years in the field and Chinese Republic."[45] Father Oster, the head of the Department of Physics "had supervised the finishing touches on a new compressor for the production of liquid air. The device is the only one in Beijing-if not in all China."[46] Dr. Edgar Taschdjian, of the Vienna Academy of Agriculture, who studied "under two famous Viennese agriculturists, Zederbaur and Tschermak-Seyenegg, gained wide experience in Brazil, the United States, France and Abyssinia,"[47] joined the faculty. Dr. Serge Michael Shirokogoroff, was elected Anthropologist of the Russian Imperial Academy, came to the faculty in 1932 as a scientist in the fields of Ethnology (physical), Anthropology and Linguistics.[48]

The superior qualities of the faculty made the university more attractive to prospective students and in good position to compete with others. Many of the Fu Ren professors were invited to give lectures in other universities. The interactions between Fu Ren and other Universities benefited all parties in their academic fields.

Statistics of the Faculty

The statistics of the faculty members kept increasing throughout the years. It was almost at the same pace as the other universities in Beijing. In some ways, it was faster than others because of the rapid growth of the university. Despite the fact of the hostile environment and of the political turmoil in Beijing, the well-educated professors still liked to work at Fu Ren University. Due to imperfect record keeping, it was hard to find all of the statistics of faculty members throughout the years, especially during the years from 1942–1945 when Japan and the United States were involved in the Second World War. Many records were missing.[49] I gathered all of these statistics from two major English magazines: *Christian Family and our Missions* and *Fu Ren Magazine*. The Divine Word Fathers regularly published these two magazines. I chose these numbers at my discretion because sometimes they don't match with each other. The following table can represent the growth of the faculty in a way.[50] These statistics are a combination of both full-time and part-time professors. I could not find materials from any archives to state exactly how many full-time professors or part-time professors over the years. There were few references mentioning that Fu Ren had too many part-time professors prior to 1930.[51]

Table I. Faculty Statistics over the years

Academic Years	Semesters	Professors Associates and Assistants
1925-26	1st T	4
	2nd T	6
1926-27	1st T	8
	2nd T	12
1927-28	1st T	22
	2nd T	22
1928-29	1st T	24
	2nd T	24
1929-30	1st T	67
	2nd T	67
1930-31	1st T	70
	2nd T	
1931-32	1st T	70
	2nd T	
*1933-34		72
1934-35		97
1935-36		106
*1939-40		189
*1947-48		225
1948-49		282
1950-51		150

I constructed the table after checking various sources: *Fu Ren Magazine*, *Christian Family and our Missions*, and Beijing Normal University archives where there were statistics.
*The years between were missing because of the unavailable information.

Summary

The quality of Fu Ren University faculty was outstanding as I have discussed. Many of them were research-oriented and the increase of its numbers was steady. Because of this, Fu Ren became attractive to many young students. Two years were significant in terms of faculty numbers: the increase of the numbers in the academic year of 1929–30 and the decrease of the numbers in the academic year of 1950–51. The reasons were simple: the first was the expansion of the university and the second was in fear of the Communists. It happened to the student numbers as well. Faculty members in the academic year of 1948–49 were the highest in the whole history of Fu Ren University. When the Communists were approaching Beijing, many non-Chinese professors left the university for fear of them. Many Chinese professors, however, either abandoned Fu Ren University for the sake of their own political stands or left the country with other missionaries. The faculty began to dissolve and the students began to leave, especially the Catholic ones. Since then, the university began to fall. Because of this, more excuses were left for the Chinese Communists to use when they tried to take over the university.

The full-time professors at Fu Ren were always less in number than the part-time professors. The rate of full-time professors kept a steady percentage. In 1934, there were 97 faculty members with 34 professors, the rate was 35% for full professors. Taking another year 1947, there were 225 professors, associate professors and lecturers on the faculty: professors and associate professors were 78; Lecturers were 104, as well as others. The rate for the professors and associate professors was about 35% and for the lecturers was about 46%.

Though there was no record to indicate how many full time professors at Fu Ren in 1948-49 when the numbers increased to 282, it was a significant growth. I am certain the rate was around 35% because of the competitive nature of the universities in Beijing. In comparison with other universities, Fu Ren was almost on the equal footing with other universities in Beijing before the Sino-Japanese War. It certainly became much better after the war started in 1937. The following statistics are the professors and lecturers who were on the faculties at some universities in Beijing that Fu Ren was competing with. The statistics were provided in Fu Ren Magazine to indicate the strength of the university: In 1934, Beijing University: 150; Normal University: 129, Qing Hua University: 193, Yangjing University: 116, Fu Ren: 97. In 1935, Beijing University: 159, Normal University: 120, Qinghua University: 215, Yangjing University: 113, Fu Ren: 106.[52]

These numbers were to compare Fu Ren University with the competing ones in Beijing. These two years' statistics certainly could not tell the future years because Fu Ren developed quickly after 1937. Also, because of the Sino-Japanese War, all other universities were affected terribly by the war, while Fu Ren rode above the turmoil.

SECTION III: STUDENT GROWTH

Overview

Student enrollments at Fu Ren also deserve detailed discussion as the faculty had. First of all, they were almost bi-lingual prior to their coming to Fu Ren because of the requirements of education in the nation. English was almost mandatory in secondary education. Overall, the trend for student enrollment was rising until the year 1949 when the Communist Party took over. In fact, the growth of student enrollment at Fu Ren University was constant and rapid throughout those years, as the table shows. The students at Fu Ren possessed interesting characteristics: they came from all over China; their family backgrounds were interesting. The Catholic population at the university was important to know because of the nature of the university, and the statistics of the students throughout the years. The years after 1949 when the Communists took over will also be discussed.

National Character

The national character is about the geographic locations where students came from. Fu Ren University was located in Beijing and attracted students from all over China. According to Fu Ren University Bulletin, in the first group of 23 students who came to the university, there already were students from Canton[53], which was far away from Beijing. By the year of 1936, Fu Ren graduates had already represented "all the provinces of China as well as Mongolia, Manchuria, and some places overseas."[54] Two years later, when Fu Ren University prepared for the occasion to celebrate its 13th year anniversary as a center of higher education and its 9th anniversary as a fully accredited university, the university had the following chart prepared. This chart shows the geographic coverage of the students.

From this table, we can see clearly the national characteristic of student population at this point. Students came from 25 different provinces in China (Manchuria was taken by the Japanese). Moreover, the university had foreign students too, although there were only a few of them. It went beyond the national boundaries, though no reasons were found why those students came to Fu Ren, neither could the references be found to indicate what subjects those foreign students were studying.

By the year 1947, Fu Ren University became the second largest university in Beijing with a student population of 2,383, which was only next to Beijing University. Expansion continued as the university tried to attract more students. As more applicants were coming from all over the country, the university decided to hold the entrance exams locally, rather than asking the prospective students to coming to Beijing. During the academic year 1948-1949 university officials did the same for the faraway students who wished to enter the Catholic University. Because of the increase of the students' population, the university administration decided to select eleven cities nationwide for prospective students to take the entrance exam. *Fu Ren Magazine* reports,

> "Students who wished to enter the Catholic University this year were able to take the entrance examinations in these eleven cities: Beijing, Tianjin, Shanghai, Jinan, Hankow, Qingdao, Pengpu, Sian, Canton, Swatow, Meixian. A glance at the map of China reveals that these examination centers are scattered throughout the land. This makes it possible for students distant from Beijing to take the required examinations without traveling too far from home. Thus the Catholic University of Peking reaches

Development: Curriculum, Faculty and Student Growth

hundreds and even thousands of students who otherwise would be without the pale of its influence."[56]

Table II.   Student distribution geographically: (1938–1939)

Provinces	men	women	total
Hopei	468	135	621
Liaoning	56	27	83
Kiangsu	58	24	82
Shandong	50	19	69
Chekiang	49	15	64
Anhui	36	17	53
Fu kien	33	11	44
Kwangtung	30	13	43
Honan	28	4	32
Shansi	22	3	25
Hupei	14	6	20
Hunan	11	9	20
Kirin	12	4	16
Heilungkiang	11	4	15
Szechuan	12	-	12
Kiangsi	10	1	11
Chahar	7	4	11
Shensi	4	4	8
Jehol	5	-	5
Kweichow	2	2	4
Suiyuan	3	1	4
Kansu	3	-	3
Yunnan	3	-	3
Mongolia	2	1	3
Kwangsi	-	2	2
Japan	9	-	9
Russia	2	-	2
Germany	1	-	1
	959	306	1265[55]

This table is reproduced from *Fu Ren Magazine*, 1939
The original names kept because of the re-division of the provinces

Though no record show how many students were accepted by the university in that academic year, the increased numbers of professors indicated the students' growth. Fifty-seven more professors and lecturers were hired by the university, which brought the number from 225 to 282. The reasons for this increase of faculty members are still unknown, whether it was solely to meet the needs of the students or because the university intended to strengthen the university, I don't intend to speculate.

The special national character of the students at Fu Ren is rather incomplete if I don't mention Saint Albert College, the school for the Chinese

Catholic priests. This group also had a national character. This college, as a special college for Chinese priest students to study Chinese literature and sciences, had students from all over the country. These students were treated differently. They had their own apartments and the professors were invited to come to this section to teach at the beginning. By the year of 1941, the college was already in its third year and the priest students began to be part of university because they were allowed to take some courses at the university men's section. At that time, they had already covered many geographic places: "33 students from 25 Vicariates: Hopeh, Shantung, Hupeh, Shensi, Fukien, Ningsi, Suiyuan, Kansu, Shansi, Kiangsu, Hunan, enrolled in the literature course and science."[57] In 1943 however, Saint Albert's College was officially reorganized as part of Fu Ren University with a four-year curriculum as the School of Arts and Letters and the School of Sciences had for the sake of cutting down expenses.[58] The priests majored in different subjects, just like other students did.

Geographically, the students at Fu Ren came from all over China. This characteristic indeed fulfilled what the Chinese founders, Vincent Ying and Ma Xiang-bo had intended to do in their petition to Pope Pius X, to make the university "be opened for our four hundred million countrymen."[59] Every place had heard about Fu Ren.

Family Background and Religion

Unlike the public universities, Fu Ren University was private with a limited endowment. Tuition was eventually required for the students who were interested in attending the university. As I mentioned in chapter three, tuition was free at the beginning when Fu Ren was first established. Vincent Ying insisted on the free education for the students. Moreover in China, eighty percent of the population was farmers who could not afford any money to send their children to go to college. Also because of the economical and political situations in China in those years, only the wealthy families would be able to afford to pay tuition. As a Catholic university, Fu Ren tried to recruit not only the students from wealthy families but also others who were qualified but financially incapable to afford their tuitions. Fu Ren tried to help these students, especially Catholic ones, with moderate financial help even when it was in financial troubles. The tuition was about $50 annually at that time. The university tried to raise money to offer as scholarships to the students, which only one reference could be found:

> 'We are glad to note that there has been a favorable reaction to our appeal for scholarships for $50 gold, the amount of tuition which a student pays to the University annually. We wish to extend this appeal to include also scholarships yielding $200 gold, the amount which the University must add annually for each and every student who studies here. $800 gold is the minimum—according the parents here who are thinking of sending

their sons to the States--for which an education can be had at American universities today. $800 Mex. is also about the minimum which we must lay out for each student, and of this the student pays but one-fifth. For the other four-fifths we must depend on those who are interested in the future of the Church in China.'[60]

Because of the economic situation in China and the structure of Fu Ren University, the students' family backgrounds were quite limited. Father Murphy, the second rector of the university reported this,

"In the matter of family background there is a wide variety, but one cannot say that all walks of life are represented. Over seventy percent can be embraced by the four classes, (1) Government employees, (2) well-to-do farmers, (3) merchants, and (4) educators."[61]

Surely, there was a reason why Fu Ren University attracted mainly these four groups. Father Murphy attributed the absence of children of physicians, lawyers, bankers and industrial engineers to the fact that Fu Ren had not been able to have those kinds of courses yet.[62] In China, the tradition was that most of the parents wanted their children to follow their footsteps into the same professions. Their children's education had to be in line with the nature of their future work. This mentality of the parents certainly indicated the utilitarian mentality in education in China.

The percentage of the Catholic student population on the campus was always small. Though Fu Ren University tried to educate more Catholics, there were simply not many Catholic youths in China. One of the reasons I discussed in chapter two was that the Catholics were mostly farmers who were not into education. The Catholic missionaries were trying to convert them and established many elementary and secondary schools to train only the catechists who would be their helpers in spreading the Catholic Faith. Over all, higher education was not an option for them, so therefore, not many Catholic youths qualified to go to college. This was the fact the motivated Vincent Ying and Ma Xiang-bo to petition Rome to establish the university. There were no systematic statistics reported on the Catholic population throughout the years, either at the entrance or graduation. However, the years from 1931–1939 were available at graduation. It is to be noted that this rate of the Catholic population was higher than the entrance time because of many conversions at the university during the academic year.

Because of the limited resources, I could not find the numbers of the Catholic students in the other years but the graduation numbers as table V shows. It is obvious to see from Table III the overall percentage of the Catholic students during these years was very small except the first year graduation. This number had been quite consistently low throughout the years. In addition, because of many student conversions at Fu Ren University yearly, the graduation percentage of the Catholic students was probably higher than the entrance rate. Statistical record of the Catholic

Table III. Statistics Concerning Catholic Students at Graduation (1931–1939)

Year	No. Graduates	Catholics	Percentage
30-31	11	10	90.90
31-32	18	8	44.44
32-33	46	14	30.44
33-34	84	16	19.04
34-35	121	18	14.87
35-36	121	14	11.57
36-37	123	16	13.01
37-38	92	8	8.9
38-39	72	17	23.61
Total: 9	688	121	17.59

This table is reproduced from *Fu Ren Magazine*, 1939

population in the university could not be found for the latter years in the archives, therefore, I am unable to discuss them. For this, Father William Ritzgibbon, the professor of Philosophy at Fu Ren University, provided general information of the student rate in overall Christian universities, which also included Fu Ren,

> "Christian universities in China, both Catholic and Protestant, have shown another aspect of education. With Christians and non-Christians, Chinese and foreigners, working side by side on the academic and administrative staffs, and with probably never more than 20% of the students as Christians."[63]

It is also noticeable in Table III that the statistics in the first few years were higher than the rest. One of the reasons was that the student population was small and the selection process at the beginning of the university was inclined to recruit Catholics. As the university developed and expanded, it entered into a more competitive arena with other universities. More qualified students who were attracted to the university were non-Catholics. The increasing of applications from qualified non-Catholics made it impossible for Fu Ren not to recruit them. The competition was in quality not in Catholic population among universities. The university was not simply limited to the Catholics.

One exception at Fu Ren University needs to be specified: Saint Albert College, and later another Saint Thomas Institute, which was established in 1947, only recruited Catholics. These students at these two schools were surely Catholics. Saint Thomas Institute was established as a minor seminary that offered philosophy. If only for the sake of the percentage of the student Catholic population, these two schools certainly could make a difference. More archival material show that conversions at Fu Ren were constant, No matter students or professors. Some of the students there even decided to become priests or nuns.[63]

Statistics of Student Growth

The increase of the student population was rather rapid. This increase demanded the expansion of the curriculum and an increase of faculty members. Its growth rate indeed surpassed all other universities in Beijing. I have mentioned earlier that other universities were established many years before Fu Ren. The following statistics contradict Sophie Lee's statement that Fu Ren University did not have many applicants and accepted almost all who applied. Table IV below can certainly speak for itself of how Fu Ren developed in those years, especially during the Sino-Japanese War era.

Table IV.   Student Enrollments at Fu Ren University (1925–1951)

Year	Students
*1925-26	23(Fall); 32(Spring)
*1926-27	37(Fall); 62 (Spring)
1927-28	36
1928-29	53
1929-30	248
1930-31	270
1931-32	519
1932-33	620
1933-34	684
1934-35	742
1935-36	675
1936-37	810
1937-38	770(Fall); 805(Spring)
1938-39	1265(959M; 306F)
1939-40	1,585(1,096M; 489F); 29 Graduate students and 29 in the Clergy College
1940-41	1950 (1224M; 726F) and 29 Graduate students
1941-42	2045 and 30 graduate students
1942-43	2054 (1253M, 801 F)
1945-46	2271
1946-47	2348 and 35 Graduate students.
#1947-48	2383 (1454M; 929F) and 25 seminarians and 12 brothers at Saint Thomas Institute and 100 priests at Saint Albert College.
1949-50	1239; Graduate students 11
1950-51	1190

Note: the two years with "*" were the students in the preparatory school before the official registration as a university. #1947–48, some other source had 2435, which was even higher. "M" for Male students and "F" for Female students. The numbers were found from *Fu Ren Magazine*, *Christian Family and Our Missions*, *Beijing Shifan Daxue* and *Fu Ren Daxue Geming Shi*.

This table makes it clear for us to see the rapid growth of the student numbers throughout the years. It is also noticeable that enrollments in three specific years were significantly higher in comparison with the previous years: 1929–30; 1931–32; 1938–39. The reasons were obvious and self-evident. The first one 1929–30 was because the university decided to meet government's registration requirement and the expansion of the university became necessary. Two more schools were required so more students had to be enrolled at the university. The second one 1931–32 was simply because of the solid development of the university that met the requirement from the Nationalist Government. Fu Ren was granted permanent registration and its increased reputation nationwide attracted more applicants.[65] The third one was because of the effect of the Sino-Japanese War. When the war broke out in 1937, many private and national universities in Beijing moved inland, except for Fu Ren University and Yan Jing University. Those students who did not want to leave Beijing and those who wanted to go a university that year only had two places to apply. Most importantly for this particular year's increase was the Women's College. This was the year when one faculty (College of Arts and Letters) of the men's section was opened to women, which attracted many more applicants. It is also noticeable from table IV, the student enrollment at the university decreased rather sharply in the year 1937–38. The reason was very simple. Many patriotic students at Fu Ren decided to stop their studies at the university; they decided to join the army to fight against the Japanese.[66] In 1942, Fu Ren became the only private university without Japanese control in Beijing because of the relationship between Germany and Japan. The rector of the university was German as arranged in 1936. The political aspect will be discussed in chapter seven as well. On the contrary, one sharp decrease of student enrollment was 1949–1950. The reason was self-evident as well. Since the Communist Party took over Beijing, many students and professors left the university for fear of persecution and loss of their family wealth. Most of them went to Taiwan.

Summary

Over the years, the increase of the student population was steady and fast. Applicants were many and steady, but because of the limitation of the capacity of the university, a great number of them could not be recruited into the university. In 1925 when the university first opened there were only 23 students enrolled, but the number of applications was larger.[67] In 1929 the student numbers rose greatly because of the expansion of the university. In 1930, the university opened with a waiting list of more than 2,000 applications for admission.[68] In the year of 1931, over 700 applied, and the university only accepted 280 new students for each and every school as following:

Three Schools

School of Arts and Letters 308
School of Sciences 158

School of Education 53

All Departments

Chinese letters 53
History 48
English 106
Philosophy 8
Social Sciences 93
Mathematics 26
Physics 39
Chemistry 53
Biology and Pre-medical 40
Education 44
Psychology 2
Fine Arts 7[69]

The reasons why Fu Ren University could attract so many applicants were unclear from archival material. However, some references made about the university can certainly help us understand reasons more clearly. (1) Fu Ren University was known as a very strict Catholic university. All students in the university "must concentrate on their studies. They are not allowed to participate in the political activities. Their gatherings need to be academically oriented."[70] Many parents in China during those days wanted their children to be academically oriented rather than politically active. (2) Emphasis on the combination of Chinese culture and Western culture. China was in time of transition from the old to the new, tradition was still strong. Chinese culture was going downward and Western science was overly emphasized. Many Chinese parents neither wanted to give up the old nor miss out on the new. Fu Ren therefore became an ideal place. (3) Religious freedom at the university was another reason. The anti-Christian movement was always a constant thing in China in those days. Fu Ren University was spared from the attacks because of the emphasis of which will be discussed in chapter seven. (4) When the Sino-Japanese War broke out in China, Fu Ren was became known in their resistance to the Japanese, which also attracted many patriotic students.[71] In those years, although the Japanese controlled universities charged no fees and tuitions, these students still did not go to there. Moreover, the fact that Fu Ren was the only non-Japanese sponsored university in north China could certainly be another reason for the Chinese students to look up to it.

The selection process of the students for Fu Ren University was basically from three resources. All these schools were registered with the government. (1) Fu Ren middle school is the first place and the middle schools nearby in Beijing who wanted to come to Fu Ren. (2) The secondary schools where the Catholic missionaries worked or recommended. Although the Catholic missionaries did not pay much attention to higher education, they did pay attention to the secondary and primary education. By 1946, only the Catholic middle schools alone: Boy schools 71 and girls' schools 57.[72] (3) The schools known to the Fu Ren or recommended by the local authorities. There is no archival proof for this, but the entrance exams for the local students were taken at local Catholic schools or in a Catholic place as both Fu Ren Magazine and Christian Family and Our Missions repeatedly mentioned.

In 1946, the year after the defeat of the Japanese empire, there were more than 4,000 students from various parts of China who applied for admission.[73] In 1948, more than 4,800 students applied to this university and one-third of the students were women.[74] With the increase of student enrollment, the quality and the capacity of the university, competition with other universities became rather obviously strong.

In addition, it is without doubt that Saint Albert College's enrollment was increasing quickly as well. Its application process was not needed because their own bishops had done the work. Though registered as part of the university, the students there were counted separately. After ten years of existence, the students rose from 12 in 1938 to 127 in 1948. On the occasion of its tenth anniversary, Archbishop Mario Zanin, the Apostolic Delegate to China said, "what began as a tiny mustard seed in the line of religious educational endeavor has become something of a sizable oak tree after ten years of growth."[75]

The development of the curriculum and the quality of the faculty, as well as the growth of the students at Fu Ren University should have some results in their efforts. In fact, the result was tremendous from the graduation statistics. Fu Ren educated thousands of students in those years.

Table V.   Graduating students over the years (1931–1951)

Year	Bachelors degree	Masters degree
1931	11	
1932	18	
1933	48	
1934	84	
1935	122	
1936	120	
1937	134	
1938 *	76 (16 loan students)	
1939 *	87 (16 loan students)**	
1940	120	2
1941	152	4
1942	431	5
1943	454	9
1944	414	10
1945	387	8
1946	352	14
1947	330	7
1948	343	5
1949	311	2
1950	326	6
1951	185	
1952	241	
Total	4746	72

Note "*" these two years when Fu Ren educated students for other universities who refused to go. The loan students were the ones from those universities.
**Loan students were the one from other universities. The 16 students: Beijing University 5; Normal University 1; Qinghua University 1; Nankai University 4; Cheeloo University 4; Minkuo College 1.
This table is reproduced from Beijing Shifan Daxue Xiaoshi (1902–1982)

Conclusion

The above three sections provide an enormous information regarding the growth of the university: the curriculum developed according to the requirements the Ministry of Education proposed for Chinese higher education institutions; the university officials secured the best professors they could, both Chinese and non-Chinese; and the student population and qualities increased and the university became the second largest university in Beijing in 1947 which next to Beijing University. It was in a fair place to compete with other great universities in Beijing and in other cities as well. In order to see the competitiveness of all universities in Beijing, the following table provides some famous universities in Beijing that Fu Ren competed with in 1935:

The youngest private university in Beijing, Fu Ren University developed gradually throughout the years with interruptions from wars and politics. In the year of 1935, Fu Ren was almost on an equal footing with other universities. Most of them had three schools, and they were similar as well.

Table VI   Competing Universities

<u>National Universities:</u>

Peiping University (1927)
    College of Agriculture
    College of Business Management
    College of Law
    College of Medicine
    Women's College

*Beijing University (1898)
    College of Natural Sciences
    College of Arts and Letters
    College of Law

*Qinghua University (1907)
    College of Natural Sciences
    College of Business Management
    College of Arts and Letters
    College of Law

*Beijing Normal University (1902)
    College of Natural Sciences
    College of Arts and Letters
    College of Education

<u>Private Universities:</u>

Franco-Chinese University (1917)
    College of Natural Sciences
    College of Arts and Letters
    College of Medicine

*Yanjing University (1870)
    College of Natural Sciences
    College of Arts and Letters
    College of Law

*Fu Ren University (1925)
    College of Natural Sciences
    College of Arts and Letters
    College of Education

This table is reproduced from *Ge Ming Wen Xian*, Vol. 56.
The universities with "*" were the competing ones, the so-called "Big Five."

Therefore, the quality of their education became crucial. One undeniable fact helped Fu Ren University immensely, though the university itself suffered tremendously as well. When the Sino-Japanese War broke out in 1937, Fu Ren University became one of the two existing universities in Beijing (the other one was Yanjing University) and became the only existing university in Beijing after 1942, until the defeat of the Japanese. All other universities had to move inland in order to survive the Japanese attack.

Development: Curriculum, Faculty and Student Growth

This certainly helped the university greatly by hiring the professors who did not want to move inland and recruiting students from these universities who did not want to go inland. Fu Ren University neither stopped operations nor suffered from a loss of many of its professors, though some of the professors had to leave Beijing because of their out-spoken views on anti-Japanese matters. By the end of the 1940's, Fu Ren added more schools, as I discussed previously. The numbers of all schools and their statistics are as following:

The Statistics of all the schools of Fu Ren University in 1947–1948,

a. Fu Ren Primary school
   Pupils 309
   Teachers 11
   Clerks 4
   Servants 3
b. Fu Ren Middle School
   Students 869
   Teachers 29
   Servants 11
c. Fu Ren university
   Students 2,383
   Professors and assist. 225
   Clerks, etc. 110
   Servants and workmen 214[77]

In fact, no other university in Beijing could compete with these numbers at this time. More importantly, no other university had all of these schools: both middle school and primary school as Fu Ren University had achieved thus far.

Certainly, the numbers could be solid proof of the university's development. But the most important thing concerns the achievements that Fu Ren University made during these years. *Catholic Family and Our Missions* reported in 1936 the departments of Chemistry, Physics, Micro-Biology and others came in for a special world of praise due to their exceptional advance. The rector had this to say about the university, "the university, especially, the College of Science, last year elicited the highest praise from government officials, and consequently this college is specially patronized this year."[78] The Department of Psychology in 1936, through unusual and quite unexpected gifts became now practically the best equipped in China.[79]

Fu Ren University was a modern, up-to-date university. In 1938, the university had made the top list of some special fields in graduate studies. *China Handbook 1937–1943* reported that departments of History and Physics were among the best nationwide, as well as the Fine Arts and education.[80] In fact, "The Department of Physics is one of Fu Ren's best developed departments. And with the last big shipment of specialized equipment from Germany, it ranks with the best that the average German university can produce. Physics equipment of the most modern kind is at Fu Ren, and many of the instruments are not possessed by any other university in China."[81] The special Fine Arts (institute) had already produced world-famous painters in less than a decade of operation, is a unique original addition to the university of the Pope's curriculum.[82] The Department of Printing became the best equipped in Beijing. The Micro-Biology Laboratory produced the vaccine to combat typhus in the early 1930's when Chinese doctors could not yet do anything about it. Moreover, a new Graduate Division for Chemistry and Biology has been opened at the Catholic University of Beijing with the opening of the fall term in the year of 1941 with excellent laboratories.[83]

Within ten years from its official permanent registration in 1931 to 1941, the achievements of Fu Ren University were certainly magnificent. Of course, more progresses were certainly made after 1941: such as, Department of Ethnology opened with emphasis on research and the College of Agriculture, as I mentioned in section one, opened as well. These developments were made into order to meet the urgent needs of China: the implementation of Western science to modernize China as all other universities were trying to do; to increase the productivity of the farm lands, to revitalize Chinese Culture and Arts. Theology, considered as the most important subject by the Church, did not have any significance in the university at the beginning. The university never had courses on theology in classrooms as required by the government. In 1938 when the president of the Nationalist Party, Jiang Jieshi realized the important works the Catholic Church had done for the nation, he rescinded the law by allowing religion to be taught in the universities.[84] Fu Ren University did not add any theology courses; neither made it mandatory for non-students to attend religious services. The university environment was already heavily Catholic because of the presence and activities of the missionaries and the Catholic discipline.

One more important issue needed to be mentioned so that we see how the Catholic Missionaries tried to make Fu Ren University a center for Chinese studies—Graduation gown. It was not a traditional Western gown but a traditional *Zhou Dynasty* gown. The significance of this dynasty was that it signified the recorded beginning of the Chinese culture and characters. This remembrance and rediscovery of the Chinese culture at the graduation of Fu Ren was certainly meaningful to all.

Faculty and student growth of Fu Ren University was certainly as obvious as the structural growth of the university. The Catholic missionaries, no matter whether Benedictines or Divine Word Fathers, determined to make the university a first rate Chinese university in every respect. Their efforts certainly met the end when they nurtured and developed the university in both structure and curriculum development. The university became one of the best universities in China prior to the takeover by the Communists. Certainly, there are more things to say about Fu Ren University that will be discussed later, which are the extra-curricular activities. They certainly brought fame to the university in a very different, yet special way. The competitive nature of Fu Ren University was certainly revealed through these activities as well.

CHAPTER SIX

Extra-curricular Activities

The nature of Fu Ren University, as both Chinese and Western Catholic, was expressed not only through its physical structure and its prescribed curriculum but also through its extra-curricular activities. It is natural to discuss the extra-curricular activities because they form an inseparable part of university life. The variety and meaningful extra-curricular activities are crucial to any university students. More importantly, they are crucial to the growth of the university itself. A well-established university, no matter in which country, must have good and well-organized extra-curricular activities. Therefore, the discussion of the extra-curricular activities at Fu Ren University can be helpful in understanding the establishment of Fu Ren University in Beijing.

Extra-curricular activities helped the university to be acknowledged both nationwide and worldwide. The university took advantage of both the traditional Chinese culture and the well-developed Western Catholic culture. The full development of the human being: intellectually and physically, had always been emphasized by both of these cultures. As Chinese, the university understood that it took time, patience and energy to educate a student as the classical Chinese culture has expressed, "it takes ten years to grow a tree, but takes a hundred years to educate a person."[1] As Western Catholic, the university "aims to develop the entire man. The faculty realizes that while the moral and intellectual sides of himself are being developed, the Chinese student has what may be called a unique need of systematic physical training."[2] This Chinese and Western Catholic nature of the university was the core of why Fu Ren University could achieve its status quo as a rather prestigious university within a short period of time despite the political turmoil. The extra-curricular activities of the students, as well as the faculty's active involvements, were evidently an outward expression of its academic life to train a person as a whole both intellectually and physically.

Extra-curricular activities were varied throughout the years. Some of the activities involved more people and efforts; some of them were simply involved all students to participate. Some were limited in numbers but had wider impacts. Each activity had its' nature and therefore carried out differently, yet, everything was for the benefit of students, university and society. It is impossible and unnecessary to discuss all the activities that the university sponsored throughout the years. I simply discuss the important ones in this chapter. All the activities are divided in three sections according to their own nature or orientation. Because of the limited archival materials, the discussions can only portray a general rather than a complete picture of Fu Ren's extra-curricular activities. Sports activities were common in most of the universities in China and were rather competitive in nature. During that time, sports in China were not for money- making purpose. All those who liked sports were certainly encouraged to participate. Fu Ren University had a variety of them: such as soccer and basketball. There were no statistics on how many students were playing sports; the university had prepared the grounds for them. Fu Ren students were enthusiastic about the sports as well. These sports showed the competitive nature of the university with all other universities and made the university known, eventually earned the title "Notre Dame of the East".

Social activities were quite unique to Fu Ren, including some that no other universities had: hosting refugees, relief services, and charitable work. Because of the nature of the university, the university felt the responsibility to take care of the poor and homeless out of the Christian charity and Confucian benevolence. These charitable activities earned praises and respects from the National Government.[3] The whole university was involved with these activities: Students, departments, professors and even the president, were all involved.

Religious activities were rather limited to Christian and secular Arts exhibitions from the Fine Art Department because of the nature of being religious. Though there were only a few painters, they brought honor to the university, which made it known not only in China, but also in the world. Some activities were opened only to the Catholic population and those who were interested in the Catholic Church, such as: retreats, the Catholic Action group and the work for the children of the poor and the neighborhood. Musical concerts satisfied and benefited all the music lovers from many places in Beijing.

The extra-curricular activities brought the university administration, the faculty and the students together. As a whole, Fu Ren reached out to a variety of peoples, both nationally and internationally. Among which, the Social Services, were the outreach of the university students and administration in light of Christian charity and Confucian benevolence. The services fulfilled the Christian charity that calls all to be attentive to the poor and the needy and the Confucian benevolence that calls for the same purpose. The Chinese professors who were non-Catholics were moti-

Extra-curricular Activities

vated by their Confucian teachings and helped the needy and helpless. The Catholics were inspired by that, as well as the Catholic socials teachings and practiced what they believed. The Social Services section shows how the university administration, faculty and students worked together to help the Chinese people who were suffering from wars and natural disasters.

SECTION I: SPORTS

Overview

Sports were an important part of Fu Ren University life throughout the years. Father Murphy who was the second rector of the university said it very well, "we are anxious to avoid that accusation, but the fact is that the sports here are as much as element in making the school known as they are in America itself."[4] As I already discussed the slogan of the university was "to buy and to sell" in any possible way. The sports helped to market the university in China. Various sport teams were formed gradually: the football (soccer) team was the first, then basketball, tennis, and track were all formed later in 1929. Having these teams would help the university compare favorably with those of the best universities in North China. These games were the popular ones in universities in China. Eventually, more teams were formed during the Sino-Japanese War era, which did not go to far: hockey and American football because there were no more Chinese controlled universities in Beijing anymore.

As the youngest university in Beijing, Fu Ren University had her eyes on the best universities and intended to compete with them from the very beginning. The competitive nature of Fu Ren showed well in sports. The teams excelled within a few years after being formed, especially soccer and basketball. The success brought the university to a new level of competition and prestige in the nation: Champions of the Big Five,[5] Champions of North China.

These teams were formed for the sports lovers as only part of the extra-curricular activities rather than training professionals. I found no information on scholarships that offered to those students who played sports. The students could not make their careers in sports in China. The competitions among them were simply to enhance the friendship and communication, to show the competitiveness of universities and to learn from each other. Most importantly, sports could educate the students who manage their time well in their studies and planning.

Soccer

Fu Ren University encouraged athletic activities from the very beginning when it was established in 1925. Although the athletics were encouraged in this institution from the very beginning, the university's extra-mural contests only began in the Fall of 1927. In order to broaden the university soccer team's horizons, the university invited a guest team to come to play against the university team for the sake of practicing. The contest between the university soccer team and the American Marines was unofficial, but it provided an opportunity for the university students to experience the nature of competition. *Fu Ren University Bulletin* reported,

> 'The American Marines stationed in Peking were the first to send a team to meet the university squad. The dates and scores of their two games of soccer have not been recorded, because these were arranged solely for the purpose of giving our boys some extra practice.'[6]

Such practice certainly had impact on the team's progress. The team experienced the competitive nature of this sport from playing against the American marines. However, because of variety of reasons, the university team never officially practiced until more games came up in 1928. The university team surprisingly defeated the Alumni team of the Sacred Heart School, which was considered the best independent Catholic team of Beijing by a score of 5–1.[7]

This starting point helped the university team to move onward to become the eventual champion in Northern China. To be competitive and well equipped, the university decided to prepare many good teams in sports: soccer, tennis, basketball, and track were officially introduced into the curriculum in 1929 that would compare favorably with those of the best universities in North China. Two hours per week of compulsory calisthenics (for which credit is to be given) would be introduced that year in all the classes.[8] The soccer team, by that time, had already received many favorable comments from the Chinese press. The famous local Chinese newspaper *Beijing Morning Post* noticed the teams' skills and potentials:

> '... The University football[9] team was formed very recently, in fact, barely two months ago. It is greatly to their credit that they dared to challenge the first squad of the ever-victorious Italian footballers. The opinion among the Chinese and Western spectators present was that all the members of the University team were promising players, and that a little more training would make them one of the most redoubtable teams in Peking.'[10]

Team members indeed fulfilled this rather prophetic prediction of the team's future by their hard work. The team did not disappoint this newspaper by becoming one of the best teams in North China within short few years. Started in the winter of 1929, the Fu Ren University varsity football team officially entered into the battlefield by playing against all other university teams, as well as the military teams from different countries. According to *Fu Ren University Bulletin*, by the winter of the year 1930, the varsity team defeated the most powerful *Chang Hsin Tien* football team and earned the title from the media: "University teams make distinctive showing in sports: Strong in soccer: leading teams of North China Beaten by Catholic Players."[11]

At this point, it is worthwhile to revisit the history of the university. From the previous chapter, the readers already know during the years from 1925 to 1930, Fu Ren University had to deal with tremendous external pressures especially in the year of 1929. The university was facing a danger of demotion from a university status to a college status because of the new requirements from the Ministry of Education at Nanjing. Under the new requirement, the university had to add two more colleges and build more buildings in order to meet the requirements from the government. In the meantime, the university administration was too busy with other administrative things, not sports. The talented students were playing on their own. They practiced and improved their skills. At the end, the achievement was prominent, "they made steady and rapid improvement and are now recognized by both the Chinese and foreign Press as one of the strongest teams in Peiping. The position in the City League has not yet been decided.'[12]

The competitive university Varsity Team went beyond the boundaries of Beijing metropolitan to Tianjin to play against the best teams of North China: Queen's Regiment, All-star teams, Nankai and the 'B' club. The following report demonstrates:

> 'During the holidays the Varsity Soccer team made a trip to Tienjin where they encountered some of the best teams in North China... They lost a very even and exciting game to the Queen's Regiment. The second game was played with an All-star team of past and present students of Nankai University whom they humbled to the tune of 3to 1. Nankai had beaten Yenching and Tsing Hua, two of the best teams of Peiping, before meeting Catholic University. On New Year's Day, they met the 'B' team of Tienjin Association Football Club. The strongest club, whether foreign or Chinese, in North China... Fu Ren lost.'[13]

By 1931, the team became more prominent and was rated as the doughtiest individual team in the North.[14] It was because of this reputation, the team received a tentative invitation to go to Manila to play (football) in a series of games with the local teams as part of the attractions at the great Charity Fair that would be held there in January of 1932. Each year one of the strongest teams in China could have this honor to participate. In 1931, another team *Chi Nan Team* from Shanghai acted in this capacity.[15]

During Easter recess, Fu Ren team went to Shanghai to challenge the strongest team there. *Fu Ren Newsletter* reported that "the occasion was the fortnight' tour of the university football team, with several supporters and members of the faculty. Shanghai is reputed to have the strongest association football teams in the Far East."[16] The purpose of this trip to Shanghai and Nanjing was twofold: the first was to compete with the best; second was to "sell" the university so the university could be known in the nation.

Within six years' period from its establishment in 1925 until 1931, "the university had been business functioning, and while the great cities of China had heard about Fu Ren they had not enjoyed those personal associations which mean so much in the creation of neighborliness and understanding."[17] Though the result of the team could not be found in the record, Fu Ren University got a lot of attention from the media and therefore, attracted many more who desired their sons to be excellent both in sports and in education:

> 'The keen interest shown in this young university and its people was at once made manifest in the newspaper attention given by Shanghai to the enterprising tour, made possible by the munificence of one of the University's good supporters in Chicago. The result of the tour was not only to establish in the minds of the Mid-China sporting fraternities a wholesome respect for the Catholic University's prowess, but also to make more widely known something of the educational activities of Fu Ren. People in Shanghai and Nanking, who gave a most generous welcome to the visitors from the North, were most eager to hear about the university, its buildings, its faculty, its students life and its progress...'

> 'As a result of the tour a great deal of desirable publicity has been broadcast among parents desirous of placing their sons in the most advantageous position for receiving a sound, modern education. It was heart-warming to see how the crowds turned out to welcome the students on arrival at Shanghai, how many great men of the city came forward to offer hospitality and to talk with the young men and their professors.'[18]

After the trip to Shanghai, the whole Fu Ren population was energized and the university varsity football team went on to beat all the four great teams in North China: the British Queen's Regiment, Nankai, Tsing Hua, and Yenching. Fu Ren won the Champion of the North in 1931.[19] Consequently, Fu Ren varsity team won series of championships in North China.

In 1935, the rivalry between the Champion of the North and the Champion of the South were in competition again. The university magazine reports:

> '... Fu Dan team from Shanghai invaded Peiping for a series of games with the leading colleges. They had won the championship among the eight universities of Shanghai. Interest was high in the outcome of the game between Fu Ren, champions of Peiping, and the visitors. Every available spot was occupied, and this applies not merely to the field itself but to every conceivable vantage point near the grounds. It ended 2–0 in Fu Ren's favor.'[20]

By the year of 1935, in Beijing, the elite circle of sports had been formed, that was the so-called Big Five: Yenching (Protestant), Qinghua (Indemnity Foundation), Beijing Normal University (National), Peking University (national), and Fu Ren University (Catholic). One article entitled *With Our Athletes* says,

Extra-curricular Activities

> 'Lately the so-called "Big Five" League of Peking entered upon its series of games with a mighty din... As for Football—winning Football championships has become something of an established tradition for our "Notre Dame of the East" booters, and our men have carried off the pennant a number of years in succession and hope to maintain that tradition...'[21]

Being known as the "Notre Dame of the East", Fu Ren University worked hard to earn that title. In fact, the real sports champion of the North was not measured by the individual teams, but the "championship is decided in favor of the team totaling the most points all around."[22] Therefore, being the Champion of the North was a combination of all the school's teams, not the football team alone. In detail, the "Big Five" Teams featured quite a variety of sports, including basketball, baseball, track and field work, volleyball, tennis, and cross-country running.[23] Doubtless, the university put a lot of effort into sports because the teams' efforts could make championship possible for the university.

Basketball

Though the Fu Ren Basketball team was formed later than the football team, it became one of the best in North China. In 1933, according to the first available record, the Fu Ren basketball team defeated the strongest Qinghua team within the "Big Five" League. More honors were brought to the university by the basketball team in later years. In 1935, the university team brought home two trophies. One was the *St. Loius Trophy* and the other was *The International Trophy*. Fu Ren won the first trophy rather easily because the Saint Loius team failed again to come up to the standard that it has set in the former years.[24] However, the international trophy did not come easy for Fu Ren team. Fu Ren's team had to be strong to win the trophy:

> The basketball league made up of local Chinese university teams and teams from the American Marine contingent. Fu Ren had won the first half without the loss of the game. The second half was considerably curtailed owing to the pending departure of the Post team for Shanghai. The Marine teams were all weakened by the selections for the general squad, and it was decided that the Chinese teams should play off their games as soon as possible and the Johnson Cup be given to the winner. Fu Ren won by default from the strong China university team, and two nights later closed their part of the schedule with a one-sided victory over a team from the Chinese Army. This gave us a clear slate for the second half in the games played and thus a clear title also to first place.[25]

Later in 1936, the so-called "Big Five" League of Peking entered upon its series of games. Every team tried its best to win. Once again,

> 'Fu Ren fought a "battle to the death' with Tsing Hua university's speedy basket-ball toters. ... Fu Ren leads all teams in points and bids fair to carry off the Basketball Championship this season.'[26]

In 1936, Fu Ren sport teams once again went beyond the national borders to play. The teams of the Catholic University of Peking were selected to represent North China in response to an invitation of the Japanese Athletic Federation. North China sent the best athletes for a series of games with the crack Japanese teams. In the meantime, they were invited to Korea to play as well.

> 'While the Seniors at the Catholic University struggled with their theses and final examinations, the Basketball and Football Teams, together with the Fu Ren's physical director, Father Peter Rushman, who hales originally from Wisconsin, Mr. E. Smithberger, a former Minnesota man, the basketball coach, and Mr. Y.S. An, the football coach, went on a three weeks tour of Korea and Japan and gave a good account of themselves in the various games.'[27]

Summary

During the Sino-Japanese War period, almost all the sports were suspended. Most of the universities in Beijing had to close their doors and moved to inland except Fu Ren University and Yanjing University who later had to move out in early 1942. They did not play with the students sponsored by the Japanese. Though no more competitions, Fu Ren added two more teams in sports, such as the hockey team[28] and the American football team[29], these teams did not go too far before they were interrupted by the terrible war.

The university sport teams could achieve the status as champions within a few years was because, first of all, the Benedictine Fathers' and Divine Word Fathers' efforts in training them. The Missionaries understood the importance of sports being part of university life anywhere. Secondly, the sports could show how competitive the university was among peers. The foresight of the Catholic principle of *a sound mind is in a healthy body* was realized at Fu Ren University. Thirdly, good sports could bring reputation to the university, which can also make the university known. Fu Ren had those teams were because the American Missionaries, as well as the Germany missionaries understood how sports could help the students in their involvements, cooperation, competitions, as well as commitment in doing things. In the meantime, sports would attract many who are physically talented. The Reverend B. O'Connor, O.S.B. who was first director of the Athletics. He was the chief force in the formation of the Five University League. Latter, E.C. J. Edwards and Peter Rushman became the directors after 1933, and they gave sport activities extra impetus and direction.[30]

SECTION II: SOCIAL SERVICES

Overview

Social service activities had always been an integral part of the university life throughout its existence. These activities helped all the students to be actively involved. Because of this, they exposed themselves to a wider society and therefore understood their own future more deeply in the world that filled with wars and turmoil. Due to the special circumstances in Beijing, Fu Ren University was involved with the world outside of the academia very early when it was established. I mentioned earlier that Fu Ren University was established in an interesting time in China where there were wars and political turmoil, which will be discussed separately. The wars occurred during the warlord era had driven people out of their homes, the political turmoil left them homeless and the natural disasters made it impossible for people to survive. These things were going on constantly around Beijing and in China. When the crisis occurred, it was then when Fu Ren decided to stretch out its helping hands to the needy and helpless, despite the fact that the university itself had its academic things to worry about and was also struggling with its own financial issues. Fu Ren University became the only university in Beijing that was active in social services and won high praises from the Nationalist Government. According to the *China Handbook, 1937–1943*, when describing the Catholic relief services, it indicated that no other university, either private or public was really involved with these things. The Catholic nature of active charity and the Chinese benevolence of the university prevailed.

These social service activities at Fu Ren University involved the whole university, the students, the professors, the President of the university. Moreover, the wealthy people in the city that the university reached to, as well as many people in the United States who were reached by the missionaries. Under the leadership of Fu Ren University, many people who were in needs received help. These services raised visibility of the university and attracted attentions from all over China. Fu Ren students benefited from participating in all these activities.

Refugees

As an academic institution, Fu Ren University did not have an obligation to host the refugees of the war. The priests and professors were there as educators not there for social services. The warlords only cared for their own political powers and ignored the ordinary people's lives. Unlike any good government, that should have taken care of its citizens first, or at least protect them, the warlords did the opposite. China, throughout the years in the modern history, proved that governments did not care much or unable to care much about their citizens. As Catholic missionaries, the

Benedictine Fathers at the beginning, and later the Divine Word Fathers, though they came as educators at the university, they felt they were obliged to help the victims of the wars. In the spring of 1926, only one semester after Fu Ren University was established, the clash occurred between Marshal Zhang Zuo-lin and the so-called "Christian General", Fen Yu -xiang in Beijing. This war left thousands of peasants in the vicinity of Peking without food or shelter. "In this emergency, the Catholic University threw open its gates to about 400 refugees and cared for them until such time as they were able to return to their abandoned farms."[31]

Moreover, on April 10, 1926, a coup of the *Kuominjun* (the army own by the warlords) compelled Tuan Qi-rui, the Chief Executive of China (residing in Beijing) to flee to the Legation Quarter. Beijing once again was filled with consternation and many of the natives sought refuge on the grounds of the Catholic University. Father Placidus wrote to Archabbot Aurelius on April 10th,

> 'Our place is now filled with refugees, who are mostly of high class. The roaring of cannons may be heard every day. Within the last week airplanes have dropped bombs on the city, but so far none have fallen on our property...God pity the poor people!'[32]

Father Prior Ildephonse again wrote to Aurelius on the 18th describing,

> 'The conditions in the *Tao Pei-le Fu* (where the university was) are somewhat uncomfortable because of the number of refugees sheltered here, most of them being women and children. Father Placidus is taking care of the housing of these and now all the buildings excepting the stables are occupied... For the last few days the city gates were kept closed, not even vegetable sellers being allowed to enter.'[33]

Another letter from Prior Ildephonse to the Rector of Fu Ren on May 1, 1926,

> "'... Thousands of upon thousands of these unfortunate people had to flock to the city and have to be taken care of, as in nearly all instances they bring nothing along with them except their stomachs and the clothes on their backs... By June 4th, 1926, those 400 refugees were almost gone. By middle of May, the available funds were consumed, they were getting 'up against it.'"[34]

Many years later, according to the recorded information later in the winter of 1948, the year prior to the Communists took over Beijing, the university again showed its hospitality and welcomed more than five hundred refugees when they seek quarters on the university ground. In fact, this was in addition to their great charitable work to feed 1500 hungry mouths each day during the wintertime, which will be discussed next. "Who could turn away the homeless and the starving from this which may well be their last resort?"[35] Such was the true meaning of Christian charity and true benevolence. The innocent Chinese civilians were hurt by the wars

Extra-curricular Activities

created by Chinese and other imperialists in China. These civilians suffered from political turmoil experienced "home and care" from the Catholic University in Beijing, an academic institution staffed by priests, kind-hearted professors and service oriented students.

Despite the fact that the university did not have enough dormitory rooms for students over the years, Fu Ren still managed to host the refugees. Meanwhile, the classes continued as usual.

Relief Service

Relief service cost a lot of money from the university. Fu Ren University had always been in financial crisis throughout the years. The university needed money terribly to develop and to expand in order to be the first-rate university in China. However, its tight budget and its ambitions did not make the university become greedy, nor prevented the university from doing charitable work. The dual nature of Fu Ren's Catholic and Chinese inspired the university staff constantly to find effective ways to help the poor and the needy in China. In 1936, when the Yellow River flooded the countryside under dreaded blanket of waves, more than 20,000 people suffered from this disaster:

> 'Villages and cities alike melted as sugar before the cutting attack of the stream. Look yonder and see those 20,000 unsheltered outcasts stretch their imploring hands heavenward in this hour of direst need! 'Fu Ren students and alumni have met the national issue and faced it squarely as any group in the land, and that, despite the labors of classroom, they have devoted themselves wholeheartedly and unflaggingly to the practical applications of the principles of Christian charity for the relief of their afflicted countrymen. We rejoice to see that our students will be bulwark to the Chinese State.'[36]

Under the leadership of Father John Fu S.V.D.[37], Fu Ren students were organized into groups to work efficiently in conjunction with Catholic Action[38] and some state authorities. The personal contributions from Fu Ren students had flowed in on the unending stream of self-sacrifice. In order to raise more funds, Father Fu organized and directed the plays consisted with a mixed cast of students and professionals in the university auditorium that attracted about a thousand people. Moreover, the students visited the scenes of desolation and also gave aid through the mediation of the missionaries where help was needed the most. Thousands of dollars had gathered by Fu Ren's handful of Catholic social workers for the flood relief.[39]

When Tianjin, the city next to Beijing and North China flooded in 1939, though the flood did not actually touch Beijing, Fu Ren University was once again in action to help the suffering people by raising money. They alone raised about $400.00 by staging theatrical performances in the university auditorium.[40] The function only took a few leaders to organize, and then the whole university body got involved. Each student contributed his or her talents to help the good cause. The students at Fu Ren were not merely bookworms, but active intellectuals who strived to make China a better place.

Charity Kitchen

Though the occasional charitable works as discussed previously were certainly worth praising, they were occasional and needed no commitment. There were two important works to which Fu Ren University really committed for many years that need to be specified. They were the so-called *Charity Kitchen* established in 1937, operated by Fu Ren students, and the *Dispensary*, established in 1939, which was in the care of the Sisters at Fu Ren Women's section. 'No living human being should be left behind' became reality through this commitment by Fu Ren.

Charity Kitchen was a regular winter service at Fu Ren. This Charity Kitchen, conducted at the university during the three winter months of distress in China, at first averaged about 600 portions of millet gruel per day, but then climbed to a peak of 1000, under the incentive of crying needs.[41] Later, the number increased to an average of 1500 daily. The Sociology Department was actively involved in finding the best way to serve the people:

> 'They investigated the poverty and employment, striving to find a better systematic mode of procedure. During coming winter, it will be advisable to enlist the support of laymen and women, and obtain Catholic volunteers to visit homes and distribute food. Cases of sheer starvation, it is felt, will be brought to light through such personal contracts. In this field of action, as in so many other points of its multiform program of "bringing Christ to China."[42]

For such great work, the university formed a relief committee and Mr. Ignatius Ying Qian-li as the manager. This committee was mainly responsible for purchasing food, and also was concerned with the clothing problem, since there were many persons in serious need, some garbed only in paper and rags.

Charity Kitchen was not a small enterprise. It cost a lot of money and needed many people to work for it. In order to keep it open, besides the committee's enterprise, and especially, the energetic management of Mr. Ying, many other people came to help the cause:

> 'To help finance the work, the secular Professors of the university have pledged themselves to give a day's salary while the students with the cooperation of their families expect also to raise some hundreds of dollars...
> 'To help the cause, the Apostolic Delegate has also offered generous assistance, Businessmen of the city with whom the university deals regularly have likewise been approached and showed themselves most willing.'[43]

Extra-curricular Activities

To the university's surprise, the original planned capacity for 500 people expanded to 800 at the very beginning. The unexpected large contributions received from the students and appeals to their friends made it possible to assist more. Many articles of clothing were also collected from various friends.[44] This charity kitchen brought all people together who had shown their real charity and benevolence: expert students from sociology department, other students who liked to help, university relief committee, the professors, as well as the Papal delegate were involved in this work.

In 1939, the Sociology Department did a survey of this great program. An estimate of the probable cost for the winter's relief work carried on here totals over ten thousand dollars. This amount of money was certainly not a small number. It came from the good-hearted people on the university property, as well as the people that the university reached to, not from the university budget. This good deed touched many kindhearted people who like to help. Some of the money was given or promised to give by various charitable organizations such as the international women's relief committee. The professors at Fu Ren volunteered important sums, each of whom gave a day's salary to this cause. The students who were raising money by their appeals among their friends and by benefit programs.[45] Most importantly, the president of the university, Chen Yuan was also actively involved. By his personal efforts, he gathered a considerable share of the amount of $20,000 to this cause. Various theatrical and musical nights of the students accounted for more. Their talents contributed to the service of China. The International Women's Club in Beijing had also busily gathered large sums for charitable distribution.[46]

The active involvement on the university part made significant progress in developing this program. The Charity Kitchen received a tremendous amount of money in the winter of 1940,

> 'Students of the University, coordinating their efforts with the authorities thereof and with the Catholic Action group and the Departments of Sociology and Economics, were able to put on a highly organized and quite effective Relief Campaign for the needy in this city during the winter months. Students and professors of Sociology investigated thousands of cases of destitution and sought funds for their relief. A total $22,259.25 was spent, partly contributed by the Peking International women's Association, partly gathered by Fu Ren groups by collection, by "charitable Night" raffles, theatrical and various exhibitions of art.'[47]

Fu Ren University continued its service to help the Chinese in conflict as much as possible. During the Sino-Japanese War (1937–1945) years, Fu Ren University remained in its location in Beijing not only to continue its academic work as before, but also continued its service to the people in needs. Education at Fu Ren had already shown its purpose from the actively involvements in the social services of the students.

Dispensary

The Dispensary was to give medical aid to the needy, especially to women and children. This had always been crucial to people during period of the wartime and starvation. The Sisters of Servants of the Holy Ghost who were teaching at the Women's College undertook the actual work of the dispensary. This was a year-long commitment besides their regular works. This dispensary for the poor of the neighborhood showed that between August and November of 1939, nearly 3,000 persons were treated, including 1,003 men and 902 women and 1,076 children.[48] Every day, the Directress, Sr. Edna, S.Sp.S. had her hands full. She had to see between 70 and 100 people daily at the dispensary who came for help. In the wintertime, however, the dispensary was connected directly with the Charity Kitchen, helping the poor ones.[49] Fu Ren University had to provide all the needs for the dispensary. It is understandable that during the wartime, many diseases would be widely spread. The preventive work had to be done effectively. The Sisters f the Holy Spirit did it at the dispensary.

Moreover, this section is not complete if this one more project is not mentioned: Fu Ren did not only care for the outsiders who were poor and needy, they also cared for the most needy ones who worked in the university. A night school was established for the university workers who were uneducated. They did this not for pure educational purposes, but for charity and benevolence,

> 'Fifty servants, laborers, and machinists of Fu Ren are receiving beneficial courses in language, mathematics and science every night under the direction of the Department of Education. They are taught by competent students of the university. Under the supervision of Mr. Hao Te Yuan, the teachers receive no salary other than the experience derived from teaching and the satisfaction of seeing progress in their pupils.'[50]

Summary

Overall, the university kept the Charity Kitchen open for 8 months each year. The dispensary however, was open year-round. The expense was quite extraordinary in consideration of the tight budget that the university had for its development and expansion. The work was not simple, but an enterprise of the whole university. The university administration exhausted everything possible means they could to provide the social services without affecting the regular academic work. Fu Ren University had been triumphant in this respect because it fulfilled the mission of the University as both Catholic and Chinese. *China Handbook 1937–1943* reported extensively on the Catholic social services which earned the great reputation within the nation[51] and caused the Nationalist Government to change its policy on religion, of which will be discussed in the next chapter. The social services not only helped those in needs, but also helped the students, pro-

Extra-curricular Activities

fessors and the university administration to grow. They worked together to make it happen. As patriotic Chinese, they loved their own people. As missionaries, they regarded the Chinese in needs as part of their duty to help. The Catholic Charity and Chinese Benevolence found home at Fu Ren University through these services.

SECTION III: RELIGIOUS ACTIVITIES

Overview

Religious activities were not compulsory at Fu Ren University from the very beginning. It was first of all because the Chinese government did not allow this to happen if the university would be seeking governmental recognition. Secondly, the missionaries who worked in the university did not come as evangelists but as educators. Unlike the early Christian missionaries who came to China to proselytize, these new Catholic missionaries, both Benedictine Fathers and Divine Word Fathers came to help the Chinese youth to study Chinese culture and Western Sciences at Fu Ren University so that they might be able to understand more about both Chinese culture and the Catholic Church. This was indeed the main reason why the religious activities were entirely voluntary for the students though services were provided. Masses were celebrated in the university chapel every day. Only those students who assisted the Masses and those who lived in the Catholic dormitory needed to be present and the rest were not forced. The environment at the university was quite Catholic and was known in China because of the active presence of the missionaries and the integration of Catholic and Chinese culture the missionaries advocated on campus. Truth be told, the power behind many of the religious activities on campus was the Association of Catholic Action, which was founded in 1927. Its members were all male Catholics. The Archbishop Celso Costantini, who was the Papal Delegate in Beijing, founded this association. He wanted all the Catholics to put their faith into practice and to live their lives according to the teachings of Faith. This association at Fu Ren wanted to utilize all the possible means to increase atmosphere of the Catholicity without imposing anything onto others. Eventually, many of these religious activities provided by the university throughout the years increased the university's reputation, especially the Christian Arts which earned praises from educators and artists.[52]

Because of the different natures of the activities in this section, generalization is inappropriate; I have to specify individually. These activities were inspired by the religious motivations, they were not purely religious for all students and professors. Religious activities were limited to certain people, but the results of these activities were broad. Some benefited only the Catholics immediately, but in a long run, these Catholics showed the identity of Catholicity of the university. Some benefited many: students, professors and many other peoples. The people who participated in variety of activities indeed were religion oriented, but the contributions that these activities had to the university were unlimited. As a Catholic university, Fu Ren was obliged to offer some special services for the Catholics but not exclusive in nature. Fu Ren utilized the Catholic tradition to benefit the whole community of having active participants.

Retreat

The first report on religious activity occurred in 1931, which was recorded in *Fu Ren News Letter*. It did not mean that no religious activities happened in the previous years. For those who know the Catholic tradition understand that retreat has always been an important part of the Catholic life. It is now and it was then:

> 'Nearly thirty-five percent of the number are Catholic students[53]. Their spiritual welfare is attended to by a Chinese priest. The attendance at daily mass is not obligatory. There is an annual retreat during which the Chinese students conduct themselves in a most edifying manner.'[54]

The annual retreat was given during the days of Holy Week. The entire school was dismissed on Wednesday and the remainder of the time was given to religious exercises. The university was permitted to provide services to the Catholic population by the government. All Catholic students were required to attend this annual retreat started from Wednesday to Easter Sunday morning.

> 'Father James Wang was the retreat master. He has but last year returned from 12 years study in Europe, the last six of which were spent in Rome where he was ordained. The Western ideal of silence among the exercitants of a retreat is fully realized among Chinese. When they set out to give their time to meditation you cannot move them to speak for any trifling matter.'[55]

Those Catholic students who would participate in the retreats strictly observed the rules. Some years when they had retreats, they would have to stay in the retreat house for the entire time and were even not allowed to go out for meals.[56]

As a Catholic institution, the university did not set a limit onto itself in terms of religious activities. It expanded its horizons by inviting all the intellectuals of the city of Beijing to have a separate retreat during the Holy Week. These intellectuals were working in various institutions. During the Holy Week of the year 1938:

> 'Separate three-day retreats were preaching during Holy Week at the Catholic University for the students and for the lay intellectuals of the city. Not fewer than seventy students attended. Thirty-six Catholic teachers of the city, including professors of Fu Ren, Yenhching and Franco-Chinese Universities and various middles schools, attended the "intellectual Re-

treat" which was preached by Very Rev. Edward Boedefeld, OFM, well-known as editor of the *digest of the Synodal Commission* and as a Retreat-master.'[57]

Catholic Action Group

The Association of Catholic Action at the university did many things to enhance the Catholic life on campus. They did pilgrimages to holy places; attendance at Mass was a regular thing for them; attending spiritual conferences for nourishment; decorating the Catholic Dormitory Oratory and chanting sacred music were their ordinary life,[58] as well as the charitable work they did behind the scenes. However, there were two things that deserve special attention here: (a) Preaching Club, (b) Night Schools.

The Preaching Club was to tend to prison inmates not in churches. Though this work did not last until the end, the students tried their best.

> 'Every first and second Saturday and Sunday from four to six of our students used to go to the General Prison to teach prisons. At times they visited also the Communist youths, who are kept in a special prison.'[59]

The Night School, however, was a long-term commitment on the students' part. It experienced the greatest development. Everything was free for students at the school:

> 'Bent on practical sociology, we started a so-called Night School. Poor pagan boys come to it who otherwise cannot afford an education. In our Night School, there are always some 80 to 90 boys. Books, paper, pens, and other school materials for this school amounted to about $250. This money is partly collected, partly asked for from the Association members, and partly donated by the University. The teachers are all members of the Association.'[60]

As a result of this teaching effort, the better students of the night school were helped to enter regular middle schools while many of others had been placed as apprentices in various shops and factories.[61] Meanwhile, conversion of the students, teachers, professors, as well as their family members had always been an on-going thing at the university. The numbers and times of the frequent baptisms were always different each year depending on the circumstances.[62] The number of conversions was increasing as time progressed.

It is worthwhile to clarify some confusing issues of having the Catholic Action Group. For those people who were politically sensitive, this association was neither political, nor evangelical, but a group of Catholic students who tried to live out the spirit of the university as both Chinese and Catholic.[63] Cardinal Zani addressed at the first Congress of the Catholic Action in Shanghai:

'The purpose of the General Congress of Catholic Action in China is to labor together. All wish to spend themselves to the utmost to promote the welfare of the country and advance the morality and all-merciful God especially in these days to take away the tribulations of China and to grant that China may prosper.'[64]

The Catholic University had been trying to be true to its nature as both Chinese and Catholic at the same time. Catholic teaching and Chinese culture inspired the university to do many things. The university was making efforts to be the center where Western Christian Culture and Chinese Culture could meet.

Art Exhibition

Art exhibition could be an example to see how the West and East could come together harmoniously. The university had this for years. Exhibitions were extremely successful everywhere. It was first opened to all the students on campus who were interested in Arts, especially the Western and Chinese style Christian Arts. The exhibitions hosted by the Fine Arts department, which made the university go beyond the city boarders of Beijing, and beyond the borders of China as well. The university was known in the circles of the Church and in the world of artists.

When the Fine Arts Department was established, it did not envision such success and the subject of the department was teaching. Under the direction of Archbishop Celso Costantini who was the Papal Delegate to China, this department was originated under the direction of Prince Pu Jin. The aim of its foundation was to use native art as a means of spreading the Catholic faith. Fu Ren University was, in fact, the only private university in China with an Academy of Native Art.[65] In 1934, after a few years of development, the dean of the department Luke Chen who was a convert[66] and its pupils who were still non-Catholics began to use Christian ideas for their paintings. This demonstrated that the faculty and students had an integrated view of the understanding of the Chinese arts and the Catholic Church:

'Catholic Church has always been a companion to art as well as a guide to science. As a companion to art she has always encouraged the artist to express himself in terms of beauty, for true beauty is of heavenly origin. From this concept of beauty the Church has never separated, she was one with it.'[67]

The first exhibition was held in Shanghai in the year of 1935, when Catholics had their first National Congress of Catholic Action. Astonishing approval was showered on this new venture.[68] The second exhibition was held a year later in 1936 in Beijing. This particular one made great influence in world of artists. The Fine Arts Department of the Catholic University prepared an exposition of Christian paintings in the Chinese style for the early days of December:

> 'Some sixty paintings by Prince Pu Chin, a great-grandson of Emperor Tao Kuang, of Professor Luke Chen, and of several of their associates and students were on exhibition for a number of days. Simultaneously, photographs of all religious pictures painted by students of Catholic University since the beginning of 1934 were shown, together with reproductions of these pictures in Chinese and European art reviews...
>
> 'The Exposition enjoyed the high patronage of His Excellency archbishop Zanin, Papal Delegate, and of the Very Rev. Dr. Wilhelm Schmidt, SVD, director of the Lateran Ethnological Mission Museum in Rome, on whose initiative the Exposition will be held at a later date in the Eternal city.'[69]

After earning its reputation within the nation, Fu Ren was invited to have an exhibition at the Eucharistic Congress in Manila in February of 1937, "where it drew throngs of pilgrims, and made the whole world aware that China was coming of age, as far as its Catholicity concerned."[70]

From that time onward, the works produced from the Fine Art Department began to make their routes internationally. Artists worldwide recognized the achievement. An international exhibition was soon arranged in France in 1937. As a result of that, "some 14 works produced by the Fine Arts Department at Fu Ren were on exhibition at the World Faire in Paris. All of them have been sold."[71] Meanwhile, another exhibition was arranged in Vienna for 1938. The well-known art dealer, Mr. K. Exner of that city, "will sponsor the debut in Europe of various disciplines of Lucas Chen's school: Wang Su Ta, Lu Hung Nien, Su Zi Hua, among others. At least twenty scrolls will be presented to the general public at this time."[72]

The saying "All roads lead to Rome" is especially true to Fu Ren University. Another exhibition of Chinese Christian art was arranged, under the special patronage of the Holy Father, to be held in the rooms of the Press Exhibit Hall at the Vatican. Many of the paintings which had won wide acclaim at the Paris Exhibit of Mission Art was going to be forwarded from the French capital for this final exhibit.[73]

Fu Ren University was extremely proud of its works after they arranged the exhibition in the Vatican,

> "It is planned that this, this display of Chinese Christian Art ever attempted on a grand scale, will thus bring to the Continent of Europe some acquaintance with the Renaissance of Christian Art now taking place in the Far East, under the auspices of the Catholic University, called by the Chinese, the University of the Pope.'[74]

Eventually, the exhibition became an annual event of the university. Every year there were new productions from the department. In May of 1938, the display was held by Mr. Li Chih-ho, a successful painter of the human figure, whose sideline was horses, a theme much loved in Chinese art. Some thirty paintings and thirty lovely Chinese fans embellished with figures were on display. At the same time, three others also presented their paintings, especially some 50 specimens of Sculptures that were done by Mr. Huang Ta Hsia.[75] In 1939, the arts department prepared a series of catechetical pictures.[76]

From 1940 onward, Fu Ren added variety of art works to its already existing ones. By this year, all who had been coming to the exhibitions expressed their keen surprise at the developments of the last ten years. It was just a decade that this modern school of Chinese Christian Art had been underway. Woodcuts became popular in the university.[77] Mr. Wang Ching-fang[78], a non-Catholic, had 4,000 woodcuts of secular art, and with the recently done 250 Christian woodcuts, attracted considerable attention. Also, specimens of woodcarving were displayed that were chiefly designed of bamboo sketched by His Highness, Prince Pu Jin—and industriously executed in wood by one of the students of the Art department.[79] George Wang Suda did the Chinese Catechetical Art series.[80] The liturgical arts were done and exhibited to the public.[81]

Fu Ren University stated that "China and art are synonymous, and the inspiration of Christian ideals has slowly brought a renaissance into existence, whose results are truly amazing."[82] In the late 1930s, the university already knew the reality of the Fine Art Department and the future influence of the Church, because of its confidence in the unique nature of the university as Catholic and Chinese. The artistic heirloom of the Chinese race was indeed enriched by Christian ideas and ideals. Doctor Chen Yuan, the president of the university, praised this in the highest terms. He also acknowledged the great faculty, composed from both East and West, for their tremendous work in this field. It was indeed the growing interest in such arts 'in intellectual circles in China is noticeable in circles other than the Catholic University's own spheres of influence.'[83]

In the article *Beauty so Ancient...* Joseph Brunet described the achievement of Fu Ren Christian arts as:

> 'The chief glory of Chinese Christian arts is that it has given new impetus to this ancient pedigreed art, has provided it with new forms, and with a whole new source of spiritual and cultural content.'[84]

The Chinese Christian arts produced from Fu Ren University attracted a lot attention from the media. Many journals and periodicals printed articles and pictures explaining the renaissance of Chinese Christian art. In every case, they met with favorable comment and encouragement.[85] As a result, a great number of people from America and Europe purchased art from Fu Ren University.[86]

Music

Another great extra-curricular activity was Church music concerts. Music has been a long tradition of the Catholic Church to draw people together. As previously mentioned, Fu Ren University hosted concerts to raise money for the relief service. That was not the sole purpose. Though those occasions indeed raised a lot of money for the poor, the university had other purposes as well: as enjoyment for the music lovers. In Beijing at that time, it was too expansive for many to go to concerts, especially for the students. Anyone who loved music was invited to come.

The concerts for students' entertainment did not really start until 1935. There was no record of why the university decided to have such concerts, but one piece of information could be found in *Fu Ren Magazine*. Though might be someone's speculation, it was probably the real reason:

> 'Clifford King has some speculation here: "Father Ruhl is opening a series of Sunday evening concerts in the auditorium, to compete, I suppose, with the highly priced concerts given at the same time in the Peking Hotel. We hope that the students will profit much by this constant attraction offered to them."'[87]

For the benefit of the student body as a whole, besides Father Ruhl's inaugurated series of Sunday concerts,[88] he invited some other musicians to come on the campus to expand students' horizons. Two separate piano concerts were featured in 1935 by visiting artists Madame Rene Florigny and Mr. Harold Scott.[89] In addition, two plays were held in the university auditorium by a professional troupe.[90]

Each Christmas since 1935, the university would have a Christmas concert. For Christmas concert in 1935, the students prepared a program for this particular occasion of poems, songs, and instrumental music. It was the first appearance of a university choir as such. In the meantime, the instrumental music was a gift of a sextet from the American Legation guard with whom the university was friendly.[91] In 1936, the university had made significant progress:

> 'The program, arranged by Rev. Theodo Ruhl, SVD, MUS. D., featured some 15 selections from various masters of the last three centuries. Besides instrumental numbers, which piano, violin cello and two violins, there were several Christmas carols and the large and appreciative audience was given and opportunity to join generally in the singing of "Silent Night."'[92]

Father Ruhl was an accomplished musician who designed the organ at the North Cathedral of Beijing. It was the largest one in Beijing and in China. For several years, he had had some organ recitals in the cathedral. In 1938, he featured another series of four organ recitals there. Music lovers who had, in the past, heard his organ recitals at the Cathedral were thrilled to learn the news. Besides the students, the public was invited to enjoy the interesting, historical series of recitals. They were all free and advantageous to the numerous students of not only Fu Ren, but also of the university-city Beijing:

> 'The aim of the four recitals was to give the audience a picture of classical organ compositions created within the last 300 years, namely from 1600 to modern times. (A) Pre-Bach music and included the composer Handel, (B) "All-Bach Recital", (C) Devoted to specimens of German and French organ compositions of the 19th century, (D) Work of Max Reger, eminent as the greatest organ composer since the time of Bach, including also a Fantasy and Fugue from the latter musician.'[93]

Such occasional concerts presented by the Catholic University had evoked favorable comments from the public. Though largely classical, these concerts had proved popular, "attracting an ever-growing number of hearers who appreciate the opportunity to listen to good music rendered by excellent artists but without 'static'."[94]

Since music became an important part of the university life, the university decided to have a concert at the beginning of the school year 1940–41 to welcome the new incoming students. One article entitled *The Marines "Say it with Music"* has it:

> 'The marine team is the best in all the metropolis. When invited to give one of their delightful garden concerts at Fu Ren on the occasion of the opening of the new school year they lent a willing ear. Colonel A. H. Turnage, commander of the Embassy guard, heartily approved their coming. A number of embassy officials, among them Mr. Smythe and Ringwalt, attended the concert. Over 2,000 students and friends of the university attended the performance, which served as a pleasant welcome to alma mater's new students.'[95]

Music is understood as a universal, which can be appreciated by all humanity at all times. The university knew its power and desired that the students and all music lovers in the city would appreciate the efforts that Fu Ren was putting into its concerts. The concerts indeed enriched the students' life and broadened their horizons by letting them enjoy the Western classical songs rather than the traditional Chinese Opera.

Summary

The variety of religious activities, though started as religious, benefited a variety of people. They did not only make the university known, but also demonstrated Fu Ren was an educational institution with the purpose of developing Chinese culture in light of Catholic Faith.

Conclusion

Extra-curricular activities are expressions of the meaningful life of a university. It certainly can tell the outside world what the particular university is. Fu Ren University's extra-curricular activities indeed achieved the purpose of making the university known not only within China, but also outside of China. These activities showed the competitive nature of Fu Ren University and brought the young university to a new level of competition with other prestigious universities in China. Meanwhile, Fu Ren University achieved its goal and mission to be the first-rate university in China, which was not only measured by academics, but also from the development of potentials of all.

Sports made the university famous in China and in Asia, which attracted many people's attentions. Fu Ren was very competitive and became the champion in sports. Because of this, many young talented students were attracted to this university. Sports then were not money-making revenue for the university, but to increase the visibility and the reputation of the university. Arts brought the West and the East together and produced 'world-famous painters in less than a decade of operation.'[96] Many talented students came to this university and studied both Catholic and Chinese traditions in painting. These painters combined the best of Christian arts and Chinese methods in painting, which produced a new type of painting style in China. Relief services of the university brought the whole Chinese people and the Catholic Church together. At the same time, the poor and the homeless benefited from the work. The students had hands on experiences in providing services, which prepared them well for the future. The musical activities nourished all who had connection with the university and helped the students who could not afford going to a concert.

These discussed extra-curricular activities indicate that the university developed all its potential as a Catholic and Chinese institution: Christian Charity and Chinese Benevolence. They cared about the students' life, the quality of the university, and the needs of China. The university intended to be an excellent university in every way, not a mediocre one was revealed through the extra-curricular activities. These activities were motivated by and meanwhile showed this unique nature of the university. These activities proved that the university administration did not only care for its own university's well-being as an institution, but also cared for the service that the university could provide for the well-being of China. This also showed the unselfish nature of the missionaries at Fu Ren. The university had accomplished its mission by educating Chinese youth in the Catholic and Chinese ways, and therefore earned its reputation as one of the best universities in China.

One must also keep in mind the efforts the university had to make to keep the university not only to survive, but also to develop and to expand. In the same time, Fu Ren had to serve the nations' needs during the wartime and the political turmoil in China because of its nature and mission. The university administration must have had to be courageous and adventurous in order to do so. The background of the affects of wars and political entanglements that Fu Ren had to deal with help readers understand the uneasiness to achieve what it had achieved in those years. Chinese politics and Japanese's imperialistic invasion in the early years were not able to destroy the university. Fu Ren University rode above all those political tides and found its ways to achievement.

CHAPTER 7

Political Entanglements

The determination to be a first-rate Catholic and Chinese university enforced Fu Ren University to utilize all its potentials to achieve its goals. The university indeed achieved its goals before it was amalgamated with other universities in 1952. During those 27 years of its existence, in the midst of wars and political turmoil, the university developed from merely a preparatory school in 1925 into a university with graduate programs in the mid-1930s. It became the second largest university in Beijing in 1945. This extraordinary growth and expansion were incomprehensible in comparison with any higher education institution, even during peaceful times. These years from 1925 to 1952 were rather strenuous for Fu Ren University's development. Its history is incomplete if the political entanglements that Fu Ren had to deal with are not discussed. Dealing with politics became almost a regular routine of Fu Ren University.

Within those 27 years, Fu Ren University went through four different governments: Warlords, Nationalists, Japanese and Communists. Each government dealt with the university differently. However, none of them was peacemaking during their reign in Beijing. Except the Warlords, the other three affected Fu Ren University greatly. The political turmoil provided opportunities for the university to rise above and to develop, to expand and to close during the Communist era. Obviously, the university was not insulated from the political arena. Starting from the very beginning, Fu Ren University made a great decision that helped the university tremendously in the long run. The decision was not to take any political stance, but to focus on what the university intended to be as an academic institution. In order to be an academic institution and to be true to its mission, the university officials had to comply with governmental laws without compromising its principles. That decision helped the university to go through the warlords, Nationalists and Japanese governments, everything except the Communists. Just before the Communists took the control over the university on October 12, 1950, the university had found it hard to comply with their demands. Two years later, the university's name was taken off the list of the universities and was divided among many universities, although the major part was taken over by Beijing Normal University and the President Chen Yuan was named as the new president of this newly organized university. Fu Ren University certainly did not exist in a vacuum, but was situated in Beijing, the political and cultural center of China for many centuries.

Fu Ren students were culturally driven, as all other university students were, and were also politically oriented. The changing situation in China certainly influenced all. The "no political stance" of the university could dissuade the students from actively involving themselves with politics in a certain way, but could not prevent them from participating them. At the opening of the academic school year 1927–28, Mr. Mu Yuan-fu, a member of the Board of Trustees who was the former Minister of Education Ministry addressed:

> '...I wish to declare that I am prepared to guarantee with my life and property that the students at the Catholic University will never participate in political agitations or street-parades, nor give the least cause for dissatisfaction to the Chinese Government.'[1]

Those dignitaries, other than the university officials, who made addresses at this inaugural also made clear in this opening, the non-political stance of the university.[2] This was indeed the reason why Fu Ren University could rise above the political turmoil and earn its great reputation in China of being strict in discipline and in academics. The students' participation in variety of protests made Fu Ren known as the strictest Catholic university in China because the administration used their discretion to make sure of the nature of the protests. The university encouraged students to make careful examination of any sort of student activities in China, especially in Beijing. In those years, there were many student agitations and sometimes, other politically oriented people used the students for their purposes. Fu Ren University did this because of the mission of the institution to be a center of learning rather than politics. When the unity of China was threatened, it was then when Fu Ren had most of its student movements. This indeed showed their strong patriotism. The university administration supported such actions.

Because of the complicated political issues that this chapter is dealing with, the issues are structured as the following: 1). Overview of the political backgrounds: Warlord, Nationalist, Japanese and Communist, 2). Fu Ren student activism, 3). Fu Ren and Warlords, 4). Fu Ren and Nationalist, 5). Fu Ren and Japanese, 6). Fu Ren and Communists, 7). Conclusion. Realizing the difficulties to categorize the political entanglements as such, I try to use historical evidence from the archives I have researched and some other authors' work to discuss them. These concrete historical evidences will certainly speak for themselves and will clarify the issues.

Overview of the Political Background

The theme is to discuss how Fu Ren University dealt with politics and the governments, in order to survive. It is therefore not my interest to argue which party was right or which party was wrong in the process of the political entanglements. The archival materials will only represent the factual information that Fu Ren University had to deal with these issues. All these four governments had impact and influenced the growth of the university greatly in the years. During the warlords' era, the university was established and was actively involved with social service. During the Nationalist period, the university expanded and grew rapidly. The students were actively involved with some protests. By the time the Sino-Japanese War broke out, Fu Ren had already become a university with a graduate program. During the Japanese period, the university also developed and expanded, with a great deal of interruptions. Fu Ren persevered and became one of the best universities in China. During the Communist period, the University did not develop but became small in terms of student enrollment and faculty. In less than two years, the university disappeared in China when the government reorganized all higher education institutions. The achievements that Fu Ren made were tremendous as far as the university development concerned. Somehow, these achievements were inseparable with the external political influences because the adaptations the university had to make helped these achievements.

Many researchers have showed their interest in the politics, education and wars in modern China.[3] More or less, they touched upon some aspects of these when they researched on other respective fields. There is not much research on Fu Ren's political aspect at all. After the fall of the Chinese Empire in 1911, China began its modernization. In the meantime, the whole country became anarchy and was divided by the Warlords. Prior to 1925 when Fu Ren was established, "The control of the modern educational system by politicians and bureaucrats caused it to be under the constant influence of changing political fortunes of the nation, which resulted in frequent changes of personnel among the higher and more influential educational officials."[4] After 1925, the situation of education and politics was intensified because of the rising of Nationalism. Students organized a variety of anti-Christianity and anti-imperialism movements.[5] Such a movement reached its height in the early months of 1927 during the North Expedition.[6] As a result, the educational system in China "became permeated with the dogmatic and intolerant spirit of modern nationalism."[7]

The warlords, who considered themselves as nationals, were fighting against each other for different purposes with the goal of taking over the whole country. However, many of them were strongly attached to foreign powers, which made it disastrous for the average Chinese.[8] The political situation was chaotic nationwide in those years before China was unified by the Nationalist Party in 1928. In 1924, the President of the Chinese Republic was thrown into jail by the warlord Feng Yun-xiang and thereafter, Duan Qi-rui became the executive of Beijing. In 1926 two warlords Zhang Zuo-lin and Wu Pei-fu ousted him, and had a joint cabinet in Beijing and established the Ministry of Education.[9] In 1927, Zhang Zuo-lin alone took over Beijing and reorganized the Ministry of Education under which Fu Ren was recognized with university status.

After the death of the Warlord Zhang Zuo-lin on June 3, 1928, the Nationalist Party took control over Beijing successfully and Fu Ren University came under the jurisdiction of the Nationalist Party, whose capital was established in Nanjing. The Ministry of Education was re-organized and Fu Ren was in danger of losing its university status because it only had one faculty.

Having taken control over China, the Nationalist Party automatically became the sole legitimate government of China and began to insert its power into all organizations, including the universities. In 1927, anti-Christian activity reached its high point.[10] Many Christian institutions came under attack. However, the government's non-resistance policy toward the Japanese invasion caused many student protests from time to time. This nourished the growth of the Communist Party because many students were turned away from it. Meanwhile, for fear of the Communists' infiltration, the Nationalist Party also caused unrest on many university campuses. Fu Ren University had to deal with the Nationalist Government constantly.

The Japanese invasion of China was to make China as its colony, to achieve its planned Far East Order. The first time they took the boldest step was in the year of Northern Expedition in 1927 and adopted its own policy of unilateral action.[11] They fought against the Nationalist Army from going north in Jinan, the capital of Shandong Province. Fu Ren Students joined other students to protest against the Japanese and against the Nationalists because of their bypassing of the Japanese without putting up a fight. Many protests occurred later prior to the Sino-Japanese War declared in 1937.

On July 7, 1937, the Sino-Japanese War was officially declared at Marco Polo Bridge[12] just outside of the city of Beijing. This war stirred up the whole country to rise against the Japanese aggression. Unfortunately, the Chinese army could not combat the powerful Japanese military and retreated inland. The Japanese took over many important cities, such as: Shanghai, Tianjin and Beijing. Many national and private universities left their "homes" and migrated to the west. In Beijing, The Japanese established a provisional government that was considered by many Chinese as a "puppet government" of the Japanese. Fu Ren University and Yan Jing University were the only two left in operation out of thirteen in total while the Japanese took control of Beijing territory. In 1941, when the Japanese attacked Pearl Harbor, Yan Jing University, which was controlled by the Americans, had to close its doors in Beijing and moved inland to join other universities. Meanwhile, Fu Ren, had been having a German rector since 1936 and a Chinese president, was left alone in Beijing. This situation lasted until 1945 when the Japanese were completely defeated and all of the universities moved back to Beijing. They closely followed the Nationalist Government.

The rise of the Communist Party caused uneasiness for many in China, such as the ruling Nationalists, the Catholic Church, and many other leaders from different countries who were stationing in China. Many schools were therefore under strict regulation from the Nationalist government in an effort to get rid of anyone who had connection with the Communist Party. The Communist Party however, basically was very secretive and infiltrated into almost every walk of life in China with the intention to recruit members to fight against all others. In the meantime, the Communist Party also threatened the Catholic Church because of its atheistic teachings and rapid growth. The Catholic Church recognized the Nationalist Party as the legitimate government of China after 1927. Fu Ren University also cooperated with the Nationalist Party, to seek out the Communist Party members within its student population. The Catholic Church, as well all other parties, misjudged the power and mobility of the Communist Party in China. As a result, when the Communists took over China in 1949, all other opposition forces had to leave China: Nationalists left for Taiwan, others withdrew from China and went back to their countries, but the Church missionaries remained staying. Automatically, Fu Ren University, as well as the Catholic Church, became major threats to the Communists' control in China. Because of the international influences of the Catholic Church, the government was comfortable to see its existence in China. In the meantime, the Communist Government accumulated all the political powers in China and was ready to face any opposition. Fu Ren University directly confronted the government by refusing to pay the salaries of some progressive professors who were appointed by the government to be on the faculty. This action angered the government. As a result, the university lost its autonomy in October 1950 and was dissolved in 1952. Fu Ren was divided among many other universities as listed in chapter one.

Fu Ren Student Activism

The statement that Kenneth S. Latourette made about the students is worth quoting. "Students are one of the most significant and important features of modern China. What is termed the student movement is the expression of their activities and of the currents of thought which have been most prominent among them. To understand the Student Movement is to understand much of the mind of China. To fail to understand the Student

Movement is to fail to enter the soul of modern China."[13] It is indeed true for readers to understand the role that students played during the anarchy and turmoil in China in order to understand the whole political situation.

Jessie Lutz has discussed in detail the nature and history of early student activism in his book *Chinese Politics and Christian Missions*. It is unnecessary to repeat what he has already discussed. However, it is necessary to add what he intended to leave out in his book which was the Catholic Church. The students from Fu Ren University, as a group, certainly were affected by the chaotic society and shared the same feelings as all other students had toward the governments and sometimes toward Christianity. They were actively involved in many protests that showed their patriotism, but not much against the Catholic Church because they understood the nature of the university. The anti-Christian aspect from Fu Ren University did not prevail until Communists gained control over the university. However, one reference on anti-foreign culture was mentioned in *Fu Ren University Bulletin*,

> 'The scholastic year of 1928-29 was opened...and the student enrollment increased...this was a year of student unrest throughout China, and of demonstrations against alleged "foreign cultural Aggression." It was found necessary to dismiss 20 students form Fu Ren University, but classes continued without interruption up to the time of the Commencement exercise held on June, 15, 1929.'[14]

This "anti-foreign cultural aggression" certainly was not discussed fully in the Bulletin. There was not much reference on this protest at all anywhere. The student activism in Beijing had its momentum over the years. Because of the students' protest against foreign culture, the Dao Ming Institute (a Dominican School which was just opened in September of 1928) had to close its doors as a result of it. The dismissed students from Dao Ming formed an association to attach Fu Ren, according to a letter from Father Ildephouse to the archabbot:

> 'The dismissed students of Tao Ming Institute formed an association against the opening of the school but they also threatened to close our school whilst we had little to fear from our students there were some six or seven who were susceptible of agitation and joined the outside association of the Tao Ming...Naturally the trouble never ceased though our loyal students ostracized the trouble-makers.'[15]

Though this was not a true large-scale student activism, it indicated that Fu Ren students were not immune to the political movements. In fact, this student agitation also caused Yan Jing University to close its doors for some days. Father Ildephonse recorded, "...but it seems their (Yan Jing's) student body is also too loyal to submit. The nationalists may be at the very bottom of such agitation, though they hide this from view. They may thereby divert attention from their own weakness in the government."[16] Fu Ren students were educated in traditional Chinese culture and with an understanding of the Catholic principle of justice. Most of them were interested in national unity, peace and patriotism, not in the university as a good institution. The first recorded student protest occurred at Fu Ren University was in 1928 when the Japanese and Chinese Nationalist troops clashed in Jinan, the capital of Shandong Province.[17] According to the recorded history, Jiang Jie-shi, the president of the Nationalist Party, decided to continue his North Expedition to unify China. When the clashes between Chinese and Japanese soldiers occurred, students were geared for action. Lutz mentioned "Shanghai students announced a three-day strike while they organized a boycott of Japanese goods, and schools in numerous cities called protest meetings."[18] He also mentioned in Beijing, though the "Beijing Student Union had been outlawed by Warlord Zhang Zuo-lin, the students staged a 24-hour walkout that led to early closure of many schools for summer vacation."[19] Beida and Yan Jing were mentioned in Lutz's book but he left out Fu Ren University.[20] The chronicle of Fu Ren University Bulletin has recorded its own involvement of May 3, 1928:

> 'Clash between the Japanese soldiers and the Chinese troops (under Jiang Jie-shi) at Jinanfu. This was the occasion of a nation-wide patriotic protest on the part of the Chinese students, in which the students of the Catholic university of Peking took a prominent part.' [21]

The Japanese became more aggressive in its Far East New Order and tried to take over all of China. On September 18, 1931, they took over Shenyang Province, containing one of the biggest cities in the northeast region of China. Jiang Jie-shi, the president of the Nationalist Party, had ordered that "under no circumstances should the Chinese army resist any attack, the Japanese occupied the entire three provinces of the region within three months. The Chinese Republic were furious about the invasion, and angered by the non-resistance policy by the Nationalist government."[22]

Facing such a national humiliation, a strong uproar among the Chinese people occurred against the Japanese invasion, especially among college and university students who were politically and culturally charged. Many students went to Nanjing to protest the Japanese invasion and called for military resistance against the Japanese. Father Hugh Wilt described the Fu Ren University students' actions:

> 'The students on account of their intense hatred for the Japanese are terribly excited. They are ready to join the army to fight against Japan. The police are guarding the city very well to keep down all kinds of student agitation... They are continually holding meetings and posting signs...'[23]

While the protests were still going on nationwide, the Japanese moved their troops inward and entered Tianjin, the seaport city next to Beijing. More disturbed by this invasion, many universities closed their doors to resist the Japanese. Yan Jing and Qing Hua students joined other students to go to Nanjing to tell the president of the Nationalist Party what he should do. In the meantime, Fu Ren continued its classes. Father Hugh wrote down this event as such:

> 'The Tsing Hua students left for Nanking last Thursday. They could not get on the train but they were determined that the train should not go without them. They simply got out in front of the train... the national university is the worst of the lot. The soldiers have been called in and they are not trying to keep the place quiet. Our students held a mass meeting last Monday. Fu Ren is the only university operating and even at that it is operating under very favorable conditions. Classes are very well attended. The students are peaceful and quiet. They are being razzed of course by the other schools and by some it is feared that the students from the other schools will attempt to pull off some demonstration here but that is hardly possible since all student gatherings on the streets are positively forbidden.'[24]

This quietness at Fu Ren did not last long. As thousands of students from many cities in the south marched to Nanjing, Fu Ren students could not stay on campus anymore and decisively joined that grand march. Father Hugh continued:

> 'The students held a mass meeting and decided to join the other schools in Peking for the grand "March" on the Capital. We were quite surprised at the outcome of the meeting for the whole affair was so well planned that we felt sure of the majority voting against going. As often happens when dealing with the Chinese just the opposite happened. The authorities at once got together thinking that they would be able to stop it but their efforts were in vain. In fact we nearly caused a strike by trying to stop it.'[25]

According to Father Hugh, Fu Ren students did very well during the protest. Many Fu Ren students who went to the protest earlier took the first train leaving for Nanjing. As of tens of thousands of students gathered in the city of Nanjing, the government got nervous. An order came from Nanjing to threaten the students, "If they (the students) left, the station master was to be punished while the engineer who would bring them to Nanking would be shot upon his arrival in Nanking."[26] As a result of this order, a very strong cordon of soldiers and police surrounded Beijing station. Many students including many from Fu Ren who missed the first train were stuck there. No one was allowed to enter, nor leave the station. Fu Ren students were the exceptions. For such a reason, all the students at the train station claimed themselves as Fu Ren students:

> 'The Fu Ren students seem to have been on their good behavior, at least they won the respect and good will of the soldiers. After the orders were given that no one was allowed to enter, the chief of police was unwise enough to make the remark to other students that the Fu Ren students could enter while the rest had to keep out. There was almost a free for all then.'[27]

In Beijing, Fu Ren students did well, and meanwhile, in Nanjing, Fu Ren students were the leaders of the protest. "They took the lead on the conservative side while a number of schools went entirely 'Red'. Nine other schools sided with Fu Ren."[28] Father Hugh continues,

> 'At Nanking the situation was about the same. Nine schools lined up with Fu Ren, wearing white bands on their arms, while the others were red. The President received our group and spoke to them for two hours. He thanked them for their good will and treated them very well. So well in fact that they think has no equal. The students were given meal tickets while in Nanking, good housing while they were there, and were accompanied part of the way back by men from the government offices who took care of their food etc. The others are openly 'red'. They didn't want to see Chiang Kai shih but were there to make trouble.'[29]

Father Hugh concluded that the successful protest put "Fu Ren University in the limelight". The majority of the Catholic students from Fu Ren were in that grand march to Nanjing. In the end, these Catholics took the lead and went far enough to bring credit upon the Church.[30]

In December of 1935, the student protests became more aggressive because, first of all, a large contingents of Japanese troops appeared in various parts of the land; secondly, the Japanese moved inland and distributed large quantities of inflammatory literature by planes all over the places; worst of all, the Japanese established a New State — Manchuria after they occupied Hebei and Charhar. The Nanjing Government was obliged to recognize its sovereignty[31]. In Beijing itself, the ancient capital and leading university city, feelings ran high. Fu Ren students once again showed their patriotism:

> 'University students, Fu Ren included, had done what they could to show their patriotism and prevent national disruption. But shortly after Nanking had been obliged to recognize the new situation, bitterness became manifest and soon all universities had temporarily or indefinitely suspended classes in order to deliberate on the national crisis. The students of Fu Ren petitioned of the University authorities a triduum interruption of classes wherein to express properly their sorrow at the nation's loss, and this petition was granted them; no indefinite or disorderly strike was declared here, but the student body on the whole manifested excellent maturity of judgment in their consultations, a quality extolled in them by many outsiders attending their discussions. The triduum was spent ideally in discussions on ideal citizenship and similar patriotic topics.'[32]

On the 9th of December 1935, the Fu Ren students marched out to join others to protest against the Japanese aggression and the compromising position of the Guomindang.[33] On December 16, 1935, when the New State officials were installed with the outlawed Chinese Emperor, another national protest broke out:

> 'A gigantic student demonstration, unparalleled in the history of Peking, began in the early morning. From every university, national or private, as also from middle schools, came huge contingents of male and female protesting marchers displaying banners expressing opposition to separation, to the northern militarists and the Japanese.'[34]

Over 5,000 students in the morning and later 7,000 students participated in the protest in order to show their opposition to the separation of China. However, the local police oppressed the students. They arrested many and over 100 were injured, some of them were rather seriously.[35] As a result of the demonstration, many universities' classes were stopped and students left for vacation early. But Fu Ren campus continued as usual, in the following months, to be filled with activities organized by students or many other people who wanted nothing but fighting against the Japanese.

As the Civil War in China intensified after the defeat of the Japanese, there were more protests occurred. According to Paul Han, from 1946 until 1948, "the demonstrations and protests organized by the students against Civil War, against Hunger and Thirst, against American Involvement, etc., broke out from time to time."[36] One particular student protest in the Fall of 1946 is worthy of mentioning at the moment. Unlike the previous protest, this one appeared to be triggered by an incident involving one university female student and two American soldiers. China was in a terrible situation when that incident occurred. The students simply poured their anger toward the Americans for variety of reasons.

After the defeat of the Japanese and at the beginning of the Second Civil War, inflation was terrible which I have described previously as "poor yet millionaires"[37]. Many people did not have jobs, and the survival level became very basic. In order to meet the expense of the university, the administration proposed to raise the heating fee for the winter, which sparked a lot of anger and hostility among the students "who were already feeling awkward with their pitiful amounts of pocket money."[38] In the meantime, the incident of the American soldiers happened which really helped the student to get their frustrations out by protesting,

> 'Right at that frustration moment, a female student of Peking University, Shen Chung, was raped by two American soldiers in the evening of December 24.39 To protest against outrageous thing, the students at Fu Ren, in coalition with many other university students in Peking, organized a huge march, asking the US government to withdraw its troops from China. Since Father Rigney (Rector of the university) was also an American, the students poured out their anger and frustration against him in relation with the matter of raising up the heating fee. In the end, the proposal to raise heating fee was aborted.'[40]

The Fu Ren University student activism was influenced by the changing politics. In the spring of 1947, as the Civil War dragged on longer and intensified, inflation grew sky high, people even could not have enough food

Political Entanglements 157

to eat. Fu Ren students again joined other university students from Beida, Qinghua and Normal and went on the street again to protest against hunger and civil war.

> 'On May 17th, 1947, Qinhua and Beida students started the "anti-hunger, anti-Civil War movement. They were on strike again. Fu Ren University Students were also joined... on the 19th, there were more 200 male students and about 200 females decided to join the strike... on the 20th, Fu Ren students had a strike and joined others in the anti-hunger and anti-civil war protest.'[41]

Fu Ren students along with all other university students were rather active in the protests, not for their own interests, but for the sake of China as a nation. Their patriotism and nationalism were beyond description and could become a window to see the needs of China at the moment of a particular protest. The Nationalist Government at this point lost its trust and loyalty from the students because of inflation and corruption. They mostly turned to the Communists for hope and leadership.

Fu Ren and the Warlords

The taking over of the governments was done mostly through war and violence in China. As indicated previously, during the rapid changes of Beijing governments from warlords to the Nationalist Party within four years from 1924 to 1928, wars occurred numerous times. Though Fu Ren University was somehow protected by the American Treaty[42] with China, it was certainly affected by the effect of the wars because of its very location in Beijing. No direct contact between the university and the Warlords can be found from the available archives, but the university was indeed a battlefield for those warlords who struggled to gain control over Beijing. Meanwhile, Fu Ren University was established and recognized as the first Catholic higher education institution with the university status when the warlord Zhang Zuo-lin took power in the city. In this section, there are only two incidents need to be mentioned. One is the clash between the warlords Zhang Zuo-lin and "Christian General" Feng Yu-xiang, which caused the university to be involved; another is the registration of the university under its reign in 1927.

The clash between Marshal Zhang Zuo-lin and "Christian General" occurred in the Spring of 1926, which was several months after Fu Ren University was established. This clash caused many refugees to flood into the campus of the university. The university became a shelter for many victims of the war of which I have already discussed. This indirect political involvement provided an opportunity for the university to be known in the society.

Before the warlord Zhang Zuo-lin took control over Beijing, no other warlords really had the opportunity to control and organize the educational institutions. These institutions were basically left alone. In 1926,

Zhang Zuo-lin became the generalissimo and reorganized the Education Ministry, and set up roles for universities to follow. Because of the anti-Christian movement and anti-Western cultural sentiment, its law forbad all the private universities who tried to seek government recognition to require: first, the university name carries the name of religion, second, the students were obliged to study religion as a core course. The worst tragedy for those non-registered private institutions at the time was that their degrees did not have much market value at all. It was under such demands, that Catholic Fu Ren University decided to comply with all the requirements that the government laid out. First, the University decided not to have any course in religion in its core curriculum from the very beginning. Secondly, the university administration decided to change its original name from *Gong Jiao Da Xue*[43] (Catholic University) to Fu Ren University in 1927 when they were seeking government's registration. This change earned more respects from Chinese intellectuals simply because the name Fu Ren was more appealing for the Chinese. Once again, the administration demonstrated their ambition to make this university a Chinese one. Father Ildephonse mentioned this process of the name changing in his letter:

> '...Registration with the Chinese authorities of the university under the new name of the Fu Ren Ta Hsueh, the Kung Chiao we had to change to the above because of its religious implications meaning the Catholic or universal church...'[44]

Chen Yuan, however, the dean of the university and the former vice-minister of Education Ministry was very instrumental in this application process. The government accepted the application and recognized Fu Ren University as a university without posing any difficulties at all.

Fu Ren and the Nationalist Government

Fu Ren University and the Nanjing Nationalist Government did not have a mutually good relationship at the very beginning. Two reasons were significant for such a rocky relationship: First of all, some students accused Fu Ren as an imperialistic institution in 1929. The Nanjing Government became suspicious of the university and sent inspectors to inspect it; Secondly, Fu Ren was caught off guard by the government's new regulation which enforced the university to comply the law to have three colleges in order to keep its status. After this difficult beginning, Fu Ren and the government began to develop a rather smooth relationship because Fu Ren earned the government's respect by striving to be the best institution to emphasize on both the Chinese culture and Western Sciences. Three strikes came against the young university after the Nationalist took control over Beijing in the summer of 1928. The first strike was a student agitation that occurred shortly after the opening of the school year. As a result, the school had to be closed for some days. The students were motivated by the Chinese newspapers and launched a violent attack against the Catholic Church and the university itself as well. I have cited this briefly in the student activism section without mentioning the following:

> '...The school but opened in September had to be closed because of the students' strike...The student body launched a violent attack against the Catholic Church, accusing her of nationalism and imperialism. Naturally agitation was rife also against us and unfortunately some five or six dissatisfied or over exuberant students in our school tried to foster discontent her and disloyalty...'[45]

The second strike against the university came in April of 1929, which was on the day of *Qingming Arbor Day* of which I mentioned briefly earlier. A group of about twenty students demanded an extra holiday. Vice President Chen Yuan refused it. The next day, one student posted a manifesto attacking the Vice President and was caught. He was expelled and "this led to sundry disturbances, which, however, were speedily quelled by the loyal students, who eventually forced the score or more of agitators to leave the school the strike ended."[46] However, the dismissed students accused the university later, which caused some aggravation for the university,

> "The agitators, who had withdrawn from the School, organized under the name of "Resistance to Imperialistic Cultural Aggression Society" and sent a telegram denouncing the University to the Central Government at Nanking." [47]

In this hostile environment, the young university was caught in the midst of anti-Christianity, anti-Western culture and anti-imperialism movements in China. Many progressive students and intellectuals were constantly attacking the non-Chinese owned institutions. This very accusation from the students was rather serious which caused the suspicion from the government. An investigation was conducted eventually and found that the university was in good standing and that students were found making false accusations. The good name of Fu Ren University was restored.

The third strike against the university came at the end of April 1929 when Fu Ren University was demoted to a college status because it did not meet the new requirements from the Nanjing Education Ministry as I have discussed.

After three strikes, Fu Ren University was not only survived, but also developed and expanded. They worked very hard to ride above the political tide under the financial strains. After that, the Nationalist Government did not give the university much trouble but checked into the university occasionally regarding the Communists' infiltration. Arrests of suspected students happened occasionally. Because of the Nationalist's policy of non-resistance to Japanese, its efforts were put into fighting against the Communists all the time which eventually caused the down fall this government. Many correspondence letters were discovered both in Beijing Normal University and Beijing City Archives in talking about these inspections of Communists on the campus.[48]

During the years from 1932 to 1938, there were 15 official documents that came from the Nationalist Government instructing the university and asking the university officials to comply with the laws by attempting to wipe out the Communist members. On December 1, 1932, a confidential letter came from the government:

> 'The Communists are preparing to organize a student strike, and trying to mobilize the city of Peiping. They attempt to disturb the universities normal life and administration... if they success, it will be harmful to the university, to the government, as well as to the Northern Provinces (Manchuria). Therefore, we instruct you to be aware of it.'[49]

On November 2, 1933, about a year later, the Nationalist government sent a letter to the university asking the students to participate in a Fighting Against Communist Week:

> 'While this government is actively destroying the Communists, the civilians are energized and enthusiastic. Therefore, we have decided to organize a weeklong conference in the City Hall of Peiking. If you have nay information on the Communists, make sure to report that immediately."[50]

This letter was posted on the university bulletin board. Many other letters, whether transmitted to the university through the Ministry of Education, Police Department, or the Office of Propaganda Commission, were posted on the university bulletin board to inform students. The Nanjing government strongly encouraged the universities to do so until almost the last minute of the its defeat,

> 'All students who are spies of the Communists should be dismissed. If they are announced by the Special Court be to of no crimes they are permitted to resume their studies.' [51]

One more confidential letter revealed how the Nanjing Government reacted toward the Communists and Japanese. It came from the Directorate of Education Ministry of Beijing, entitled *The Books on Anti-Japanese and Communists*:

> 'All anti-Japanese books or those of the Communist theories should be sent to the Directorate before the end of October. It is, therefore, all the books, (1) anti-Japanese; (2) Communism; (3) socialism; (4) Marxism; (5) those books whether directly or indirectly talking about these themes, should be listed as forbidden books. This is an order to Fu Ren University.'[52]

The anti-Communists and non-resistance to the Japanese were very consistent in the Nationalists' policy. Mostly, the Nationalist Government dealt with the university through the transmission of documents and cables, either prior to the Sino-Japanese War or the postwar period. There was no constant physical presence from government officials on campus, which was unlike the Japanese and Communist's who dealt with the university through a physical intrusion into the university.

Fu Ren and the Japanese

The relationship between Fu Ren University and the Japanese was rather confrontational. The aggressiveness and the arrogance, as well as the brutality of the Japanese offended most of the Chinese population, especially the university students. Fu Ren students were no exception at all. Their nationalism and patriotism were expressed clearly during their protests against the invasion of the Japanese. The university officials, in their support for student activism, demonstrated their anti-Japanese sentimentality as well. The tension between the two was enormous.

Trying to occupy the whole country and to destroy all the oppositions,[53] the Japanese became more and more aggressive in China after 1937. It is necessary to mention once again that while the Japanese were trying to take over China, they did not attack the places where were occupied by their allies. Since the Opium War 1880–1882, many countries forced the Chinese Emperors to sign the unequal treaties with their governments so that certain places would be under their control rather than the Chinese. After the World War I, things changed, but many countries remained, such as Japan had its allies in China such as Germany, Italy, France and even the United States. Fu Ren and Yan Jing could open in Beijing were because of Fu Ren had a German Rector and Yan Jing was owned by the Americans. After the Japanese attacked the Pear Harbor in 1941, Yan Jing became a target of the Japanese and had to move out of city and Fu Ren was fortunate enough to remain there.

In order to fulfill their dreams in China, the Japanese took control over all the mines, railways, telephones, factories and banks, etc. More importantly, they tried to reconstruct schools in the occupied areas by enforcing very school to teach Japanese as the second language, and all textbooks should be modified to praise and glorify Japan. All schools must hang Japanese flag; students and their teachers must attend the celebration of Japanese victory over their enemies.[54] Experiencing this unspeakable shame and humiliation of the nation, Fu Ren University confronted all these requirements. There was no Japanese flag at the entrance of the university, no changing of the Japanese textbooks and curriculum, the students and professors refused to participate any Japanese celebrations in Beijing. The Japanese were not happy with it.

In early May of 1938, after many months of treacherous fighting, China lost another important city Xuzhou in Jiangsu Province to the Japanese. In order to celebrate this important victory, the Japanese ordered all the schools and various entities to celebrate this occasion voluntarily:

> 'When the order came to Fu Ren University and Fu Ren Middle Schools, it stated that if the schools did not organize their students to take part in the celebration, they would be closed...the celebration was held on the first Sunday of May. All of the schools in Beijing went to the celebration except for Fu Ren. The teachers and students who went to the celebration had to have two flags in their hands: one Japanese and one of the New Regime's five provinces controlled by the New Regime.'[55]

As a result of this resistance, the university and the middle schools were ordered to close the next day. Fortunately, the university was closed only for three days, but the middle schools were closed for a longer period of time until after the Fall semester started.[56]

Since Fu Ren University refused to participate in the Japanese celebration, Father Fu S.V.D. and some other priests were arrested. Some Fu Ren students, out of their patriotism, could not tolerate the Japanese cruelty toward the Chinese and decided to join the army. Father Fu and Father Kroes S.V.D. from Holland helped them go inland. They were caught and arrested. Luckily, Father Kroes was released soon, but unfortunately, Father Fu was severely tortured,

> 'The Japanese became furious...at the end of the first trial, which lasted about eight hours, Fr. Fu was already beaten half to death. Yet, the worst was still to come. The next day, the trial lasted even longer. Form seven o'clock in the morning till seven o'clock in the evening without ceasing, the Japanese officers took turns to question and torture him...'[57]

Father Fu was abused and tortured to the point of half death. "He was tortured to such an extent that his clothes were stained with blood and got stuck into his flesh. The Japanese had to have his clothes torn off and dressed in with the prison uniforms."[58] After many weeks of disappearing, many people at Fu Ren thought he was dead. The news of Father Fu's imprisonment reached the Shanghai. An Italian Franciscan who was a friend of his and also befriended with Benito Mussolini in1910s, petitioned the Italian and German governments to ask the Japanese to release Father Fu. Consequently, he was released weeks later and was sent to the United States for medical treatment.[59]

Because of these incidents, the Beijing puppet government condemned Fu Ren University as anti-Japanese. Fu Ren was hated by the government officials because of this. The Japanese sent their undercover detectives[60] onto the university property to seek opportunities to make arrests. Quite frequently, students and teachers had disappeared.[61] Despite the threats, the university continued its operation; President Chen Yuan and Rector Father Rahmann of Fu Ren were trying all they could to bail the professors and students out.

The president of the university although, originally discouraging the students from being involved in political matters, presently was active in resisting the Japanese. He was a true patriot and an anti-Japanese activist.

Political Entanglements

He was convinced that the Japanese were going to be defeated and encouraged the students to be strong, to be patriotic, vigilant and not be trapped by the Japanese. In the meantime, he strongly discouraged the student not to work for the Japanese. On four special occasions, he addressed the graduates on their graduation day along the same lines.[62]

In the Fall semester of 1942, the whole school had a sports competition. During the opening ceremony, the president noticed many officials who worked for the Japanese, some betrayers, opportunists and some sloppy students who were wasting time on campus, he addressed the following, entitled *Confucius Attending Sports Ceremony*:

> 'Many people attended a shooting arrow ceremony. When the ceremony about began, Confucius asked his disciple Zi Lu to address the people: *those people, such as, the defeated marshals, the betrayers, the officials whose country has been destroyed and rehired by the new regimes and those opportunists, should not be present at the ceremony.* At the end of the address, only half of the people left at the ceremony. At the end of the ceremony, the disciple once again said: *the young ones who love their brothers; the older ones who love the rituals; those who have principles and even die for their own dignities should sit at the head table.* Another half left at the end of the talk. Finally, Confucius asked the disciple to raise his glass, saying: *those who love to study, those who love the rituals, even at age of eighty or ninety, they still remain righteous, should sit at the head of the table.* As a result, only a few people left at the ceremony.'[63]

Those who were named in the president's address were extremely angry and indeed left the ceremony quietly. They knew the president was criticizing them, but they could not do anything to him because he quoted his speech from the *Analects* of Confucius. This indeed showed how patriotic and courageous the president of Fu Ren University was who also encouraged the students to do the same. Even during the terrible financial crisis of the university in 1941, the university turned down the offer from the provisional government of Beijing, which was under the direction of the Japanese.[64]

Fu Ren and the Communists Government

The relationship between Fu Ren University and the Communists was rather complex. The archives in fact have conflicting versions of the stories. Many missionaries wrote articles on the terrible things that the Communists had done to the Church: missionaries were killed and many schools were closed where the communists occupied.[65] The opposite side claimed that the Communists tried to protect people's lives and to keep the original status of all.[66] Over all, because of atheistic teaching of the Communism and the nature of this party were to change all others, which made Fu Ren University and the Communist Party never become friendly. Actually, they were hostile and intolerable toward each other from the very beginning when the Communist Party was founded in China in 1921.

In October 1948, the Communist military had already surrounded the city of Beijing and was trying to take over. They took over the major passes about 20 miles away from the city so that any moves in the city would be stopped. The Negotiation began between the Communists and the Nationalists in finding ways to take over Beijing, principally in a peaceful manner so that these two parties could make the transition. In Beijing, Fu Zuo-yi, the Nationalist commander decided to end the war by surrender in December and Beijing was peacefully taken over by the Communists on January 31, 1949 without shedding a drop of blood. The communist military moved into the city and the Nationalist military surrendered.

In early November of 1948, the American consulate in Beijing warned all the Americans to leave the city of Beijing. The Divine Word Fathers at Fu Ren began to move university's valuable staff out while of the communists addressed to all the universities in Beijing through radio, especially to Fu Ren " Fu Ren must change its entire policy."[67] The Church "up to this time has been entirely opposed to the communists and their students. Since no compromise is likely, I foreseen the closure of Fu Ren and the possible loss of the facilities there," wrote Auer.[68] This Divine Word priest had sensed and expressed the hostility that the communists had toward Fu Ren.

Fu Ren University, as a Catholic institution after having been established for so many years in China, had its own understanding of its mission and of Communism. In the meantime, had its own unique feeling toward the Communists:

> 'The Communist, unlike the Christian, cannot co-operate whole-heartedly with the traditional Chinese culture. There is no community of interests between the Chinese way and the Communist way of life: Communists do not preserve, but abandon, the traditional moral virtues of the Chinese.'[69]

As the Communists continued their victories over the Nationalists, many missionaries left the territories where the Communists took over. They came to Beijing and were sheltered at Fu Ren University.

> 'Almost every week the university receive a missionary bishop or priest who is seeking refuge and help for his mission which has been ruthlessly devastated by the onslaught or inroads of the Communists.'[70]

These Catholic missionaries who came to Beijing for refuge had experienced the ways communists had attacked the Church and themselves. One article entitled "the True Story of Chinese Communism" in *Fu Ren Magazine* discussed extensively how the communists attacked the Church. In the article, Father Raymond De Jaegher said, the methodology that communists used was "to seduce-to compromise-to pervert-to destroy." He continued,

> 'To discredit the Church in order to destroy it!...the continual tactics perfected by the Reds. Hence the communist's definitions: the priest? A use-

less being getting fat at the expense of the people. The priest? A parasite, living outside of society without a family. The priest? What does he produce? Where is the work of his hands?'[71]

Not only the Catholic priests were threatened by the attacks from the Communists, Fu Ren University, as well as many non-Chinese institutions, were all threatened by the progress of the Communists. In order to avoid direct confrontations with the Communists, the American consulate in Beijing issued another warning for all Americans to leave the city as soon as possible.[72] Fu Ren University was prepared for it. The rector, Father Rigney, already told the missionaries to make sure to have enough trunk space for things:

> 'Our university libraries are being packed in high ship crates for removal to Formosa or Shanghai and the general plan at present is for our latest group here in Peiping to move out first with these crates. The University boat, the LEE Kung just left Tianjin for Shanghai and will immediately return by the 20th of the month to leave thereafter with the most valuable books etc. belonging to the university...'[73]

Evidently, the university staff was instructed and prepared to move before the Communists even took over Beijing. All the valuable books from the libraries and scientific equipments were shipped to Shanghai and Taiwan before the confiscation, while the university itself continued in operation even during the "Communist occupation if that should occur. Americans and Germans who were in charge of departments would remain to staff the place although they would be working with fewer instruments and books."[74] The Communists, however, wanted to prevent this from happening, but unable to do so at that time. They could only tell the university through the radio address asking the university, "Fu Ren must change its entire policy".

Prior to taking control over the university, the Communists had announced their proposed rules that Fu Ren administration should follow. After the Communist Party took over Beijing, life at Fu Ren became tense, cautious and suspicious,

> 'The university made sincere attempts of good will and cooperative negotiations and co-existence with the new communist government, but these were ignored or rejected. False accusations were made; phones were tapped, and father Rigney was under constant surveillance.'[75]

The curriculum began to change right after the spring semester started. New courses were forcibly added onto the core curriculum: *New Democracy Theory, Dialectic Theory and History of societal development*. In the meantime, all the courses that had to do with Catholic Church[76] were forced to drop out, even some philosophy courses: *Metaphysics, Introductory Philosophy*[77] were dropped. To be more exact, all schools and departments of the university had to make changes to study the Marxist theory, and the government directly appointed some professors onto the faculties to teach course against the Catholic Church:

> 'In March of 1949 when the Spring semester started, some new courses had to be added on to the curriculum: *New Democracy Theory, Dialects, history of Social development* were the required courses. *Teachings of New Democracy* was required in the Department of Education. *Study of Capitalism* was added in the department of Economy. Juniors at sociology department had to take *Politics of New Democracy* and the *Organization of British and the US governments,* Sophomores had to study *Marxist and Lenin's Theory on Economics.* Ji Tao-da, Zhu Zhi-xiang, Du Ren-zhi, Liu Da-zhong, Zhou Zuo-ren, Li Jing-han and Zheng bo-bin were appointed by the government to come to teach courses.'[78]

This caused great tension between the two parties because of the interference of both the administration and faculties of the university. The government inserted its power on the university by appointing professors and forced the changes of courses. The autonomy of the institution was threatened and almost destroyed. On one hand, the Communists insisted that the Church should continue to finance the university, and at the same time, should comply with the government's roles. On the other hand, the government continued to have the right to appoint and fire professors while the original university professors who remained in positions had to comply with the government orders. Because of the uncompromising natures of both the university and the Church, Father Rigney, the rector, warned the government about the consequences and refused to finance the university unless it remained Christian as it was before.[79]

In the summer of 1950, the communist government tried to re-organize the whole curriculum and appointed more Communists on the faculty. Father Rigney, as the rector and a representative of the Church, confronted this very act, but did not succeed.[80] He wrote a letter to the Premier of China Zhou En-lai to protest the government's treatment to the university. He wanted the Premier to tell the education ministry to help Fu Ren to re-install the Board of Trustees, and fire those newly appointed professors, otherwise, he would cable Rome to stop sending Fu Ren any money.[81] The answer came back from the Premier:

> 'Rigney's letter proposed threat and it is nonsense. The Education Ministry needs to rebuke his activity. The Catholic University has to obey the government laws and regulations for its continuing operation. The relationship between Catholic Church and the University is that the Church should provide financial support and its offerings of religious courses, but its doctrine and education should not be intertwined, although the courses on religion can be permitted. The Divine Word Fathers can stay at the university, but they don't have anything to do with the university administration. The church can excommunicate the professors but can not take them away from their teaching positions.'[82]

As a result, on October 12, 1950, the government seized the university and all the priests were expelled from the teaching staff. Father Rigney was arrested because of his resistance to the government and put in jail on July 25, 1951.[83] He spent the next fours years in a strictly confined prison. Fu Ren University was completely under the Communist control from that point onward.

Fu Ren University became completely involved in political movements since the break out of Korean War, and education became completely politicized as well. Chen Yuan became pro-Communist and stayed on at the university. In May of 1951, President Chen Yuan led a large group of students, intellectuals, professionals of all kinds to Southwest part of China for re-education, and later in August of 1951, most of the students from all universities in Beijing were sent to the faraway countryside for land-reform movements. When they finished participating in the Land Reform Movement in the early summer of 1952, the amalgamation process started and Fu Ren was dissolved.

> 'The students from all departments at Fu Ren University, who were Sophomores, Juniors and Seniors, should participate in the Land Reform Movement in the Fall of 1951. Only from two departments Sociology and Economics alone, Fu Ren had 239 students spend one year in Guanxi Province.' [84]

Conclusion

Fu Ren University and political entanglements were not coincident in history. Ever since the opium War in 1840–1842, China began to grope after the ways and measures of nation building, of making the country "wealthy and strong."[85] After the fall of the Qing Emperor in 1911 and establishment of the Republic of China, China began to experience some dramatic movements: nationalism, democracy and socialism.[86] The warlordism became widely spread in China. These warlords divided China and fought against each other. The May Fourth Movement changed the people's understanding of the traditional Chinese culture. The anti-Western, and anti-Christian movement began to rise. The Catholic Church always became a target of attacks.

It was in the midst of wars and turmoil, Fu Ren University was established. It was unavoidable that Fu Ren became a target of any movement. Its basic survival became extremely apparent. This hostile cultural environment was caused by the young Chinese intellectuals who began to take the initiative in an effort of building up a new China. As a result, the intellectuals and the political parties were all intertwined. Lutz in the preface of his book *Chinese Politics and Christian Missions* referred to this "the alliance between political parties and student movements remained, even so, an uneasy one, with intellectuals retaining a degree of autonomy."[87] This was certainly true before the Sino-Japanese War. Starting from 1937, almost every one who had a sense of patriotism became political, including the intellectuals.

In 1925 when Fu Ren University was established, the anti-Christian, anti-Imperialism and anti-Western movements became more aggressive in China. Fu Ren was left alone because the warlords were too busy fighting for their own territories. They never intended to establish a coalition to work together. Complying with the government made Fu Ren become competitive because without government's recognition, the diplomas granted from Fu Ren could not carry any market value. For the sake of the students' future, Fu Ren complied with its rule from the very beginning by also not teaching theology.

The Nationalist Party gained legitimate recognition as the official government of China after 1927, but the power to control China was never consolidated by this party. However, the party affected Fu Ren University tremendously. Every year, the inspection of the university was carried out from Nanjinig to see whether the university was in good standing. When the Communists became a threat to them, the Nanjing Government supervised the university more closely. Constantly, they were checking out the university attempted to wipe all the members who joined or had connections with the university. The regular campus life was constantly interrupted. A special Anti-Communism Bureau was established in Beijing in order to keep all the universities inspected. They made the campus become an anti-Communist battlefield rather than resisting the Japanese.

The Nationalists offended Fu Ren professors and students because of their patriotism and hatred toward the Japanese. The students' strikes and protests against the Nationalist party from time to time. However, the Nationalist Party never threatened the university administration. Eventually, the president of the nationalist party praised the Catholic Church because of the social services that provided during the wartime and allowed the private school to teach religion. Religious freedom was then found on Catholic campuses though Fu Ren never enforced the students to study religion throughout the years.

The Sino-Japanese War provided an opportunity for Fu Ren to excel. Though the Japanese constantly harassed Fu Ren University, it remained in operation because the Rector was a Germany. Overall, the university was greatly disturbed but education continued. Just as the whole nation was united to fight against the aggression of the Japanese, the Fu Ren faculty and students were also active during these years. They became more and more patriotic and political. In 1942, when Fu Ren became the only university in Beijing to resist the Japanese invasion, Fu Ren kept its tradition and the model of the higher education system and trained many students throughout those years. The active involvements in the resistance of the Japanese earned respect from both Nationalists and the Communists during those years. In fact, many students joined the communist party secretly though the nationalist party was public.

Political Entanglements 169

During those eight years of the Sino-Japanese War, the university persevered and insisted on its patriotism and nationalism. More importantly, as a university, it in fact developed and expanded quite well during these eight years. Many students, who did not move inland and stayed in Beijing, joined the university; many famous professors joined the faculties at Fu Ren. The women's college expanded and shared the curriculum at the man's section during those years. One important reason for the university's growth was the strong emphasis of the university on patriotism and nationalism. The Germany rector should not be ignored of course. Many young high school students in the north who were unable to go to the freeland where Nationalists had control, meanwhile, those who did not want to go to the Japanese controlled universities, decided to be enrolled at Fu Ren University. For some, it took them a couple of years to get in because of the competitiveness and the limited numbers that Fu Ren could recruit yearly.[88] As a result of this particular war, Fu Ren rode above the war tides and became very selective in its enrollment while others that moved out Beijing suffered greatly.

After the defeat of the Japanese in 1945, Fu Ren campus became another battle place for both the Nationalists and the Communists. Under the law enforcement, the university administration had to work hard to calm the students down not to be involved with the demonstrations because most of the students were anti-civil war and many students were politicized by joining the two political parties. Fu Ren University became politically instable. The original non-political stance became politically active because of the wars.

In 1949, the Communists made Fu Ren comply with its rules, which caused resistance because of principles that would not be compromised. Since the Catholic Church merely became a finance resource for the university, the university administration could not fire its faculty members on the basis that they were against the Church. It is to be noted also about the president of Fu Ren, Chen Yuan was proactive in accepting the Communist government in Beijing. When the Communists' People's Liberation Army was marching into Beijing on January 31, 1949, Chen took two students and walked to Xi Zhi Men Street to welcome the Army. He became very friendly with the Communists. He was instrumental in adding the Marxist Theory courses in the university.

The Communists changed the life of Fu Ren University completely, as well as all Christian Universities. Throughout the years, as early as 1935, the Communists had already infiltrated in the university[89] and utilized every possible device to win the students' mind. According to Bush that all students in universities where the Communists controlled had to participate in intensive discussion groups where the Communists quickly gained control.[90] Fu Ren was almost the same to have those discussion groups, but secretly at the beginning. Many student organizations were formed on the campus, especially after 1949, "Fu Lian" and "Xin Wen Jian" associations changed to "Xing Minzhu Zhuyi Qingnian Tuan"(new democratic youth association) and acted publicly to promote communist theory. Almost every department in Fu Ren had its own "Association," which gradually became politically charged against the school administration.[91] As a result of the political involvement of Fu Ren and the growing power of the Communist, Fu Ren University was taken over by the Communist Government in 1950 and was dissolved in1952 along with all the private universities. Though Fu Ren University survived all other governments and war, simply could not pass the test from the Chinese Communist.

CHAPTER EIGHT

Conclusion

Fu Ren University in Beijing was both Western Catholic and Chinese in nature and structure. Its mission, establishment and development, as well as its interactions with politics, had demonstrated this dual nature completely. As the youngest university in Beijing and the youngest among all Catholic universities,[1] Fu Ren showed its competitive nature from the very beginning until its demise in striving to be a first-rate university in China. In those 27 years of existence, Fu Ren University achieved its goals to be a center for Chinese studies and to demonstrate its dual nature as Catholic and Chinese. Its extremely rapid development and expansion led the university to surpass almost all other universities in Beijing and became one of the best universities in China. This chapter intends to analyze and draw conclusions how Fu Ren University achieved its goal to be a prestigious university and the roles that Fu Ren University played in the Catholic Church and in the field of higher education in China. The demise of Fu Ren University was certainly a loss to China and to the Catholic Church.

From its establishment in 1925 to its demise in 1952, Fu Ren University operated through political turmoil and war years, such as: through the power struggles between the governments, from warlords to Nationalist Government, to the Japanese, and eventually to the Communists; through the wars between the warlords, between Nationalists and the Warlords, between China and Japan, between the Nationalists and the Communists. Although all thirteen universities in Beijing operated through these political turmoil and wars, Fu Ren University was the only one stayed in Beijing and survived the Japanese control without migration or change of its curriculum. Without doubt, Father Rahmann, the German rector of Fu Ren, and the German priests in the administration helped the university survive. This benefited from Germany's allied relationship with Japan during the Second World War.

The Japanese invasion terribly affected the new Chinese educational system. In their occupied territories, the Japanese forced all schools to change the textbooks and to follow the Japanese model. Fu Ren University did not follow this rule. The university was not only survived the Japanese attacks without making changes in its curriculum, but also continued its expansion during the years of the Sino-Japanese War. After the Japanese attacked Pearl Harbor in 1941, Fu Ren became the only university left in Beijing and still had its own autonomy without flying the Japanese flag. Surprisingly during these years, the faculty was strengthened and student enrollment increased steadily. Fu Ren University rose above the political turbulence and excelled in its quality and patriotism. As a result, after the Japanese surrender and during the Chinese Second Civil War (1945–49), Fu Ren University became the second largest university in terms of student enrollment in Beijing, just behind Beijing University in 1947. In the Spring of 1949, the Chinese Communist Party began to insert its power onto the university because the curriculum had changed and the administration began to change. On October 12, 1950, the government officially took over the university. Fu Ren thus became the first private university to lose its control in China. In the Summer of 1952, Fu Ren University was divided and absorbed by five other universities in Beijing. The saga of Fu Ren University in Beijing continues in the works of the researchers.

From its establishment to its demise, Fu Ren University's very existence and its education of students made great contributions to China. This university did not only change the Catholic missionaries' attitude toward China and the Chinese Church, but also changed the attitude of the Catholic hierarchy as well. Missionaries once again began to respect Chinese culture and the Chinese clergy. Through their education at Fu Ren, Chinese Catholic youth at the university also grew in quantity and quality as they mastered the understanding of Eastern and Western cultures. The development and expansion of the university had certain impact on Chinese higher education and therefore influenced it, especially in the Arts and in women's education. The encounters with political situations demonstrated the university's patriotism and anti-imperialistic nature throughout the years. The demise of the university was certainly a loss to the Catholic Church and to Chinese higher education as well.

In order to clarify these issues, this chapter is structured as, 1) Overview and analysis of the university, 2) Fu Ren University marked a new beginning of the Church and China, 3) Fu Ren University in the context of Chinese higher education, 4) Fu Ren University and the Catholic Education in China in general, 5) Legacies of Fu Ren, 6) Future research directions, 7) Conclusion.

Overview and Analysis of Fu Ren University

The rise and fall of Fu Ren University proved that the Catholic Church's intension in China was to build up the university as one of the best Chinese universities. The Catholic missionaries who worked at Fu Ren University did not have any intention to build up the university as a tool for American and European imperialistic acts in China. Though they were Catholic religious members, they came to Beijing as educators to make Fu Ren University a center for Chinese learning and Western sciences. They followed the proposal of the two Chinese co-founders, Vincent Ying Liang-zhi and Ma Xiang-bo, who were well known in the world of Chinese intellectuals.

Inspired by these two Chinese Catholic scholars and patriots, the Catholic missionaries from both the Congregation of American Benedictine Fathers and the Society of Divine Word Fathers understood their work in China. They wanted to make the Catholic Church more indigenously Chinese to win over the Chinese intellectuals. They understood the success that the early Jesuits had in China by winning over Chinese intellectuals. Those early missionaries showed Chinese intellectuals the Western sciences, technology and mathematics. This attracted many Chinese intellectuals to convert to Catholicism. The average Chinese citizen then followed the road to conversion because of their admiration of the intellectuals. As a result of their work, even the Emperor of China showed interest in the Catholic Church.[2] Though those Jesuits did not establish any schools of higher learning in China, they had influence in the highest academy in China, which was called *Hanlin*, a school only for officials in the imperial court. These new Catholic missionaries understood the importance of establishing the university as the center for the study of Chinese and Western sciences in Beijing under the sponsorship of the Pope in Rome. In order to attract Chinese intellectuals, the Catholic Church had to make an effort to think and to work as the Chinese intellectuals did. Both the Benedictines and Divine Word Fathers tried to adopt this method. This approach was successful and appealed to Chinese intellectuals at the time. Under their administrations, Fu Ren University developed very successfully, despite all of the political problems.

Unfortunately, their efforts were unappreciated and even misunderstood, whether intentionally or not, by some Chinese after the founding of the People's Republic of China. Many Chinese writings and in particular, *Beijing Fu Ren Da Xue: Ge Ming Shi (Beijing Fu Ren Da Xue: Revolutionary History)* by Xu Nai-gan and *Beijing Shi Fan Da Xue Xiao Shi (History of Beijing Normal University)* by Beijing Normal University, attacked the Catholic Church in general, and the Catholic missionaries at Fu Ren as well. They accused the Catholic missionaries as spies for their own countries, and also accused them acted as spies of American and European imperialistic agents in the name of God.[3] This became obvious in early 1950's before Fu Ren was closed. Many people who accused Fu Ren University were certainly politically oriented. They didn't want to remember that Fu Ren was co-founded by two patriotic Chinese scholars who were instrumental in the establishment of the university. Neither did they want to know that Fu Ren University was highly praised as being patriotic through its resistance to the Japanese invasion. The following analysis lists the reasons I claim the nature of Fu Ren University as both Western Catholic and Chinese. This very dual nature of the university as Catholic and Chinese can also dispute the false accusations.

Petition and the Mission of the University Showed the true Nature of Fu Ren

The petition to the Holy Father spoke clearly about the Catholic and Chinese nature of the future Catholic University in Beijing. Vincent Ying Lian-zhi and Ma Xiang-bo petitioned the Pope to establish a Catholic university in Beijing in 1912 with the intentions, first of all, to compete with the Protestant Church and secondly, to promote Chinese culture and to introduce Western scientific knowledge. Two crucial reasons motivated these two Chinese Catholic scholars to petition the Pope which can be found in the *Letter to Pope Pius X*: First, the Catholics were unable to take responsibility to be in charge of the National University when it was offered by the Chinese government. "Catholics have voluntarily eliminated ourselves"[4] from participating educational institutions. The Protestant Church took it over without hesitation. The Protestant Church at that time already attracted many Chinese educated people who were considered as upper class. For years, Protestant missionaries had been active in sending men and money to schools in China. "By the time the Chinese Empire of the Manchu's fell in 1911 they had six major universities and upwards of 20 reputable high schools leading young China along the paths to the modern world."[5] Vincent Ying and Ma Xiang-bo cared about the Catholic Church and understood the urgent needs of the Church in China. They made their petition rather bravely and decisively. Secondly, "Unhappily for us, the number of missionaries or of seminarists devoting themselves to the pursuit of science is pitifully small. In fact, we see none thus engaged."[6] As a result, Chinese priests spent much time studying Latin, Western philosophy and theology rather than mastering Chinese literature. Even such, they were still considered as the second-class citizens in the eyes of the missionaries. The Chinese intellectuals didn't treat them well either. The Chinese general population regarded the Chinese clerics as *Yang He Chang* ("China-made foreign monk"). This was considered a terrible insult. Though the missionaries tolerated it, the two Chinese patriotic scholars could not take it. They tried to persuade the Pope to help them to enter into the competition with the Protestants in order to rectify the Chinese priests' name.

These two simple reasons laid out in the petition letter demonstrate why these two Chinese scholars wanted the Catholic Church to reconsider her mission in China by becoming friends of Chinese intellectuals. Evangelization merely for the low-class people was not effective enough for the Catholic Church to be well rooted in China. Therefore, "A Catholic University here would see large numbers of students, both Christian and pagan, flocking to its doors; it would constitute a strong bond of union between Catholicity and the nation at large..."[7] This also became the mission of Fu Ren University:

> 'The aim of the founders is to supply the demand of the large group of the younger Chinese for higher education under Christian auspices. The University, as planned, is not intended to be primarily a professional school, but rather is intended to lay special emphasis on general culture and learning, which seems to be most needed in China at the present time.'[8]

Vincent Ying, in his 1907 article entitled *Exhortation to Study*, re-emphasized the importance of higher education for Chinese Catholics to be truly both Chinese and Catholic. This was specifically necessary for the Chinese clergy. "Unhappily for us Chinese Catholics, however, we are the only people who fail to appreciate truism. Receiving, as we do, a hybrid education, partly foreign and partly Chinese, we form our country today what may be termed a group of moral half-casts."[9] Knowing the reality, Vincent Ying emphasized, "Our contempt for national literature and thought is proverbial."[10] In promoting Catholic higher education in China, Vincent Ying fearlessly criticized Church authorities who were responsible for the humiliating situation of the Catholic Church in China:

> 'May we be permitted to speak clearly—for now silence is impossible-our superiors are responsible for this serious situation. Devoid of clear and broad ideas, they do not pursue ideals in harmony with the spirit and role of the Church; hence scarcity of talents, smothering of merit, general retrogression, such are the humiliating characteristics of the general stagnation and voluntary barrenness of Catholicity in China.'[11]

Rome and the Benedictine Fathers' Interests Confirmed the Nature of Fu Ren

The *Exhortation to Study* from Vincent Ying had a profound impression on Rome. Pope Benedict XV decided to look into this matter and appointed Msgr. De Guibriant as Apostolic Visitor to China, "and the report ultimately made by the latter was substantial agreement with the representations of Mr. Ying, especially with reference to the imperative need of a Catholic university in Northern China. The Holy See, accordingly, was very anxious to have such an institution established in the capital of the Chinese Republic..."[12] Evidently, the Pope confirmed the intention of the Chinese founders to make the university a Catholic and Chinese one.

No matter how interested in China the Pope was or how enthusiastic he was in establishing a Catholic University in Beijing as petitioned by the two Chinese scholars, the Pope was rather powerless at the time. He could not reach China without the approval from the French and Italian governments. This blockage from France and Italy indeed helped the Benedictines to be the chosen religious order to establish the university in Beijing. The reason was rather simple. First, before 1908, the United States was still considered as a mission territory. According to Latourette, "it was only in 1908 that the Pope withdrew the United States from the jurisdiction of the Propaganda and thus proclaimed that it had ceased to be a foreign mission field."[13] This meant that in the Catholic Church, the American Church was able to send her own missionaries to work in other countries. The Pope paid attention to the U.S. Catholics since. Second, Doctor O'Toole's initiative to visit China and to petition Rome became instrumental for the Congregation of the American Benedictine Fathers to be the candidate for China. The Primate of the Benedictines was also interested in this mission who had close relationship with the Congregation of the Faith. The connection and interest that the Benedictines had made everything possible for them to co-found Fu Ren in Beijing. Rome was convinced the necessity to compete with the Protestant higher education in China by choosing the American Benedictine Fathers to work in China.

The difficulty to establish the Catholic university in China was also reflected in the letter to the entire American-Cassinese Congregation from Cardinal Van Rossum, Prefect of the Propagation of the Faith. This letter also reaffirmed that the Rome consented the competitiveness of the higher education situation in China, in the meantime the nature of the Catholic university in China to be Chinese was reassured:

> 'Conditions peculiar to the Church in China demand that no human means of furthering the propagation of the Faith among the cultured and educated classes should be neglected....
>
> 'Now among means of this sort none is more important than a superior school or college, in which Chinese Studies of an advanced type will be cultivated. For some years past, a Catholic University has been contemplated for a city of Peking, but hitherto nothing has been done to put this project into execution...'[14]

In the Fall of 1920, while Msgr. De Guibriant, the Apostolic Visitor, was still in China, Dr. Barry O'Toole, who was a Saint Vincent Seminary professor, went to China to explore the educational situation. He acquainted himself with Mr. Vincent Ying. "His own observations of the situation in China corroborated Vincent Ying's estimate of educational situation in China, and he became convinced that a solution of the problem must follow the lines that proposed by this eminent Chinese layman."[15] As a result of this visit, he became a very instrumental lobbyist for the establishment of a Catholic University in Beijing. The Benedictine Fathers' congregation also showed interest in by doing everything it could to make the Catholic university in Beijing a first-rate Chinese university. Without any doubt, the establishment of Fu Ren University was due to the two Chinese Catholic scholars' vision for the Catholic Church in China. Their vision motivated them to action. Their action, in turn, influenced Rome and the Benedictine Fathers who eventually answered the petition with an affirmation to "preserve and Christianize Chinese literature, art, and philosophy."[16]

Curriculum Development Showed the Nature of Fu Ren

The development of the curriculum explicitly illustrated the very nature of Fu Ren University as both Western Catholic and Chinese. The original curriculum was designed before the Benedictine Fathers went to China. They designed it according to their experience with the general American curricular norms of the day. Since the founding administration from St. Vincent Archabby had both a seminary and a college, the envisioned curriculum for Fu Ren may have been based on these two existing models. In any event, they understood that the curriculum was rather ambitious, even if it was only tentative. "Regarding the proposed Faculties and Courses of the new University, it would be premature to draft any definite prospectus at the present moment. Such a program must be based on a careful survey of local educational needs, and cannot be drawn up until this has been made."[17] Since there was an emphasis on the local educational needs, the Benedictine Fathers understood that the curriculum was subject to change. The first curriculum at Fu Ren University was purely focused on Chinese studies because Dean Vincent Ying designed it for a specific purpose for the newly-established *MacManus Academy for Chinese Studies* or *Fu Ren She*, to prepare students for college-level Chinese literature studies.

The Benedictines understood the situation in China fairly well. The educational system in China was heavily influenced by the American system. In 1905 the old Chinese system of civil service examinations was abolished, and the "Ministry of Education was created and to it was entrusted the organizing of a new school system in which both western and Chinese subjects were studied."[18] This requirement coincides with the petition of Vincent Ying and Ma Xiang-bo in 1912. Many youth went abroad to acquire Western knowledge, either in Europe or in America after 1905. Latourette pointed out that as a result of Westernization and modernization, "many younger scholars began to write extensively in a dignified form of the Mandarin instead of in the less easily understood classical style."[19] The intellectual and educational changes during those years paralleled the political revolution that led to a complete change in China. "The hold of Confucian philosophy upon the nation, especially upon the younger classes, was, accordingly, weakened."[20] In order to ensure that the Chinese culture was not destroyed, the Benedictine Fathers knew the educational needs in China. The Catholic University decided to focus on the studies of Chinese literature and classics.

"That the Order of St. Benedict, which during the Middle Ages saved Latin and Greek literature from certain destruction, should found in the city of Peking an institute of higher Chinese studies as the most apt means of fostering a more vigorous growth of our Holy Religion in the vast territory of China."[21] The Benedictines helped the Church to keep the culture in the Middle Ages. Presently as non-Chinese, they were trying to be the keepers of traditional Chinese culture at Fu Ren. There was simply no room for the Benedictines to have an imperialistic mentality as they worked in China.

Another educational need in China was to follow the government's requirements to train students for the country's different needs. The Benedictine Fathers obeyed the government's law not to make religion and theology required courses. When the university was registered with the government in 1927, the university took the name Fu Ren University, which appealed to many Chinese intellectuals. It had only one School of Letters, with strong emphasis on Chinese culture and Chinese philosophy. The academic degree granted from Fu Ren University became marketable because of the government's recognition. The graduates could work anywhere in China. This was quite opposite of many other Christian universities including the Catholic ones, which educated students for their own immediate purposes within their own institutions. Fu Ren University kept her eyes on China as a whole.

The Women's College at Fu Ren developed and had a special curriculum from the very beginning. That curriculum was specially designed for them according to their prestigious family backgrounds. Fu Ren Women's College was the first and foremost Catholic school for women. Its contribution to China was certainly immeasurable. The Chinese nature of the university shined through this particular action of Fu Ren University's administration. Saint Albert's College for Chinese priests was also the first in China to emphasize studies of Chinese literature and sciences. Those Chinese priests who were trained in the enclosed seminaries could not converse well with the Chinese intellectuals, neither could they write Chinese well. Saint Albert's College at Fu Ren was meant to bring the Chinese clergy to an equivalent level with the intellectuals. The Institute of Christian Arts was more prominent in bringing the Western and Chinese Arts together. All the religiously oriented productions from this institute exhibited the talents of the professors and students through a unique amalgamated Western and Eastern style.

I have not found any criticism of the curriculum of Fu Ren University as being designed for imperialistic purposes. Everything at Fu Ren met the governments' requirements, except for the Japanese requirements during the Sino-Japanese War period and the Communists. Fu Ren University's curriculum was too Chinese, which threatened the Japanese rule in Beijing. Though Fu Ren's refusal to change its curriculum to the Japanese model caused some trouble for the university, the Japanese could not force Fu Ren to cave in because Fu Ren had a German rector. The diplomatic relations between Germany and Japan helped Fu Ren in this aspect. The Communists succeeded this.

Faculty Showed the Nature of Fu Ren

The cosmopolitan character of the Fu Ren University faculty indicated the collaboration of all the professors. Chinese professors always formed the majority of the faculty. Catholic missionaries, no matter priests, religious sisters or lay people who represented more than ten countries, were constituted as a minority throughout the years. These professors came together to work for the university with the purpose of making the university a first-rate institution in China. There are no references accusing these non-Chinese professors as being imperialists. As much as can be gleaned from available sources, the non-Chinese professors dedicated themselves to teaching and research at the university. From the Warlord time to the Japanese occupation in Beijing until the Communist Party took over Beijing, not even one professor was accused as being imperialistic, or as a spy. It is therefore difficult to understand that as an institution, Fu Ren was accused of being an instrument of western imperialism by Communists. The last rector, Father Rigney was an exception. He was the only one identified as a spy by the government because of his stance for the Church's principle and his disagreement with the Communists.

Political Entanglements Revealed the Nature of Fu Ren

Fu Ren University was not insulated from China's political reality. Though Fu Ren University had a non-political stance policy from the very beginning, which discouraged students from participating in the political movements, Fu Ren was still actively involved with politics when the threats to the nation as a whole became evident. The political entanglements showed Fu Ren University's patriotic nature. Students protested against the Nationalist military as early as 1927 when they showed their non-resistance attitude to the Japanese invasion of Shandong Province. With support from the university, the students protested against this government again when they allowed the Japanese set up Manchuria (Manzhouguo) as an independent state. The unity of China as a nation was threatened on both occasions. Even during the Sino-Japanese War era, Fu Ren refused to comply with the Japanese rules to change the curriculum, to fly the Japanese flag at the gate and to bow to the flag whenever the student had to go by.

The university did not only resist the Japanese, but also tried to safeguard the patriotic professors and students whose lives were threatened by the Japanese. On many occasions, the university sent them inland secretly for safety reasons. For such reasons, some priests such as Father John Fu and Father Kroes were harassed or arrested, and the university was invaded many times by the Japanese soldiers.

Could Fu Ren University have avoided the Japanese attacks during those years? The answer is positive. It could have avoided them. The university decided to stay in Beijing to confront the regime. The administration wanted to continue to offer education to Chinese youth and placed a greater emphasis on Confucian culture. On many occasions, the President Chen Yuan of Fu Ren University attacked the Japanese invasion. Fu Ren University did not give up, just as the Catholic Church never gave up in its proclamation of the truth, no matter what happened in history. Fu Ren University also never gave up, just as the Chinese Confucian culture always found its ways to flourish in China.

The survival of Fu Ren University under the Japanese government from 1937 to 1945 was not coincidental, especially after the Pacific War broke out. The German Divine Word Fathers certainly were instrumental to the survival of the university because of Germany's relationship with Japan. There were other elements that contributed to its survival. First of all, Fu Ren University was intended to be an American owned university. Therefore, the changing of the administration indicated that the Americans would lose control of the university, both in terms of administration and physical property. The willingness of the American Divine Word Fathers to give up the posts so that the German and Dutch priests could take over the university in 1936 was pivotal in the survival of Fu Ren. Secondly, Fu Ren's emphasis on the study of Chinese traditional culture also contributed to its survival. The role that Vincent Ying played at Fu Ren was crucial, though he only spent half a year there before his death. As a well-known scholar in China, the Japanese Emperor also honored him for his scholarly work in the revitalization of Chinese Confucian culture. Despite their efforts to colonize China, the Japanese soldiers still respected the Chinese culture that helped their own culture tremendously in the past.

In summary, Fu Ren University was established and developed as a Western Catholic and Chinese university. This dual nature of the university reinforced its growth to be true to the Catholic Church's mission in China to preserve and develop Chinese culture by introducing Western sciences. The university kept its mission and fulfilled its mission in China because the faculty, students and administration in total, collaborated to make Fu Ren a first-rate university. The curriculum emphasized the integration of Chinese culture and Western science; the social service activities showed the universities care for the innocent victims of war and natural disasters; the students' activism showed their patriotic zeal and their efforts in fighting injustice in China; the non-political stance of the university did not carry imperialistic actions. More importantly, Fu Ren remained in Beijing, the heart of Japanese control, to battle against its invasion during the Sino-Japanese War era. This showed the university's Chinese nature of combat and Catholic nature of justice. Any threat that occurred against the Chinese culture or against China as a nation caused Fu Ren to protest.

Therefore the accusations that the university was established as an imperialistic tool for the Americans, and that the missionaries acted as spies for their own countries were simply groundless. Since the beginning of Communist rule Fu Ren University was made suspicious in China, not because it was financed by the Catholic Church, but because the very nature of Communism made the university suspicious and intolerable. It was not the foreignness of the Catholic missionaries that caused the university to be closed, but it was the foreignness of Communism in China that used guns to take over and caused the university to cease its existence. Fu Ren University survived all other governments except for the Communist government. Moreover, no private university could survive the Communist government. Even the national and provincial universities that were owned by the government could not maintain their original missions and structures. They were all subjected to change under the Communist' government's new regulations on higher education. Amalgamation[22] of the universities in 1952 clearly demonstrated the new Chinese government's way of dealing with higher education institutions. As a result, all universities were publicized and academically specialized. This followed the Soviet Union model.

Additional Findings and Speculations

There are two more interesting findings that need to be reviewed at this time. I have mentioned these two in different chapters without discussing them in detail. They represented some similarities with the history of the Church in China. They can also broaden our understanding in the rise and fall of Fu Ren University.

First of all, the Benedictines failed to cooperate in financing Fu Ren University. This failure was crucial since it caused them to transfer the university to the Divine Word Fathers. At the very beginning, the financing of this university was a joint effort of the Congregation of the American-Cassinese Benedictines, as well as the American bishops. In his letter to all Benedictine monasteries, Archabbot Aurelius Stehle of Saint Vincent Archabby mentioned: "we draw inspiration and confidence from the glorious past of Benedictinism, but we may not rest upon the laurels earned by the sweat of those who have preceded us. Rome admonishes us that a mighty task, one that is assuredly difficult, lies before us, and has, in consideration of this fact, authorized us to appeal for aid not alone to our Benedictine confreres, but likewise to all the Bishops and all the faithful of America... Under such circumstances, the monks of Saint Vincent Archabbey might well be appalled at the magnitude of the task assigned to them, were it not for the consciousness that they bear a commission from the General Chapter, backed by a promise of co-operation on the part of all the abbeys of the American-Cassinese Congregation."[23]

The records show that Archabbot Aurelius Stehle did not get much financial support from the rest of the Benedictine monasteries. He singlehandedly financed the university from the beginning. The Stock Market Crash of 1929 indeed brought this hidden un-collaborative spirit of the Benedictine monasteries to light. When the economy was good in the United States, Saint Vincent Archabbey was able to finance the university alone. When the economy was down, every single monastery's contribution became crucial in the finance of the university. In order to meet the university expenses, Doctor O'Toole, the rector of the university also visited many bishops in the United States to plead for help during the financial crisis of the university. Some records from Saint Vincent Archive showed this. The result was limited because many bishops did not respond to his plea.

The transfer of the university in 1933 was another incident that showed the same flaw that the Catholic religious communities had. They were unfriendly toward each other. First, they could not agree with each other about the debt Fu Ren had to pay. The Benedictines insisted that the Divine Word Fathers should pay the debt. The Divine Word Fathers resisted to pay it, but only agreed to take over the university. Secondly, the Divine Word Fathers stopped the Benedictine Fathers when they tried to take some books and instruments that they thought belonged to them. This was not rare and unfamiliar in the Catholic Church. Many religious communities in China were divided either by their nationalities or by their religious orders. From the sixteenth century mission of Matteo Ricci, religious orders accused the Jesuits as heretics by their use of enculturation in evangelization. This hostile spirit remained until the transfer of Fu Ren University to the Divine Word Fathers in the twentieth century. Numerous similar incidents happened within the religious orders in China.

In spite of the fact that the Divine Word Fathers refused to pay the university's expansion debt of 1929, they did something similar to the Catholic missionary history in China as pointed out by Vincent Ying and Ma Xiang-bo in their petition letter to the Pope. I quote again, "...The Catholics, however, were unable to accept, and the institution fell into the hands of the Protestants, who have succeeded in insinuating themselves into all branches of government administration. They have not failed to make rapid progress in the race from which we Catholic have voluntarily eliminated ourselves, without having been excluded."[24] The reason I mention this is because the Divine Word Fathers did the same thing in 1948. When the Communists took over the city of Beijing, the Divine Word Fathers shipped many books and scientific equipments out of the university for fear of the Communists' confiscation. This was done after receiving advice from the American Consulate in Beijing. Many Chinese as well as foreign professors left the university at the same time. Though some American Divine Word Fathers remained on the faculty at the request of Rector Rigney, the university was never the same again.

Conclusion

These two findings about those Catholic missionaries who administered Fu Ren University certainly presented a miniature look at Catholic missionaries in general. Traditionally in China, the missionaries were not friendly enough toward each other. Each group had its own interest. When there was trouble, they simply moved out of the place in order to avoid confrontation with the government or people. It is certainly not my interest at the moment to fully explore these two findings. In my opinion, they would not minimize the two religious orders' contributions to the Catholic Church in China, to Fu Ren University, as well as to the Chinese higher education.

Fu Ren Marked the New Beginning of Church and China

The founding of Fu Ren Catholic University changed the whole attitude of the Catholic hierarchy and Catholic missionaries' attitude toward China. The founders of the university were inspired by the early seventeenth century Jesuits who appreciated Chinese culture. Under the leadership of Matteo Ricci, they tried to learn and utilize Chinese culture in their evangelical work. They associated themselves with the Chinese literati, trying to be friends with them. They tried "consciously to adapt their methods to Chinese prejudices."[25] The Chinese Emperor Kang Xi, but not the Church herself, appreciated their efforts in China. Ever since the Rite Controversy[26] in the early seventeenth century caused the condemnation of the Jesuit missionary activities by the Holy Father Clement XI in 1715.[27] Until the early part of the twentieth century, the Catholic Church had always been suspicious of China and of Chinese culture. The foreign missionaries did not treat the Chinese clergy equally.

French Catholic missionaries were the most aggressive ones in all of China. The French mission in China dominated not only religion, but also politics and culture. Bob Whyte stated that the majority of foreign priests and bishops in China at the time were French. He also provided the statistics of the French domination in China: in 1922, there were 680 French priests out of 1438 in China; there were 24 bishops out of 56 in China.[28] Vincent Ying was very familiar with this situation, which he mentioned in his *Exhortation to Study*. The Vatican tried many ways to seek direct relations with the Chinese government as early as 1886, but France intervened to thwart any Vatican moves. Both France and Italy even opposed the Chinese president's 1918 request to have a direct diplomatic relationship with the Vatican.[29] The French looked down on the Chinese just as they looked down on the Vatican. They discarded Chinese culture as well. Their aggressive, arrogantly hostile attitude confused the minds of Chinese of both the government and the ordinaries. Jachques Leclercq described this well in his book, *Thunder in the Distance*. The old image of "scholars from the West" was transformed into an image of agents of imperialism and oppressors of non-Christians. In general, Catholic missionaries coming with the gunboats of the Opium War did not appear to appreciate Chinese culture and Chinese people. For them, the civilization meant having a white skin—any other color was a sign of racial inferiority. The poor people unfortunate enough not to possess it were simply "natives" and "baboons."[30]

Not only were the French Catholic missionaries doing such, but also the early American Christian missionaries were doing the same. Flynt and Berkley described similar activities that the American missionaries did in China. "The missionaries tried to force their culture views of women, marriage, alcohol, individualism, health, education and medicine onto the Chinese. They did not take the deeply rooted Confucian culture seriously. The Westerners imagined themselves alone to be civilized."[31] Overall, all missionaries from the West were the product of their own place and age, who shared their fellow European's enlarged ethnocentric ego. They came to China to change the culture and to change the people. They simply equated the Christianity with the white race.[32]

Missionaries looked down the Chinese people as both "odious and ridiculous" as Leclercq stated in his book. "Their pride as Europeans made them look down upon the Chinese people as both odious and ridiculous. Their whole civilization was ridiculous; and as pagans they had all the vices."[33] According to Leclercq, the European missionaries' attitude toward Chinese Christians was rather that of a father towards his children. Coming from an inferior race, these Chinese Christians were inevitably children. Chinese priests might be quite all right to co-operate with, so long as they were kept under, but they still had to be treated as children. "They were likable children, sometimes very touching with their good nature and simple outlook and straight forwarding, but still children. Civilization was a European matter: if the Chinese priests and lay people were allowed the slightest independence, the result might easily be all kinds of errors, especially schism."[34] The missionaries were haunted constantly by the fear that pride would drive the Chinese to revolt, and so they thought the best thing to do was to keep these priests in a state of humility.[35] In order to do so, the Europeans dominated them and kept them in low positions in the seminaries. Chinese priests could only pursue a far less advanced course of study than did the clerics in Europe.[36]

Vincent Ying expressed this also clearly in his *Exhortation to Study*.[37] The missionaries did not treat the Chinese seminarians and their culture respectfully. The founding of Fu Ren University indeed was necessary to change such an attitude among the Catholic missionaries who tried to convert the Chinese. The university served as a bridge to connect with the great Jesuit missionaries of the past:

> 'Under the Ming dynasty, science proved an excellent means of attracting the Chinese to the truth of the Gospel. Following upon the miracles of St. Francis Xavier came the science of the Jesuit Fathers Ricci, Schall, Veribest, and Aleni, whose scholarship conduced to the self-same result;

for science, far from being opposed to Revelation, gives support to the latter—it, too, comes from God and leads us back to Him.'[38]

This eloquent letter to the Pope clearly stated the results of the missionary work in China's recent history. Chinese intellectuals on the other hand, mostly despised the Catholic Church because of the missionaries' work. They thought the Church could only attract "the tillers of the soil, small shop-keepers, fishermen, and canal boat-men."[39] Dom Peter Celesine, OSB, former premier of the New Republic, Lu Cheng-hsiang declared, "the failure of the missionaries to take into account Chinese culture and scholarship explains the fact that the Chinese nation as such has not yet been influenced by the Catholic Church."[40]

This concern also appeared strongly in the petition letter to the Pope from Vincent Ying and Ma Xiang-bo:

> 'The missionaries of our day confine their instruction to those emanating from the lowest ranks of society; those even who receive such elementary instruction as is given, and who become able to read and write their mother tongue correctly, are the rare exception. New China does not see any Catholics capable of sitting in Parliament, or in provincial and departmental assemblies.'[41]

Dr. O'Toole, the first rector of Fu Ren University, also mentioned the bridge that Fu Ren was about to set up and the disasters of the Catholic missions in China,

> 'It is now, in fact, very generally recognized that, in departing from the educational policy of the early Jesuit missionaries to China, our Catholic missions made a sad and serious mistake. There are, it is true, many extenuating circumstances, such as poverty and persecution, but an evil, even though it can be explained, is still an evil, and must be cure by remedies rather than exculpations. To expect the Church to thrive on intellectual darkness and illiteracy in china, a country where literary culture and scholarship are universally esteemed as the highest excellence, is doubly fatuous.'[42]

Eventually, many of the Chinese clergy who were trained in the European style seminaries in China did have an opportunity to study Chinese literature, as well as other subjects at the Catholic University in Beijing. Saint Albert' College was the place where the priests resided and did their studies.

Because of the letter, the Vatican began to change its attitude toward China. By 1915, the Vatican showed its concern for China, though it still was powerless at the time:

> 'By 1915, officials of the Vatican's mission, propagation of the faith, were clearly worried about the missions in China...France was still in control of the mission and Rome, so to speak...if the Vatican could recruit Irish and American missionaries, it would still have to deal with the govern-

ment of France, which claimed to be the secular protector of the China missions and used them as an excuse of political activity in China.'[43]

Eventually, the Vatican bypassed France and ordered many missionaries to go into China with a different attitude toward the Chinese and their culture. These were the ones that really obeyed the Pope such as the Benedictines. On October 28, 1926, Pope Pius XI consecrated six Chinese bishops for the first time since the seventeenth century[44]. Most importantly during the 1930's, the Holy Father Pius XI reversed Pope Clement XI's decree *Ex Illa Die* by allowing Chinese Catholics to resume what Matteo Ricci and his fellow Jesuits insisted on in the late sixteenth century the respect of Chinese civilization and Chinese culture. The Catholic mission in China began a new phase.

This reversal of *Ex Illa Die* did not come easily. Father Paul Yu Pin joined Fu Ren University after he finished his graduate studies in Rome. He emphasized Chinese tradition and Chinese culture, as intended by the Chinese founders of Fu Ren. He was instrumental in this effort. Moreover Rome was very supportive to Fu Ren as well. One apostolic delegate had always been present in Beijing. Archbishop Celso Costantini was the first who encouraged the Benedictine Fathers to establish the university in Beijing. Bishop Zanin who came after Costantini as the apostolic delegate. These two helped Fu Ren along the way in its development.

Fu Ren in the Context of the Chinese Higher Education

It is rather difficult to discuss the role of Fu Ren University in the context of Chinese higher education. As a young university, Fu Ren did not influence Chinese higher education as the Protestant ones did. However, its interactions and contributions to Chinese education were worthy of discussing. Fu Ren was not an isolated university but was a university with an open mind and a broader mission. The archives did not have much material on this aspect, but some special areas could reveal the important role that Fu Ren played in the context of Chinese higher education.

Fu Ren invited many professors from other universities such as Beijing University, Beijing Normal University, Yan Jing University and others, to come to teach or to give lectures. In turn, many Fu Ren professors were invited by Beijing University to give lectures as well. According to the available archival materials, Fu Ren professor Father Franz Feinler was invited by Beijing University to address the Mathematical Society as early as 1931. Father Feinler, who was known to the American Mathematical Society, the Cambridge Mathematical Society and various European societies, was the first foreigner to be invited.[45] Fu Ren University was actively engaged with intellectuals from other universities. Doctor Hu Shi had close relationship with Fu Ren and its president Chen Yuan to promote Chinese culture.[46] He was one of the greatest Chinese scholars who once was the dean of the School of Liberal Arts at Beijing University and later became the president of Beijing University. Dr. Hu Shi was a member of Fu Ren's Board of Trustees for many years until Fu Ren lost its control to the Communists.

On many occasions, Fu Ren joined with other four universities, which formed the "Big Five" in Beijing to sponsor thesis writings and speech competitions for students. The themes were selected from the Chinese classics, Chinese philosophy, Morality, etc.[47] The topics were scholastic and intellectual rather than rhetorical. The purpose of these competitions was for students to seek ways to improve the chaotic situation in China by rediscovering the Chinese culture.

More importantly, Fu Ren University became a sanctuary for many universities in Beijing after the Sino-Japanese War broke out in 1937. Many universities migrated inland to escape Japanese control. While they were in the free land, the Nationalist government reorganized many universities in order to meet the needs of nation. *China Yearbook* described the following:

> 'The work of Christian colleges has largely been redirected along the lines of medicine, agriculture, applied science and engineering, comparative culture, economics and the like, so as to meet the national needs.'[48]

The Chong Qing Nationalist Government organized all other universities differently, no matter they were national, provincial, or independent universities. They became more vocational rather than liberal arts in nature. *China Yearbook* once again relates:

> 'Following the mass migrations of China's institutions of higher learning, there have been amalgamations, reorganizations and dissolutions.'[49]

As a result of these amalgamations, reorganizations and dissolutions, most of the original universities changed their original missions and became specialized schools.

> 'Besides Tsinghua, Peking and Nankai Universities which jointly form the National Southwest Associated University, and National Peiping University, National Peiping Normal College and Peiyang Engineering College which form the National Northwest Union University, the schools of fine arts from Peiping and Hangchow were merged to become the National school of Fine Arts. The College of Railway Administration was incorporated into the Engineering College...'[50]

Fu Ren University however, remained unchanged throughout the years while the Japanese controlled Beijing. Fu Ren kept its nature as a liberal arts university in China, and developed into a research university according to the standards of the time. Only a few universities in China could do this. One more important contribution Fu Ren made to Chinese higher education was that it became a host for many prominent professors from Beijing University and others, as well as a haven for many students who declined to go inland. These professors performed much research, resulting in many written works at Fu Ren University during these war years.

Statistics state clearly the prominent role Fu Ren University played. After the amalgamation of the universities in 1938, there were 108 universities in the whole of China. For graduate studies alone, there were 35 graduate departments with 62 courses in 17 public and private institutions. By this time, Fu Ren university already had two departments: History and Physics, which were able to grant Master's degrees.[51] The School of Christian Arts was the only private school that harmonized both Western and Chinese style paintings. It became known both in China and in the world, and especially in the Catholic Church.

During the Sino-Japanese War years, Fu Ren kept developing without major interruptions. Though criticized by some progressives that Fu Ren did not change its curriculum as others did in order to meet the national needs, Fu Ren indeed met the national needs in a very different way. It courageously resisted the Japanese enforcement to comply with their curriculum. In a long run, Fu Ren contributed more to national needs by keeping its tradition. All Chinese higher education institutions should have done this as well, but they didn't. Eventually after the Cultural Revolution in the late 1970's, many Chinese universities changed from the Soviet model and adapted to the liberal arts model again.

Fu Ren and the Catholic Education in General

Fu Ren University was the only Pontifical University in China out of three in total. Though this university was the youngest among Catholic universities and among many seminaries,[52] Fu Ren was the first to be granted university status by the government. Unlike any other schools, such as Aurora University and Heute Études (which were controlled by the French Jesuits), and seminaries (which were controlled by different religious orders with same nationalities), Fu Ren was administered first by American Benedictines and later by Divine Word Fathers from different countries. Fu Ren was quite unique in its nature and structure to be Catholic and Chinese at the same time, which no other institutions had. Somehow, Fu Ren had connections with all of these schools and seminaries in certain ways.

Fu Ren was connected with Aurora University because of Ma Xiang-bo. The co-founder of Fu Ren was also the founder of Aurora University. Fu Ren achieved the will of Ma Xiang-bo, but Aurora University did not. Ma Xiang-bo had a vision for Aurora University, which was to be modern, yet truly Chinese in its spirit and ethos.[53] He invited the French Jesuits to help with this vision to build a "new style university that would keep pace with western universities"[54] to teach European sciences and Chinese culture. Because of his rich experiences in Western universities[55] and his deep appreciation of Chinese culture, he gave all his family property to the Jesuits in 1900 to establish the university. In 1903, Aurora University officially opened its doors to the talented students. The Jesuits, however, had their own ideas about their education in China because they were convinced that their French Catholic education was the best, and therefore they tried to create a French Catholic University in China. Because of the irreconcilable differences in approaching the mission of the university, Ma Xiang-bo and most of the students walked out of the university.[56] This provided an opportunity for the future birth of Fu Ren in Beijing. Aurora University then was under the complete control of the French Jesuits and eventually developed into an elite university in China. It became nationally known for its schools of medicine and law.

The relationship between Fu Ren and Heute Études, the Tianjin College of Industry and Commerce that also was established by the French Jesuits, was not obvious. Only a few references in the archives indicated that some professors and priests from this college would occasionally go to Fu Ren for lectures or visits. Besides this, these two schools shared a similar goal to train Chinese youth in specialties such as business and engineering for the modern China. Because of the nature of Heute Études, the curriculum was specially designed for training students in Engineering and Commerce. The school was also well equipped with research facilities.

Fu Ren University was an ideal place to study Chinese literature and sciences for graduates from the seminaries. Though there were many seminaries in China that also offered studies in Chinese literature and philosophy, their education was quite limited. This did not earn the respect of the Chinese literati. Surely, the professors at the seminaries did not want to train the Chinese priests as intellectuals. After all, they should only be the second-class citizens in the Church. Moreover, no seminary was registered with the government and therefore, their educational degree was not recognized by the government. These were the very reasons that prompted Vincent Ying and Ma Xiang-bo to petition the Pope to establish the future Fu Ren University. In fact, from the summer school for Chinese priests to the establishment of Saint Albert's College, Fu Ren was fulfilling its mission to emphasize Chinese culture within the Church. Eventually this college provided an opportunity for the priests to study Western sciences, which they never had a chance to explore in the seminaries.

Legacies of Fu Ren

It was unfortunate that Fu Ren University had to close in 1952. Yet its heritage continues both in Beijing and outside of China. Three legacies are in need to be specified. First, over its 27-year period in Beijing, Fu Ren educated about 5,000 students. Those who stayed in China as professors after 1952 transferred to the prestigious universities. Those who left China and worked overseas also had good jobs. This was especially true of those who moved to Taiwan. Most of the professors remained teaching. This promising university reached its high standard prior to the Communist take over of Beijing by striving for excellence. It met its end in Beijing in 1952. Although Fu Ren University was dissolved in Beijing, another university was re-established in Taiwan under the same name with many of the same professors who taught in the previous Fu Ren University in Beijing. This university was established as an joint efforts of three parties: Divine Word Fathers, Jesuits and Taiwan bishops—each had its own school within the university. It is not my intention to investigate the transition and the new university in Taiwan at this time. However it is important for some future researcher to do this work in order to make the university's history complete.

Moreover, Fu Ren University's legacy continued in Beijing. In the early 1990's, the Fu Ren Alumni Association was established with the government's recognition. Its office is located at the old Fu Ren University campus, the so-call *Tao Pei Le Fu,* which was the first palace purchased by the university. Beijing Normal University's Chemistry Department and the School of Continuing Education for Adults currently occupy this campus. Beijing Normal University is known as one of the best universities in the nation. It is my hope that the establishment of the Alumni Association may be the beginning for researchers to re-evaluate Catholic higher education in China. In a way, future research will rectify the position and mission of Fu Ren University in Beijing because the Communists had made many inaccurate accusations in the 1950's. These misconceptions still have some influence on the younger generation in China.

Finally, a scholarly journal from Fu Ren is still being published in Germany. *Monumenta Serica,* one of the scholarly publications was inaugurated at Fu Ren University in 1930s remains alive today. This polyglot scholarly journal of Oriental studies, edited and printed at the University Press in Beijing was published in English, French and German. It now finds its home in Germany.

Future Research Directions

The rise and fall of Fu Ren University in Beijing has proved the nature of this Catholic university as both Western Catholic and Chinese. This book, though as extensive as it is, has not covered and will not be able to cover all aspects of the university. Several more areas concerning with the university deserve more extensive studies.

First of all, the transition from the Benedictine Fathers to the Divine Word Fathers certainly deserves more research. As I indicated a number of times, because of the financial crisis, the Holy Father asked the Benedictine Fathers to transfer the university to the care of the Divine Word Fathers. Thought the debt was eventually paid off by a joint effort of some parties, some archival materials indicate the transition was not as smooth as it appeared to be. Some Benedictine monks who worked at the university decided to take everything they thought belonged to the Benedictines, while

Conclusion 191

the Divine Word Fathers who were on campus before the transition thought everything belonged to the university. Moreover, the Benedictine Fathers thought the debt of the university should also be transferred with the university to the Divine Word Fathers. As a result, the Divine Word Fathers refused to inherit the debt while inheriting almost all the Benedictine property in Beijing. These unfriendly exchanges also indicated that Catholic missionaries were not very friendly toward each other when there was dispute. This phenomenon had existed in China for many centuries. It could go as far back as to the sixteenth century when the Jesuits, Dominican and Franciscans had to deal with the Chinese culture that led to the Rite Controversy. This caused the Pope to condemn the Jesuits and to despise the Chinese tradition. More study on this aspect can certain reveal more church politics.

Secondly, the Benedictine Sisters established the Women's College as a secondary school. It was the first Catholic school for girls in China. This school officially reached college level in 1936 after spending four years doing the preparatory work. When the Holy Spirit Sisters took it over in 1936, they soon organized its special curriculum for those high-class young ladies who attended the college. The Women's College was a separate section of Fu Ren University. Though the women had their own core curriculum, they were allowed to take some courses given by the men's section professors. This enabled the women to fully pursue their academic degrees. I mentioned that the professors went to the women's section to offer the courses after the first year 1938 when women were allowed to take men's courses in the School of Education in order to cut down the expenses. No further archival materials are available to indicate how the professors did from 1939 onward, when women were allowed to take the required courses from all three schools. Since Fu Ren University was not a co-ed institution, it certainly would be interesting to ascertain how the professors managed to teach the two sections at the same time. Future research on the might shed light on questions that if answered, would yield a more complete history of the Women's College. Questions posed might include: Were the professors paid accordingly or did they go without additional pay when they had to teach the women? Did the Divine Word Fathers finance the Women's College completely? How much responsibility did the Sisters have to finance the college?

Also importantly, it was the Protestant missionaries who first started the schools for women's education. According to Anthony Li's study of the privately controlled colleges and universities, there were only four women colleges in China. Two were Catholic[57] and two were Protestant.[58] Therefore, an extensive study of Fu Ren Women's College will contribute tremendously to the field of general higher education for women in China.

Thirdly, Saint Albert College, also known as *Collegium Sinicum*, was a school for all Chinese priests who had been ordained. Its location is currently used as the headquarter of the Chinese Catholic Bishops' Conference. All rectors of seminaries and priest teachers of middle schools were invited to take advantage of this place. The archival materials did not mention much about this special college. A private collection I found during my research has some limited information regarding the tenth anniversary of this college. It is therefore important for further research to be done on this college so that the life of this college and its contributions to the Church could be preserved.

Fourthly, additional research on the Catholic students who came to study at Fu Ren in comparison with the non-Catholics needs to be done. Catholic education for Catholics is generally a common intent for all Catholic schools. Although Fu Ren University was established to educate non-Catholics as well as Catolics, its Catholicity certainly could have attracted many Catholics to this university. Unfortunately, the Catholic population at Fu Ren always had been very small. The graduate rate of the Catholic population indeed was higher than the entrance rate because of the many conversions on the campus. This number varied from year to year, as shown in the available archives. It would be interesting if some future research could be done to compare Fu Ren with all other Catholic universities in non-Catholic Asian countries, such as Korea, Japan, and India. Were they similar or quite different? Fu Ren was well accepted by the society prior to 1949 and earn its respects from Chinese intellectuals. The Catholic Church's influence on student education and its enculturation in different countries are in need of further exploration.

Conclusion

Education always has been an important part of the Catholic Church's mission through the centuries. As the Catholic Church has insisted, "Genuine education must aim not only at developing intelligence and imparting knowledge but also at forming character. Its object is to train one to live both here and hereafter. To attain this goal one must study not only literature, history, art and science, but most important of all, one must learn morality and religion."[59] Fu Ren University indeed achieved its mission as both Catholic and Chinese, as the founders of the university intended in their petition to the Pope. Thousands of students received their education and developed their moral character here at Fu Ren. If not for this university, these students would not have any opportunities to expose themselves to Catholic teachings and moral development. For those who did attend Fu Ren, its influence pervaded its students' lives. In one instance, its influence was manifested during the Cultural Revolution of the 1960's when government officials who were Fu Ren graduates refused to persecute intellectuals and Catholic clergy on moral grounds.

Fu Ren University was established and developed in accordance with the government requirements to train the Chinese students. Despite the fact that Fu Ren experienced financial difficulties and influences of wars and

Conclusion

political turmoil in its 27 year history, it developed into a rather elite Chinese Catholic university. The patriotism and student activism that the university showed during these years confirmed Fu Ren's efforts of educating the students as both ethical and learned Chinese. Though the short-lived Fu Ren University could not fulfill its ambitious plans to add more colleges onto the university and continue mission in China before it was closed, it indeed made a difference both in the Catholic Church and in China. Most importantly, those thousands of graduates from Fu Ren who took variety of important jobs[60] in China greatly benefited from this fine institution.

Fu Ren University became a focal place between the Church and China in 1949. Its prominence once more was revealed when the Communists tried to take over all privately owned institutions. For the sake of the unification of China, the government decided to take over this university first, as a preparation of taking over all private universities, secondary schools, as well as hospitals.[61] The Chinese Communist government showed its totalitarian nature by unifying all institutions. Everything was under the direct control of central government of Beijing. Without intending to compromise its Catholic principles, the existence of this prominent university in Beijing came to an end. Yet, the takeover by the Chinese Communist government should not, in any sense, be a measurement of Fu Ren University's nature as anti-Chinese. On the contrary, Beijing's Fu Ren University indeed showed its nature as being both Chinese and Catholic. Though disappeared, it certainly left an interesting history behind which will attract many more researchers.

APPENDIX A

Letter to Pope Pius X

Father and Doctor Universal:

The intention of the Apostolate of prayer for the current month (July, 1912) is prayer for the conversion of the lost sheep of the Chinese nation, so that there may be but one fold and one shepherd.

This benevolent intention comes at a moment when a great change is sweeping over Chinese society; for China has just seen proclaimed freedom of worship, abolition of superstitious rites and the cessation of most of the obstacles which hitherto impeded the progress of the Catholic religion—is not this a time like that of which the Gospel speaks, when God can raise up from the very stones children to Abraham?

We believe it to be so, and that God's Spirit which breatheth where He will and which does not discriminate between the Orient and the Occident, shall from these hard stones choose and raise up for Himself an elect.

During the period which followed the introduction of Catholicity into China under the Yuan or Mongol dynasty, the newly-planted Church suffered from a dearth of priests, and this continued for more than two centuries. Then, from the end of the Ming dynasty up to the Opium War, the ministers of the Gospel succeeded one another, without interruption, indeed, but still only in small numbers. Throughout all this long stretch of years, our country resembles the paralytic of the Gospel, deprived of the use of his members, impotent to cast himself unto the healing waters without the help of an alien hand. The motion of the water was telling him that salvation was nigh, but his infirmity precluded all personal effort. It required a great miracle to restore him to health.

The Yuan dynasty, being favorable to foreigners, welcomed the missionaries (i.e., the Franciscans). But of the latter little is known and we are left to pure conjecture as regards the works and wonders of salvation which they undoubtedly achieved.

Under the Ming dynasty, science proved an excellent means of attracting the Chinese to the truth of the Gospel. Following upon the miracles of St. Francis Xavier came the science of the Jesuit Fathers Ricci, Schall, Veribest, and Aleni, whose scholarship conduced to the self-same result; for science, far from being opposed to Revelation, gives support to the latter—it, too, comes from God and leads us back to Him.

But what do we see to-day? While the Protestants of England, Germany and America are building schools and universities, we note with sorrow that the Catholic Missions alone remain indifferent to the educational movement. In this capital of China, the Catholics have no university; no secondary schools; not even primary schools. The sole exception being a Franco-Chinese school at which the board is so expensive that pagans are the only ones able to attend it; besides the students who graduate from it can only enter the service of Frenchmen.

During the last years of the Ts'ing (i.e., the recent Manchu) dynasty, the government had under consideration the idea of giving the direction of the National University to the Catholic Mission. The Catholics, however, were unable to accept, and the institution fell into the hands of the Protestants, who have succeeded in insinuating themselves into all branches of government administration. They have not failed to make rapid progress in the race from which we Catholics have voluntarily eliminated ourselves, without having been excluded. Unhappily for us, the number of missionaries or of seminarists devoting themselves to the pursuit of science is pitifully small. In fact, we see none thus engaged. For lack of seminaries giving higher education, our students are forced to seek such education in the Eternal City. And those who thus acquire a superior education do not emulate the example of Ricci and his colleagues who enriched our country with all the European sciences of their times, from astronomy to the latest applications of mechanics; who formed a veritable galaxy of outstanding figures, of which we do not see the slightest trace or shadow to-day.

The missionaries of our day confine their instruction to those emanating from the lowest ranks of society; those even who receive such elementary instruction as is given, and who become able to read and write their mother tongue correctly, are the rare exception. New China does not see any Catholics capable of sitting in Parliament, or in provincial and departmental assemblies.

We have heard that the Holy See proposes to found a Catholic University at Tokyo. Many think that the step has been taken too late. But, in China, there is yet time. A Catholic University here would see large numbers of students, both Christian and pagan, flocking to its doors; it would constitute a strong bond of union between Catholicity and the nation at large, whereby advantages immeasurably superior to those, which mere treaties of protection pretend to guarantee, would be secured for the Church—this University, in a word, would carry on, in its own way, the beautiful mission of St. Peter, by becoming a fisher of men.

We make bold, therefore, to beseech Your Holiness to hearken to this petition, and not to leave us a prey to heretical doctrines. Send us learned men, meek and humble of heart, that they may become our leaders; men of divers nationalities, that Catholicity may be spared the reproach of being the religion of any particular nationality; men of different religious order, in order to do away with all exclusiveness, all jealousy, all party spirit. For if it be in man's very nature to prefer his compatriot to foreigners, it is also, unfortunately, the tendency of religious to hold secular priests in lesser esteem, and to arrogate for their own undertakings a domination which never seems to them exclusive enough.

There is one more point of prime importance. It is this: that the prosperity of the church is intimately bound up with the establishment of an indigenous national clergy. It is the same with the Church as with a family, which can only survive when it manages to find within itself and not outside the means necessary for its own existence.

To-day we see disorders in administration, illiteracy, incompetence and insincerity prevalent in every quarter. The nation's reaction against these evils has taken the form of a universal desire for progress—it yearns for the blessings of European civilization as the farmer, at the sight of his parched fields, sighs after the beneficent rain. Meanwhile, the educated classes realized that religion alone can maintain the prosperity and morals of the people.

This is the reason why, from the bottom of our hearts, we implore you, our Father and teacher, to have pity upon us and to send us missionaries, virtuous and learned, to found in this great capital a university open alike to Christians and pagans, a university that will be a model proposed to the entire nation, preparing an elite among Catholics and bringing true enlightenment to pagans. Thus will the way be opened for our four hundred million countrymen to become a consolation to Your Holiness, thus will they be enabled to respond to your benevolent intentions and, especially, to the intentions of the Sacred heart of Him Who is truly the Savior of all that enter into His fold.

Ying Lien Chih
July, 1912.

APPENDIX B

Exhortation to Study
By Vincent Ying, K.S.G.

Among the interesting questions connected with the propagation of faith in our country at the present hour, the most urgent is incontestably the one of instruction. A witness for about ten years of the imperfections and deficiencies that impede the advance of the Catholic Church in China, we have not ceased to warn our brethren in Christ, and to exhort them, to give serious in attention to the national literature and to the various branches of science.

Various answers have greeted these exhortations. Some evade the question by means of an elusive formal; others give as reasons the hardness of the times and the pressure of the struggle for life; others, finally, and they are a majority, deny the truth of the contention altogether. To their mind, the study of the national literature is of no practical utility, when a few years devoted to the study of European idioms enables persons to fill remunerative positions in commerce or in various administrative capacities. In default of loftier motives, such a point of view can justify itself by appealing to short-sighted utilitarian considerations.

As to the students of our seminaries, whose noble ambitions it is to bring about the conversion of the nation, most of them cite, against the necessity of study, the fact that the apostles chosen by our Lord were personas without instructions; that the saints of the following epochs, though living in the deserts, have done work of essential fervor in the service of God and of their neighbor without ever pretending that the lack of instruction closes for anyone the celestial gates. Thus Saint Vincent de Paul, they say, excelled in simplicity and obedience. It was through charity and humility and not through learning that he did great things. These reasons and others similar were once used to impress our minds, and we did not formerly venture to question their validity. But an already ripe experience, combining a knowledge of human nature with the lessons taught by events have since mad us aware of the error that is mixed with the truth in such palliatives, of specious words concealing a poverty of ideas, of ingenious excuses for making narrow the Church's horizon, casting reflections on true merit, and fostering obscurantism and prejudice.

The sad consequences of the principles are obvious, and it would be rather easy to enumerate them. As to the errors, they contain, if we neglect to point them out, we fear the superficial minds may be deceived, and that the evil many grown worse through lack of resistance.

On the other hand, to refute them singly and in order would involve us in a task both tiresome and interminable. We shall therefore content ourselves with calling your attention to a few vitally important points, hoping thus to succeed to some degree in dissipating prejudice and in counteracting the further spread of this evil so fatal to the propagation of the faith and to the good reputation of the Holy Church.

It is true our Lord, chose most of his apostles from an uncultured and ignorant medium, but did not the Holy Ghost make them on Pentecost day doctors of eminent wisdom and learning. There is no need of insisting on this point.

It is true that the Saints of the church were not all canonized on account of their learning, but is it not also true, on the other hand that the Church glories in the wisdom and learning of such men as Saint Augustine and Saint Thomas Aquinas, and has bestowed upon them the venerable title of "Doctors of the Church"? Not for a moment would I contend that the Church was founded solely for the wise and the learned, but surely no one in his senses will maintain that none but the ignorant and the illiterate are entitled to the care of the Church! It is undeniable that Saint Vincent de Paul was canonized for his humility and charity, and not for his learning; but we must bear in mind that it was for a particular purpose that he founded his congregation, namely, for the diffusion of Christian Doctrine and its benefits among the poor and the lowly, just as it was the intention of the Jesuits of his time to exert a similar influence upon the upper classes. And we must remember that Saint Vincent in establishing his congregation, had no intention of supplanting or condemning the principles upon which other religious societies had been founded.

Those who oppose higher education in our seminaries usually bring forward the plea that for the service of God and the salvation of souls prayers and sacrifices are far more important and efficacious than studies and literatures. I should only like to ask such men whether they are willing to subscribe to the conclusion which logically descends from their premise, namely that it is impossible to serve God and save souls otherwise than by affecting a profound contempt for learning and culture.

And here, lest there be any misunderstanding let say at once that in exhorting my brethren in Christ to take steps to improve the instruction given to our seminarists, I did not mean that our ecclesiastical students should be made to devote long and laborious years to study and to mastery of the intricate grammar and syntax of the Chinese *wenli* or literary language, in the hope of some day becoming so many pedantic and rhapsodizing literati. I was contending for something far more simple and elementary than that. I was merely urging that our seminarists should receive sufficient instruction in the vernacular to enable them to speak and write their native tongue correctly when they emerge from the seminary at the time of their ordination to the priesthood.

How, indeed, we should like to know, can anyone unable to read or write his native tongue correctly aspire to a respectable social standing or to any intercourse with the educated and intellectual members of the community? The question needs no answer; for it is evident that this is the very minimal requirement. Unhappily for us Chinese Catholics, however, we are the only people who fail to appreciate truism. Receiving, as we do, a hybrid education, partly foreign and partly Chinese (but which does not deserve to be called wither the one or the other), we form in our country today what may be termed a group of moral half-casts. Our contempt for national literature and thought is proverbial. Those who ask what wisdom and knowledge our occidental education has brought us are usually put off with the excuse that Western philosophy and science are too abstruse and subtle to be expounded through the medium of Chinese. But alas! This is not true. Let me cite but one instance to the contrary. You have surely heard, gentlemen, of a book called "Lin-Yen-Li-Shao". It is a Western work translated into Chinese by Hsu-Kwang-Ch'I and Pi-Feng-Tsi. Its theme is highly abstruse and metaphysical and its reconditeness is acknowledged by all. Does not the bare existence of such a work in Chinese refute the foregoing contention and stand as a glaring example of our own ignorance of the resources of our national literature?

If we admit for one instant that the Chinese language is inadequate to convey ideas of a higher realm. We shall be forced to conclude that china can never be converted to the Faith until, and unless, each and every Chinese shall have abandoned his native tongue and mastered some Western idiom; for that premise being given, under what supposition could philosophical and theological notions be propounded and explained to the Chinese who seek after Truth?

I freely acknowledge that, owing to the fact that our people do not know the true God, our morals, both social and political, have the contempt and ridicule of the whole world. We must remember, on the other hand, however, that China occupies and immense expanse of territory, embraces within its confines nearly one-fourth of the entire human race, and can boast of an uninterrupted history of 4,000 years. It is extremely improbable that such a country will disappear within a few years from the map of the world. And even if we suppose this possible, it would be just as unlikely that the teeming millions our countrymen could either be annihilated or completely assimilated within the space of a few decades.

The language question, therefore, cannot be evaded, and the present hour is the acceptable time for its solution. Now or never our clergy must put forth their utmost effort to fulfill the demands of their sacred calling, to animate themselves with the genuine spirit of the Church, to spread far and wide the Sacred Doctrine of our Holy Religion. And, gentlemen, we have no more time to lose!

You know the recommendation recently given by the Holy See to missionaries: "in going to foreign countries do not introduce Italy, France, England or Germany! Go as messengers of the Catholic Religion." And what do we see, what do we hear in China? Do not missionaries everywhere sing the praises of their respective countries of France, England, and Germany? Nay, worse still, their zeal is satisfied only when they have succeeded in making submissive subjects of their own countries out of the Catholics of our China. Their own supreme fear seems to be that we might be lacking in respect to their various fatherlands. We have even heard the following contention voiced: "Whoever does not like such or such a country is unfaithful to the Catholic Church, because he is rebellious to his superiors."

Alas! The great duty of the missionaries is to preach the love of God and of one's neighbor. It is to fulfill this that they have sacrificed all, and every man with a human heart admires them without reserve. And yet a small number of men without nobility or disinterestedness have succeeded in making them serve as tools and agents for the benefit of the foreigner. And this effectually closes for pagans, unable to see the real state of affairs hidden beneath these external facts, every avenue of approach to the Catholic Religion. Alas! Gentlemen, out of the Church of all beauty and truth, you have made a road strewn with thorns and hemmed in with precipices.

Recently after the invasion of Belgium by Germany, Cardinal Mercier published a celebrated pastoral on Patriotism-love of the native soil, of the country of one's fathers-such was the theme that he developed in the document wherein the clearness of exposition is on a par with the nobility of the doctrine expounded, and all accordingly, both learned and ignorant, have been moved by it to the very depth of their souls.

As for China, I vainly rack my memory in order to recall ever having heard a missionary exalt patriotism. Does this mean that the Catholic Church exacts of the Catholics of China alone the duty of loving the foreign countries rather than their own? The explanation of this phenomenon escapes us. What we are the witnesses of, however, is the haughtiness and domineering spirit of certain personages without either sincerity or magnanimity, whose perpetual fear seems to be that our fellow citizens should escape their tyranny or resist them openly. They have not read the lines wherein the philosopher Mong-Tze teaches that "one gains men by affection and not by force", and their efforts are vain and their pains sterile.

But, someone will say, your "Exhortation" deviates from its object, and in your temerity you venture to attack your superiors. Is this not violating the laws of the Church? No! No! Our absolute conviction resulting from many years of observation and reflection is the fowling:

Appendix B

"Our Catholics of China do not value study, and this evil has very deep causes; whoever desires to study them must avoid a double peril, the one of only pointing them out without going to the root of the evil, and the other of drawing them down upon himself, if he desires to speak out clearly and openly, the accusation of insubordination of lack of respect towards his superiors."

We Catholics regard respect towards superiors and obedience to their orders as a matter of prime importance and, in point of fact, all of us are faithful to this duty of respect and obedience. This habit is so strong that, although we are constant witnesses of many abuses and errors, we not only repress within ourselves all reflections concerning them, but we bear them patiently and resignedly saying that such is the will of God.

And it is preciously for this reason that our fatherland is deteriorating daily, that to-morrow threatens to be worse than today, and that the situation is without remedy. As for us, we think that the duty of obedience does not absolve us from the duty of personal effort toward good.

Our own submission to spiritual superiors is irreproachable and in our veneration for them, we do not yield to any. But the very sincerity and depth of these selfsame sentiments show us an imperious duty the need of devoting our poor services, without any thought of the personal consequences, to so great a cause.

The Changes that China has undergone within the past few years have left in their wake a society disabled, without guidance and without support. This is for the church an Unparalleled opportunity the like of which ahs not been offered during the past ten centuries. We have tried within the limits of our powers, to profit by this providential hours, to mix intimately with a society given to the hazards of uncertain doctrines, in order to point out to others the way of salvation; and we have reaped only criticism and disapprobation for our pains. And now it is with sorrow in our souls that we raise our voices to recall the true principles to those who ought to serve as our leaders and models in these matters. For the enlightened citizen, for the ruling classes of our country, it has long since become a commonplace that the Catholic Church does not encourage study and does not commend instruction. May we be permitted to speak clearly—for now silence is impossible—our superiors are responsible for this serious situation. Devoid of clear and broad ideas, they do not pursue ideals in harmony with the spirit and role of the Church; hence scarcity of talents, smothering of merit, general retrogression, such are the humiliating characteristics of the general stagnation and voluntary barrenness of Catholicity in China.

This racial narrowness and lack of clear conceptions come from their won lack of education. Add to this, the pride race and fatherland, and an *esprit du corps* carried to an extreme degree, and you will understand why this sort of intellectual poisoning has also progressed to an extreme degree.

An exaggerated attachment to the fatherland and to a particular religious society leads inevitable to intolerance of the merit of others. Where this tendency exists, one does not want to give up to others that which one is incapable of doing one's self, and one is unwilling to acknowledge one's own incapacity. Under such conditions, it is necessary, by all means, to keep the minds of one's subjects in ignorance and deform their characters by favoring the habit of acquiescent flattery and servility.

How true is this word of an ancient! "The jealous man cannot suffer merit which surpasses his own; he contradicts and annihilates the merit that promises but which might be later lacking in compliance." Does not this remark seem to be an anticipated picture of or superiors?

These observations should suffice. The sentiments, they express, are conformable, we are sure, with the natural law and uprightness of conscience. If we do not insist further, if we are silent about many known facts and solid proofs, we are not deterred by considerations of human prudence, but by fear of passing for sowers of discord, as discouraging pessimists, or even as enemies of Holy Church. In reality it is not the Church we fight, but rather the conduct of men with partial and personal views.

If having received from God the grace to understand these things that make for discernment between good and evil, between that which edifies and that which ruins, if having reflected many years on this matter, we preferred to buy, by a silence and a patience out of place, the good name of humble and simple submission, would we not be acting against our conscience, and would we not be despising the gift of God?

Some will think, perhaps, that these declarations savor of the spirit of revolt, and that we are following the footsteps of Luther. We beg them to spare themselves this charitable anxiety. Without powers or orders, we are among the least of the faithful, and does not history teach us that those who raised against Rome the standard or revolt were always from among the ministry? As for us, our only fear has been that of getting away from Rome. Those who, faithful to the Holy See in the open, resist it in secret; those who openly violate its directions and address to it without scruple lying reports, these have high places in the Church. Fore them, Gentlemen, your solicitude would not be misplaced; but one is not a rebel for denouncing the rebellion of which one is a witness.

Others say: "If the superiors command the errors or injustice, their responsibility lone is involved, and there is merit for us even here in conforming to their order; a simple faith does not permit itself to judge them." This theory changes the criterum of morality by placing it in the will of the superiors and no more in the commandments of God and the testimony of conscience; It is a theory favorable to lying and illusions, contrary to the sentiments of all mankind, and such is not the "simple faith" our conscience can admit.

You ignore, others say, the difficulty of the superior's position. Seeing things from the outside, you criticize them without measure, and this is a perilous procedure. You are forgetting that on earth good and evil are mixed, as well as usefulness and nullity, and that only a superior intelli-

Appendix B

gence can choose aright. This is really true; but we may remark that, in the pursuit of good and the exercise of virtue, that which imports above all is the general good: this is the paramount consideration, and not a few personal and particular advantages, involving as a manifest result, a serious dishonor to the Church, and falling back upon the cowardly excuse of reigned impotence: " There is nothing to be done". Here lies for spiritual, as well as for temporal things, the true rule of discernments.

As for that which is now decorated with the name of propagation of the faith, it is well-known that the recruits acquired thereby for the Church are as so many festering wounds, and as a leprosy infecting a healthy body; they taint and enervate the true faithful and inundate the Church like a swam o unclean insects. Any man endowed with felling suffers and groans under this shame, but the feat of a domineering authority restrains the outward expression of his grief which finally resolves itself into smothered groans.

Kindly remark, gentlemen, that the defects to which we allude and which our sorrow cannot pass over in complete silence, are very real, and that discretion alone prevents us from divulging them with great precision.

We do not dare attribute to ourselves either merit or virtue, nor any great knowledge of the Catholic doctrine, but our conscience tells us that the virtues which the Church preaches to us are an enlightened and loving faith, a perfect obedience to the orders and directions of the Holy See, and not an acquiescence confused in its principles and blind in its essence, which admits without hesitation thing contrary to conscience and morality and which decks itself with the name of obedience.

To return to our subject, and enquiry into the matter brings the following facts to our support: At the closing period of the Ming dynasty, Father Ricci fired with an intrepid zeal and an immense love of souls, gifted with a great intellect, and equipped with vast knowledge, crossed the seas to come to China. Studying incessantly and scrutinizing deeply for more than twenty years the literature and history of our country, he composed works that exercised a great influence on the lettered men and ministers of his time and which are still the admiration of posterity. Other missionaries of great intellect followed him, Fathers Schall, Veribest, and Aleni, all of whom published works as noteworthy for their beauty of composition as for their solidity of doctrine. What was not then the position of the Catholic Church in China? When later the Emperors proscribed it, when the governors and other mandarins were banded together against it, then the men of influence that it had known how to gain for Christ, saved it from a complete extermination.

Today, what do we see? The era of religious freedom has run the knell of old restrictions, and obstacles of all kinds have disappeared. Is it not the occasion to announce without restraint the good news of the Gospel? Alas! Opposition and obstacles come no more from without but from within. We would not dare to enumerate before pagans the obstacles of all kinds that paralyze the evangelical preaching—the pride of race pushed to an extreme, the prestige of a European country, the hostility toward the other congregations—such are the fraud lines of the program! This affirmation, although it seems daring and emanating from a mind given to criticism, is supported by facts and we shall cite two or three.

Under the reign of Hsuan T'ung the government requested the Catholic Missions here to provide professors for the National University; not being able to furnish them ourselves, we preferred to abandon these posts to persons foreign to the Catholic Religion rather than to call in members of another religious society. This is past history, one may say, and these details may not have a sure foundation.

Here then is another example, very recent, and of which we ourselves have been actual witnesses. A certain missionary desired to found a university in a great city; the opposition of our superiors baffled his designs, for it could not be possible that other religious should gain footing among us. This, indeed, is the sole motive. Recently another missionary publicly disparaged in his writings Fathers Ricci and Adam Schall; his tactics or restoring to offensive words and lies have only revealed his own baseness, and his sentiments deserved nothing but silence and scorn.

We have spent ourselves in conjectures as to the possible purpose of such a manner of acting, which seeks to revive ancient quarrels long since settled by the Holy See, and which represents to say the least, a useless expenditure of energy, from the standpoint of Christians no less than of pagans. The mystery becomes clear when one reflects that Ricci and Schall did not belong to the same nation nor to the same society as the author. That suffices to explain his animus in the attack and his joy in humiliating a rival.

At the base of all this, however, is an aversion to study, a horror of all superiority. That is the root out of which all this *esprit du corps* springs, and this aversion explains many things...

If such is the invariable program, and such the strength of this opposition to culture, what then are the results. While priests able fitly to compose a letter in Chinese are as rare as the morning starts, do we find any pagans remarkable on account of their intellect and knowledge attracted to the Catholic Religions? No! not a single one. And yet so sad condition does not seem to suggest to our superiors the idea of a change of methods. They exult, on the contrary, in declaring that it is more difficult for a rich man to enter into the heavenly realm than for a camel to pass through the eye of a needle...and all the while they forget our models who by their teachings have converted men of all classes.

Ask them what examples they themselves have given, what serums they have produced, what doctrines they have expounded to convert men such as the celebrated literati as Su Koang Ts'I (Xu Guang-qi)and Li Chih Tsao (Li Zhi-cao). With the actual method now in vogue, if are to count on the conversion of a member of the ruling class, it will be necessary first that

Appendix B

this adherent fall from heaven, next that he be endowed with a certain number of indispensable virtues: i.e. with an humble disposition to become submissive and respectful subject of foreign men; to recognize the transcendent merits of the superiors, on whom he will be called upon to lavish reverences, genuflections and prostrations; it will be incumbent on him to renounce all science and instruction, and above all, the love of his native country.

Again, the accusations of boldness and insubordination address themselves to us. Whence does such regulation emanate and on what authority do you lay such ideas at the door of our superiors? It is true that these regulations are not written, but which one of you gentlemen will deny that in practice they do enforce such rules and principles, and that their manner of acting is sufficient of itself to close to the enlightened and ruling classes all access to Christianity; and that, far from opening their eyes to this sad reality, they are entirely satisfied with it.

Such are the serious obstacles which confront the propagation of the faith in China. The remedy? You will ask. We answer that it is very difficult to cure those who are deeply infected with the malady, and whose understanding is, as it were, poisoned therewith and who support themselves on material strength, and not upon God.

We would propose that our youth gifted with energy and disposed to sacrifice all for the salvation of their brethren be asked to make a quarter of an hour daily prayer for an entire year with the aim of begging the God of all kindness to procure for China the gift of faith...to enlighten and change whose who are an obstacle and a dishonor to the Church, that He grant them the courage of change of orientation, that he may help them to repress their too great attachment to race, fatherland, and factions, that he may give to us all a heart like the Sacred Heart of Jesus, and a mind docile to the direction of the Holy See.

After a year of fervent prayer, we will gather anew to kneel before our Bishop and beg him in all sincerity and respect to prolong the studies of the seminary to six years, so as to give the future priests and opportunity to get a deep knowledge of both European and Chinese Culture. It will be necessary to procure the services of professors of high standing and a great reputation in order to revise the program of study, and so bring nearer to perfection the course of studies, instead of being satisfied with a superficial knowledge. Salvation is to be gained only at that price.

Many of our young native priests are, unable so much as correctly to compose a simple letter: their embarrassed and awkward style would be unworthy of an ordinary clerk in commerce.

Useless to insist on other points; the forgetfulness of the Holy See is the cause of great harm to the reputation and dignity of the Catholic Church in our country.

We pray you, gentlemen, to look upon continuous applications to study as a duty of state. An if, in unfolding our ideas on this subject, our language has been imperfect, and the tone of it a little brusque, the word of an ancient reassures you: "Thought the expression may be harsh, it comes from a sincere heart."

Kindly read and meditate on this exhortation, and familiarize yourselves with it; but we protest beforehand against all incomplete and detached quotations from the text that would disfigure our thought.

Kindly excuse our badly strained emotion, having regarded to the sadness of our heart, and to not consider us a rebel to Holy Church nor as a sower of condemnable doctrines.

Ying Lien Chih
June, 1917.

APPENDIX C

Terminology

Beijing—Pei Ching, Pei ping 北京，北平，

Beijing Union Medical College—Peiking Union Medical Colleges 北京医大

Da Xue—Ta-hsue 大学

Feng Yu Xiang—Feng Yu Hsiang 冯如祥

Fu Ren—Fu Jen 辅仁

Gong Jiao—Kung Chiao 公教

Guomindang—Kuomintang 国民党

NanJing—Nanking 南京

Qing Hua University—Tsinghua University 清华大学

Sun Zhong-shan—Sun Yat Sen 孙中山

Shen Chong—Shen Tsong 沈崇

Tianjin—Tientsin 天津

Wu Pei Fu—Wu P'ei Fu 吴佩服

Xuan Tong—Hsuan T'ung 宣统

Yan Jing University—Yen Ching University 燕京大学

Zhang Zuo lin—Chang Tso Lin 张作霖

Notes

CHAPTER ONE NOTES

1. The name Fu Ren University was officially used in 1927 in China. The official English name of the University was *Catholic University of Peking*. Formerly, the Chinese name of the university was *Kung Chiao Ta Hsueh* and the Title *Fu Jen* was confined to the Preparatory School, which was also called *Fu Ren She* or *MacManus Academy of Chinese Studies*. This was the first and the foremost establishment of the Catholic University. The name Fu Ren is taken from the Chinese classics and makes a powerful appeal to the mentality of the Chinese. This name, as already stated, was adopted as the official Chinese title of the Catholic University of Peking when it was officially registered with the government in 1927 and dropped off *Kung Chiao* because of the religious implications.

   Moreover, it is necessary to understand where the name Fu Ren came from. A few words of explanation seem to be appropriate. These two characters are taken from a sentence in the 24th chapter of Book XII of the Confucian *Analects*, which is ascribed to the philosopher *Zeng Shen*, a disciple of *Confucius*: *"Jun Zi Yi Wen Hui You, Yi You Fu Ren"*, which translates, "the superior Man on grounds of culture meets with his friends, and by their friendship help his virtue." More details see *Fu Ren University Bulletin*, #4, 1929, 29.

2. Full text see appendix A.

3. The student enrollment record that kept was very incomplete. It is difficult to possess the numbers throughout all the years. Chapter five has detailed numbers of all the available years.

4. See chapter five for the numbers and details.

5. ASVA, Leon McNeill, "Benedictines and University of Peking," in *The Grail*, July 1927, pre-folder, 115.

6   There were thirteen Colleges and Universities already existed in Beijing when Fu Ren was about to be established. Those universities were either Christian controlled private ones or government controlled national ones. Anthony Li in his book *The History of Privately Controlled Higher Education in the Republic of China* (Washington, D.C.: Catholic University of America press, 1954) listed all of them. Fu Ren was the youngest university in Beijing.

7   ASVA, Dom Michael Hanbury, O.S.B. "The Catholic University of Peking", in *Pax* No.89, Winter, 1928, 354.

8   Propagation of the Faith is established by the Pope to oversee the Catholic Mission in the world missions. All the missionaries should have to report the this congregation.

9   SJS, *Fu Jen University Bulletin*, #1, 1926, 60.

10 Appendix A.

11 Ibid.

12 Appendix A.

13 He Jian-ming, in his essay, "Chen Yuan and Fu Ren University" in Zhan Kai-yuan, ed., *Wenhua Chuanbo yu Jiaohui Daxue* (culture transmission and Christian Universities) (Hu Bei: Hu Bei Chubanshe, 1996) made a reference to this as well.

14 Vincent Ying Lianzhi's whole life can be found in Saint Vincent Archabbey archive, Donald Paragon, "Ying Lien-Chih (1866–1926) and the Rise of Fu Jen, the Catholic University of Peking," in *Monumenta Serica, Vol. XX*, 1961 has details of him. He was recognized by both the National Government of China and the Japanese Government for his achievements.

15 Ma Xiang-bo, who was an ex-Jesuit priest. Together with Vincent Ying, were the only two well-known Catholic Scholars in China among many intellectuals. He founded two Universities: Aurora University and Fu Dan University, both in shanghai and also served as the grand councilor to the President Yuan Shi Kai. He left the priesthood because he could not tolerate the way the French Jesuits treated the Native Chinese priests. Ruth Hayhoe & Lu Yongling have details of him in *Ma Xiangbo and the Mind of Modern China 1840–1939* (New York; London: M.E. Sharpe, 1996).

16 Details are discussed in chapter two in the Catholic higher education section.

17 Paul Varg in his book *Missionaries, Chinese and Diplomats* (New Jersey: Princeton, 1958), described how Rome attempted to have a relationship with China, but the efforts were blocked by France and Italy.

18 Such as selecting the location, buying the properties, and renovation and finding professors for the school, etc.

19 There are conflicting references on the government registration because the *Fu Ren University Bulletin* mentioned that Fu Ren was the first private university registered with the government in the city of Beijing. The clarification is that Fu Ren was in the City of Beijing, and Yan Jing was in the Metropolitan of Beijing. Yan Jing was registered with the government in 1926.

20 ASJA, *Fu Ren University Bulletin* #8, 1931, 106.

21 Anthony Li, *The History of Privately Controlled Higher Education in the Republic of China* (Washington D.C.: Catholic University of America press, 1954), all three Catholic Universities stayed where they were during the Sino-Japanese War, all the American Protestant Church run universities moved inland after the broke of Pacific War.

22 Ibid., 117.

23 According to a well-known scholar and historian, Zhang Kai-yuan, a professor at Hua Zhong Normal University in China, there are no available materials in China for scholars to write on the Catholic Higher Education. He and many scholars from both Mainland China and Hong Kong have done tremendous studies on Protestant higher education. Details can be found in the introductions in Xu Yi-hua's book *Jiao Hui Daxue he Shenxue Jiaoyu* (Christian Universities and Theological education) (FuJian: Fu Jian Jiao Yu Chu Ban She, 1995), preface 1 & 2.

24 W. Lawrence Neuman, *Social Research Methods: Qualitative and Quantitative Approaches*, 4th edition, (Boston, London: Allan and Bacon, 2000), 396.

25 A copy of the bounded *Fu Ren University Bulletin* #1–#5 can be found at Saint John's Seminary, the future reference will be mentioned specifically. Fu Ren University Bulletin is also called *Fu Ren Da Xue Bulletin*.

CHAPTER TWO NOTES

1 John Fairbank and Ssu-Yü Teng, *China's Response to the West* (Cambridge: Harvard University Press, 1961), 205.

2 Kenneth Scott Latourette, *A History of Christian Missions in China* (New York: the MacMillan Company, 1929), 529.

3 Ibid., 528.

4 Ruth Hayhoe, "Towards the Forging of Chinese University Ethos: Zhendan and Fudan, 1903–1919" in *The China Quarterly*, No.94, (June, 1983), 324.

5   Ibid., 325.

6   Ibid., more details see 325–326.

7   Ruth Hayhoe, *China's Universities 1895–1995: A Century of cultural Conflict* (New York and London, Garland Publishing Inc., 1996), 31–32.

8   Ibid., 37.

9   Marianne Bastid, "Servitude or Liberation" in Ruth Hayhoe and Marianne Bastid, ed., *China's Education and the Industrialized World* (Armonk, N.Y.: ME Sharp, Inc., 1987), 6.

10 Wang Zhong-xin, *Ji Du Jiao yu Zhong Guo Xiandai Jiao Yu* (Christianity and modern Education in China) (Hu Bei: Hu Bei Jiao Yu Chu Panshi, 2000), 101.

11 Zhang Kai-yuan, ed., *She Hui Zhuan Xing yu Jiao Hui Da Xue* (The Changes of the society and Christian Universities) (Hu Bei: Hu Bei Jiao Yu Chubanshen, 1998); Zhang Kai-yuan & Ma Mei, *Ji Du Jiao yu Zhong Guo Wenhua Congshu* (Christianity and Chinese Culture Series), (Hu Bei: Hu Bei Jiao Yu Chubanshe, 2000). Xu Yi-hua, *Jiao Hui Da Xue yu Shen Xue Jiao Yu* (Christian Universities and Theological Education), (Fu Jian: Fu Jian Jiao Hu Chubanshi, 1999).

12 "Republican China 1912–1949" in John Fairbank ed., *The Cambridge History of China*, Vol. 12, (Cambridge: Cambridge University Press, 1983), 167.

13 Ruth Hayhoe, "Toward the Forging of a Chinese University Ethos: Zhendan and Fudan, 1903–1919" in *China Quarterly*, No. 94, June 1983, 329.

14 Ibid., 331.

15 Ruth Hayhoe, Lu Yongling, ed., *Ma Xiang-bo and the Mind of Modern China 1840–1939* (Armonk, New York: M.E. Sharpe, Inc., 1996). In this book, they discussed quite extensively on this dispute.

16 Ruth Hayhoe, "Toward the Forging of a Chinese University Ethos: Zhendan and Fudan, 1903–1919", 333.

17 Anthony Li, *The History of Privately Controlled Higher Education in the Republic of China* (Washington D.C.: the Catholic University of American Press, 1954), 61.

18 Ibid.

19 Kenneth Scott Latourette, *A History of Christian Missions in China*, (New York: the MacMillan Company, 1929), 559.

Notes

20 Ibid.

21 Anthony Li, *The History of privately Controlled Higher Education in the Republic of China* (Washington D.C.: the Catholic University of American Press, 1954), 69–72. Aslo see, Latourette, *A History of Christian Missions in China*, (New York: the MacMillan Company, 1929), 731ff.

22 Latourette, *A History of Christian Missions in China*, (New York: the MacMillan Company, 1929),338.

23 Ibid. , 560.

24 Ibid. , 550.

25 Ibid. , 338.

26 Ibid. , 338.

27 Once again to name these three Catholic higher education institutions in China: Aurora University (*Zhen Dan Daxue*) of Shanghai (1902); Tientsin College of Industry and Commerce (Hautes Étudies) (*Jin Gu Daxue*) of Tianjing (1923), which later became a university; Catholic (Fu Ren) University of Peking (*Fu Ren Daxue*) (1925).

28 Wu Xiao-xin, "A Case Study of the Catholic University of Peking During Benedictine Period (1927–1933)" (Ed.D dissertation, University of San Francisco, 1993). A copy of the dissertation can be found in Saint John's Seminary Library, Brighton, MA., with a title *Peking University* on the cover. This was a printing mistake, I believe.

29 This article can be found in *Tripod* (Hongkong: Holy Spirit Center, 1991). This article is not a research paper. It is only a description of the university, in which he points out that Ma Xiangbo joined Vincent Ying to write the petition letter to Pope Pius XI, see Appendix A.

30 Sophie Lee, "Education in Wartime Beijing: 1937–1945", (Doctoral Dissertation, Michigan, Ann Arbor, 1996). A copy can be found in Harvard *Yenching* Library, Cambridge, MA.

31 He Jian-ming, "Fu Ren Guo Xue he Chen Yuan"(Fu Ren Chinese Literature and Chen Yuan) in Zhang Kai-yuan, ed., *Wen Hua Chuanbo yu Jaohui Daxue* (Culture transmission and Christian Universities) (Hu Bei: Hubei Chubanshe, 1996), 233–265.

32 Sophie Lee, "Education in Wartime Beijing 1937–45" (Doctoral Dissertation, Michigan: Michigan University, 1996), 201.

33 Ibid.

34 He Jian-ming, "Fu Ren Guo Xue he Chen Yuan", in Zhang Kai-yuan, ed., *Wen Hua Chuanbo yu Jaohui Daxue* (Culture transmission and Christian Universities) (Hu Bei: Hubei Chubanshe, 1996), 265.

35 Ibid., 240.

36 Ibid., 245.

37 Ibid., 248.

38 Wu Xiao-xin, "A Case Study of the Catholic University of Peking During Benedictine Period (1927–1933)" (Ed.D dissertation, University of San Francisco, 1993),119.

39 Ibid., 133.

40 Ibid., 134.

41 Ibid., 147.

42 Sophie Lee, "Education in Wartime Beijing 1937–1945" (Doctoral Dissertation, Michigan: Michigan University, 1996), 146.

43 After the break of the Sino-Japanese war in 1937, the Japanese took over Beijing, and set up its own government which was called "Provisional Government" or the "Puppet Government" in some Chinese writings. The Nationalist Government moved to inland, and set up its wartime Capital in Chengdu, Sichuan Province. Many government universities moved to inland after 1937 to avoid the Japanese control. In Beijing, only Fu Ren and Yan Jing remained during the years from 1937 to 1941. In the end of 1941, Yanjing University had to move because of the Pacific War.

44 Sophie Lee, "Education in Wartime Beijing 1937–1945" (Doctoral Dissertation, Michigan: Michigan University, 1996), on pages 202–205, Lee presented her "evidence" that Fu Ren was sponsored by the Puppet Government when the Japanese took over Beijing after 1937.

45 Ibid., 203. She uses "Conventional Wisdom to conclude that Fu Ren was less "pure" of being patriotic in comparison with Yanjing University.

46 Ibid., 148. Lee is convinced that Fu Ren University was under the total control of the Japanese during their occupation. Her conclusion was drawn from Lutz's reference on pages 371–372, in his book *China and the Christian Colleges1850–1950*, "Schools in areas taken over by the Japanese were not permitted to operate if they were registered with the Kuomintang Government in Chungking." Without doing further research, she uses Yan Jing University's record to draw a conclusion of Fu Ren University: "Records of Yanjing University, Fu Ren's purported comrade in these endeavors, contain no confirmation

Notes

of this secret directive, but the official history of the university also makes similar claims for unimpeachable behavior during the time between the *Luogouqian Incident (*Marco Polo Bridge*)* and the attack on Pear Harbor." This statement is rather speculative because the author ignored the status of the University Administration were Germans. Since Germany was still the ally of the Japanese, and Fu Ren was not destroyed.

47 ASJA, *Catalogue of the Catholic University of Peking 1936–37*. The graduation requirements mentioned both Chinese and English were the official languages in writing.

48 Ibid. , 147.

49 Ibid. , 205.

50 Harold Rigney, SVD, *Four Years in a Red Hell* (Chicago: Henry Regnery Company, 1956). He described his experience of his imprisonment of 50 months in Beijing.

51 Jessie Lutz, *Chinese Politics and Christian Missions—the anti-Christian Movements of 1920–1928* (Notre Dame, Indiana: Cross Cultural Publications, Inc., 1988), 101.

52 Ibid. , 101.

53 Ibid. , 139.

54 Paul Varg, *Missionaries, Chinese, and Diplomats* (Princeton, NJ: Princeton University Press, 1958), 51.

55 Jessie Lutz, *Chinese Politics and Christian missions—the anti-Christian Movements of 1920–1928)*, (New York: Cornell University Press, 1971), 238–252. See also Kenneth Scott Latourette, *A history of Christian Missions in China*, 698.

56 I learned more about this through a phone conversation inquiring of his books on Christian higher education in China.

57 Thomas Breslin, *China, American Catholicism, and the Missionary* (University Park, PA and London: the Pennsylvania State University Press, 1980), 104.

CHAPTER THREE NOTES

1 SJS *Fu Ren University Bulletin*, #1, 40.

2 The full text of this letter can be found in the Appendix A. *Letter to Pope Pius X, 1912.*

3   SJS *Fu Ren University Bulletin*, #1, 40.

4   The full text of this article can be found in the Appendix B. *Exhortation to study, 1917*.

5   Kenneth Latourette, *A History of Christian Missions in China* (New York: the MacMillan Company, 1929), 705.

6   According to Thomas A. Breslin, *China, American Catholicism and the Missionary* (University Park and London: Pennsylvania State University Press, 1980), "By 1915, officials of the Vatican, especially the propagation of the faith, were clearly worried about the missions in china. France was still in control of the mission and Rome... Rome wished to avoid a direct confrontation with the French government over the issues of replacing French missions." 21–25.

7   Kenneth Latourrette, A History of Christian Missions in China (New York: the MacMillan Company, 1929), 705. In fact, in this year, Yüan Shi-kai, the president of China gave formal reception to greetings sent by Benedict XV at the hands of Bishop Jarlin, Vicar Apostolic in Peking. 713.

8   Jessie Lutz, Chinese Politics and Christian Missions ((Indiana: Cross Cultural Publications, Inc., 1988), 87.

9   ASVA, Box #7, For details of Vincent Ying Lianzhi, read Donald Paragon, Ying Lien-chih (1866–1929) and the Rise of Fu Jen, the Catholic University of Peking. Reprinted from Monumenta Serica (Hua Yi Xue Zhi) Vol. XX, 1961. This series of books is still publishing in Germany under the direction of Divine Word Fathers. Vincent Ying was the first to convert. Later his wife became a Catholic, then his mother, brothers and sisters. His father was the last one to convert.

10 Ibid. , 177–8.

11 For details of Ma Xiang-bo, read Ruth Hayhoe & Lu Yongling, ed. Ma Xiangbo and the Modern Mind of China 1840–1939 (Armonk, New York/ London: M.E. Sharpe, Inc., 1996).

12 These two universities are: Zhen Dan University (Aurora University) in 1903; and Fu Dan University in 1905. He used his own money for the endowment. The latter one was a public school from the very beginning. They both became famous. The first one was famous for its medical school; the later was famous for its patriotic movement and political science.

13 See Appendix A, Letter to Pope Pius X, 1912.

14 Ibid.

Notes

15 Ibid.

16 Ibid.

17 Appendix B, Vincent Ying, Exhortation to Study, July 1917.

18 Eric Hanson, Catholic Politics in China and Korea (Maryknoll, New York: Orbis Books, 1980), 21–22.

19 ASVA, Box #8, The Catholic University of Peking (Beatty, PA: the Archabbey Press), 6. This article is undated and without an author.

20 ASVA, Box #7, Paragon, Ying Lien-chih (1866–1929) and the Rise of Fu Jen, the Catholic University of Peking, 207.

21 ASVA, Box #8, The Catholic University of Peking (Beatty, PA: the Archabbey Press), 6–7.

22 ASVA, Box #8, The Catholic University of Peking, 8–9.

23 As I mentioned briefly in the same section about the political entanglements within the Church were complex. It will also be analyzed in chapter eight when I analyze Fu Ren University's contributions.

24 G.B. O'Toole, "The Spirituality Lineage of the Catholic University of Peiking", in the Fu Ren University Bulletin, #1,16ff.

25 ASVA, Box #8, The Catholic University of Peking, 7.

26 Ibid. , 9.

27 ASVA, Box #1, folder #7, Letter to the Abbots, by Archabbot, Aurelius Stehle, September 18, 1923.

28 Jerome Oetgen, Mission to America (Washington, D.C.: the Catholic University of America Press, 2000), 285.

29 Ibid. , see 285–286 for more details.

30 ASVA, Box#1, folder #9, Letter to the Abbots, by Aurelius, Stehle, September18, 1923 for more information about the procedural structure.

31 ASVA, Box #1, folder #9, Roman documents, June 27, 1924. Protocol N. 2244–24.

32 ASVA, Box#1, folder #9, Letter to Monsignor Stanilaus Jarlin, dated February 2, 1922.

33 ASVA, Box#1, folder #9, Letter to Rev, Monsignor Stanislaus Jarlin, dated November 20, 1923.

34 ASVA, Box #1, folder #7, Letter to Rt. Rev. Archabbot Aurelius, Dated on July 17, 1924.

35 Francis X. Clougherty was a secular priest and was running an American-style high school in Kaifeng. Later he became a Benedictine monk and eventually succeeded Aurelius as the second chancellor of Fu Ren University. For details, see Fu Ren University Bulletin, #2.

36 Jerome Oetgen, Mission to America (Washington, D.C.: the Catholic University of America Press, 2000), 290.

37 ASVA, Box#1, folder #9, Letter to the Rt. Rev. Abbots of the American-Cassinese Congregation. By Aurelius Stehle, October, 5, 1924,

38 ADWM, Clifford King, SVD, "The 'Why' of the Catholic University of Peking", in Fu Ren Magazine, 1935, 12.

39 SJS, Fu Ren University Bulletin #1. "Chronicle of Events," 66–67.

40 Ibid., see "Buildings and grounds" for details of the property purchasing and the description of the Palace.

41 Ibid. 12.

42 Ibid. 12.

43 Ibid., "Pei-Ching Kung Chiao Ta Hsueh", in Fu Ren University Bulletin #1, 7.

44 Ibid., more details see the whole article "Pei-Ching Kung Chao Ta Hsueh". 7–9.

45 For details of the explanation of the name Gong Jiao and the background of the name of the university, see Fu Ren University Bulletin #1, 6–9.

46 ASVA, Box #7, Paragon, 200–201.

47 For details see "the MacManus Academy of Chinese Studies" in Fu Ren University Bulletin #1, 39–45.

48 ASVA, Box #7. The information can be found in Pragong, Ying Lien-chih (1866–1926) and the Rise of Fu Jen, the Catholic University of Peking, 1961. 207–208.

49 Anthony Li, The History of Privately Controlled Higher Education in the Republic of China (Washington, D.C.: the Catholic University of America Press, 1954).

Notes

50 SJS, Fu Ren University Bulletin #3, 1928, Dom Callistus Stehle, "Glimpse of China", 23–24.

51 Ibid., Fu Ren University Bulletin #1, 1926, 13.

52 Appendix B, Vincent Ying, 1917, Exhortation to Study.

53 ADWM, Fu Ren Magazine, 1935, 17.

54 ASVA, Box #1, folder #9, Aurelius, Letter to the Abbots, Feburary 22, 1926.

55 Ibid.

56 SJS, Fu Ren University Bulletin, #1, 1926, article, "A General Prospectus of the Institution", 13f.

57 Ibid. , 19.

58 More information on the linkage of the Benedictines and China, see O'Toole, "The Spiritual Lineage of the Catholic University at Peking", in Fu Ren University Bulletin #1, 1926.

CHAPTER FOUR NOTES

1 I have found conflicting references in terms of the location and registration of Yan Jing University, which was owned by American Protestant Church. The references are unclear about the city boundaries of Beijing: City of Beijing and Metropolitan of Beijing. Fu Ren was in the city of Beijing, and Yan Jing was in the outside of the City of Beijing. Whether Fu Ren was the first or second, it depended on the location of the city, not year.

2 SJS, See "the MacManus Academy of Chinese Studies", in *Fu Ren University, Bulletin,* #1, 39–42 for details. It is needed to clarify that the currency names were sometimes confusing. Some documents have Yuan (Chinese currency); some documents have Dollars (US currency); some use gold (international). It was hard to define which was which when they referred to. I try to use Dollars as much as possible.

3 ASJA, Prior Basil, "Suggestions of drafting the Statues of the Catholic University in Peking" 1933, #71–12.

4 ADWM, *Fu Ren Magazine,* January, 1935, 3.

5 The amount of the contribution from the Holy See is varying from record to record. The archival information from Beijing Normal University has $16,000.00 annually. Some records from Saint Vincent's and St. John's abbeys have either $10,000.00 or $25,000.00 variably. I chose $15,000,00 is because

this number appeared more than once in the official letters written by Archabbot Aurelius Stehle, the chancellor of the university.

6 Sir Theodore F. MacManus was a personal friend of Dr. O'Toole, the rector of the university. He contributed $100,000 to the newly established university as endowment to secure the best professors for the University. *Fu Ren University Bulletin* #4 had this to attribute, "His services to the Church in the missionary field have not been less outstanding. The Catholic University of Peking owes to this munificent benefactor an enormous debt of gratitude." The interests depended on the stock market. Later, the income from the interest dropped down to $6,000 annually. After the Divine Word Fathers took over the university, the endowment was never mentioned; probably the Benedictine Fathers withdrew it as well.

7 SJS, "Building and Ground", in *Fu Ren University Bulletin*, #1. 1926, a detailed description of how the Palace looked like. It is necessary to provide something information here: the Palace Court, flanked by the *Da Men* or Ceremonial Gate on the North connected by a central driveway. This drive divided the premises into two main sections: South and North. Southerside was called "the Garden Gate" with a "Vegetable Garden" where the first building was erected, and North part was the Palace Proper where later converted as classrooms, library, dormitories.

8 Ibid. , for details of the whole renovation process.

9 Ibid.

10 ASVA, *Letter to the Rt. Rev. Abbots and Rev. Fathers of the American –Cassinese Congregation*, October 5, 1924. Box#1, folder #7.

11 Ibid.

12 Ibid. , *Letter to the Rt. Rev. Abbots and Rev. Fathers of the American –Cassinese Congregation*, February 22, 1926. Box#1, folder #7.

13 Ibid.

14 *Gong Jiao Da Xue*, is called "Universal Religion University". I have explained it in Chapter Three.

15 ASVA, *letter to Archabbot Aurelius*, Dated August 15, 1927. Box#2, folder#2.

16 1927 was the year, when the Southern Nationalists' North Expedition with the intension to defeat the Warlords in the north and unify the country. The Warlord Zhang Zuo-lin from Manchuria controlled Beijing.

17 ASVA, Aurelius Stehle, *Letter to the Abbots of the American-Cassinese Congregation*, December 10th, 1927. Box #1, folder #7.

Notes

18 Beijing Normal University Archive, folder #702, *Finance reports: 1929–1930*.

19 These articles can be found in *Fu Ren University Bulletin*, #8,105–106.

20 This New Hall was designed in a Chinese style as well. Fu Ren Newsletter has this description: It is in harmony with all other buildings of the Palace. It is built in the form of the Chinese character for the sun (»') two squares placed side by side, and of all the prospects of the future the omen symbolized in this building is the most consoling. It augurs the hope of a sunny day for the university and its destiny to become a bright light in what was once the Celestial Empire. The quadrangle New Hall's southern front was 400 feet long and a side elevation 220 feet in breadth.
In St. John's Abbey, Minnesota, *Fu Ren News Letter*, March 1931, 1.

21 ASVA, *Letter to Abbot Lambert*, Box #5, folder #1.

22 ASJA, *Fu Ren News Letter*, March 1931, 5.

23 Ibid. , Colman Barry, *Worship and Work: St. John's abbey and University 1856–1992*. (Collegeville, Minnesota: The Liturgical Press), 1993, 307.

24 ASVA, Hugh Wilt, *The History of Fu Jen Catholic University of China*, April 29, 1966. Box #2, folder #9.

25 Ibid., *Letter to Bruno Schmid*, dated on March 21, 1960.

26 Ibid., Columban, *Letter to Edmund*, March 12, 1930. Box#1, folder#5.

27 Ibid., Hugh, *Letter to Val*, December 30, 1930. Box#1, folder #5.

28 ASJA, *A letter from Fr. Boniface*, Feburary1, 1933. #71–11; 1926–1933.

29 ASJA, Colman Barry, *Worship and Work: St. John's abbey and University 1856–1992*, 308.

30 ASJA, *Fu Ren News letter*, October, 1931, 1.

31 Ibid., *Letter from Rome to the American Cassinese Benedictines*, dated on July 28, 1932,

32 Ibid.

33 Ibid., Father Basil, *Letter to Father Abbot*, January 2, 1933, #71–10.

34 Ibid., Alcuin, *letter to Abbots of American-Cassinese Benedictines, Abbots*, February16, 1933 which called for a general meeting on the February, 22.

35 Ibid., *O'Toole's letter to Alcuin Deutch, abbot of St. Johns,*' February 9, 1933.

36 ADWM, Father Fritz Bornemann, *A History of the Divine Word Missionaries*, (Rome: Apud Collegium Verbi Divini, 1981). The new Abbot of Saint Vincent Abbey was no stranger to the Divine Word Fathers because he was one of them before he became a Benedictine Monk. In 1932, he visited Beijing, and on his way back to the US, he went to Rome to report to the Holy See, meanwhile, he visited the General Consultor of the Divine Word Fathers. He convinced the General to take over the university from the Benedictines.

37 He Jian-ming, "Fu Ren Guo Xue he Chen Yuan"(Fu Ren Chinese Literature and Chen Yuan) in Zhang Kai-yuan, ed., *Wen Hua Chuanbo yu Jaohui Daxue* (Culture transmission and Christian Universities) (Hu Bei: Hubei Chubanshe, 1996), 247.

38 In *Fu Ren University Bulletins*, readers can find different names of his titles. Though Chen Yuan was registered as the president of the University, he was referred as Vice-rector occasionally. This lasted until 1929 when Fu Ren was reorganized under the requirement of the Nationalist Government.

39 ASJA, #71–12.

40 Ibid. , 311. Their fears were for their benefactors. The superiors and treasures thought that new appeals for Fu Ren University would be sent to their benefactors, who were still suffering from the effect of the great Wall Street crash of "Black Friday", 1929.

41 ADWM, Joseph Murphy, "The SVD in the old Capital of China", in *Christian Family and Our Missions*, 1934, 62.

42 ADWM, *Short-biography of Father Ralph Tyken*.

43 Ibid.

44 ADWM, this can be found in both *Christian Family* and *Fu Ren Magazine*.

45 ADWM, *Christian Family and Our Missions*, 1937, 398.

46 ADWM, *Christian Family and Our Missions*, 1941, 76. This new building was in traditional Chinese style, in harmony with other Original buildings in the Palace. See also *Fu Ren Magazine*, 1941, 55.

47 ADWM, *Christian Family and Our Missions*, 1941, 39. See also, *Fu Ren Magazine*, 1941, 55.

48 Ibid.

49 Ibid.

50 ADWM, *Christian Family and Our Missions*, 1940, 239.

51   There are mixed references to this one. Some places refer to it as a department, and some places refer to it as a school. I chose school because in the Chinese version, Fu Ren University refers to it as school, when this part of the university was taken over by the University of Agriculture of Beijing. One more reference in the Divine Word Father's archive refers the same.

52   ADWM, *Christian Family and Our Missions*, 1939, 239.

53   Ibid., 1942, 39.

54   *Beijing Shi Fan Daxue Xiaoshi (1902-1982)* (History of the Beijing Normal University) (Beijing: Beijing Shifan Daxue press, 1984), 266.

55   Ibid. , 267.

56. ADWM, *Fu Ren Magazine, December* 1947. The numbers of students will be discussed in chapter five.

57   Ibid., *Christian Family and our Missions*, 1943, 6.

CHAPTER FIVE NOTES

1   Elliot Eisner, "Invitational conference on the hidden consequences of a national curriculum", in *Educational Researcher, 22 (7), 1993*, 38–39.

2   There are some disputes here on the number of colleges within Fu Ren University. I think Fu Ren had four colleges in total because in the history of Beijing Normal University stated this. Some articles say that Fu Ren had only three colleges; some others say there were four colleges. The College of Agriculture was also considered as the Department of Agriculture by some authors. In fact, it is rather confusing from reading the archival materials both in Chinese and English. In addition, I also am saying that the University had more than four. It had another, St. Albert's College and Women's College. Though the students took almost the same courses, they had their own deans, with only one president of the university. All the archival materials confirmed these were colleges.

3   ASVA, *Plan of Studies*, Box# 1, folder #9; see also *Fu Ren University Bulletin* #1.

4   SJS, "Preparatory Schools" in *Fu Ren University Bulletin* #1, 15.

5   "The Inauguration and Registration of the School of Arts", in *Fu Ren Da Xue, Bulletin* #4, 15.

6   A variety of subjects were studied within the departments. The subjects were itemized specifically in different departments. *Fu Ren University Bulletin* #4

has details of all the subjects. In fact, the curriculum was just like the ones that any Liberal Arts College would have.

7   ASJA, *Fu Ren News Letter*, February, 1932, 8.

8   ASJA, *Fu Ren Da Xue, Bulletin* #8, 107.

9   ASJA, *Fu Ren University Bulletin*, #8, 108. In a letter to the Minister of Education, Dr. O'Toole literally begged the ministry to allow Fu Ren to keep the status. He emphasized on the exclusivity of studying Chinese that Fu Ren was doing. "As the first president of our Academy, Mr. Ying carried out this policy of stressing the importance of Chinese letters to the extreme of excluding everything else from the curriculum...his successor, Mr. Chen Yuan liberalized this policy by introducing Western subjects..."

10 Ibid., 111.

11 Ibid., 110.

12 Ibid., 113.

13 Department of Fine Arts was also called Institute of Christian Fine Arts in some writings. I use both as the text requires.

14 *Zhong Guo Wen Xian: Kang Zhan Qian zhi Gaodeng Jiaoyu*,(Revolutionary document) vol. 56, editor, Huang Ji Lu, 79–97.

15 *ASBC, Fu Ren Da Xue, Bulletin, #7,* 1930.

16 ASJA, *Letter to the Abbot*, dated on February 10, 1933.

17 Zhong Guo Wen Xian: Kang Zhan Qian zhi Gaodeng Jiaoyu,(Revolutionary document) vol. 56, editor, Huang Ji Lu, 152–153.

18 It is not easy for me to make the changes of the currency of the time because of the exchanging rate was uncertain to me. However, there is no reference in the Fu Ren Magazine 1947 mentioned that the exchanging rate was $1=2 Yuan.

19 Ibid., 154–5.

20 ADWM, *Fu Ren Magazine*, 1935, 157.

21 ADWM, *Fu Ren Magazine*, September, 1948, 42.

22 Ibid.

23 Ibid., 42–48. A whole story of the development of this department.

Notes

24 Ibid., *From the Tenth Anniversary Memorandum of the Collegium Sinicum Ecclesiasticum.*

25 College of Agriculture in some places is also called as Department of Agriculture.

26 This material is taken from a private collection. Paul Han, S.V.D., who is studying in Chicago Theological Union, and has been collecting certain amount of materials of Fu Ren University. The Curriculum was from one of his collections, which is called *Collected Historical Materials of Peking Fu Jen Catholic University.*

27 Some places mention that there were seven languages taught in the university without specifics. Once the rector of the university mentioned seven in his address. I cannot name the last one if there had been one.

28 ADWM, *Fu Ren Magazine,* 1940, 239.

29 ADWM, *Christian Family and Our Missions,* 1939, 119.

30 *Beijing Shi Fan Da Xue Xiaoshi* (History of Beijing Normal University), 246.

31 He Jian-ming "Chen Yuan yu Fu Ren Guo Xue" in Zhang Kai-yuan ed. *Wen Hua Chuanbo yu Jiaohui Daxue* (Hu Bei: Hu Bei Jiaoyu Chubanshe, 1996) 254. Chai De-gen, Qi Gong, Mu Ruen-sun, Shi Shu-qing, Shi Nian-hai, Liu Nai-he, Zhou Zu-mo, Guo Yu-heng, Lai Xin-xia, Zhao Guo-xian, Wang Shu-min, etc.

32 ADWM, *Fu Ren Magagine,* 1940, 46.

33 Appendix A, *Letter to Pope Pius X.*

34 He Jian-ming "Fu Ren Guo Xue yu Chen Yuan"(Fu Ren Chinese culture and Chen Yuan) in, Zhang Kai-yuan, ed. *Wen Hua Chuan Bo yu Jiao Hui Da Xue*(Culture transmission and Christian Universities) (Hu Bei: Hu Bei Jiao Yu Chu Ban She, 1996) 238–240.

35 ADWM, *Fu Ren Magazine,* 1939, 55. Among the very last acts of Pope Pius XI, the Pope of the Missions, in the week of his death, he honored three from Fu Ren: Chen Yuan, president of the University and famous historian and scholar, was named "Commander of the Order of St. Gregory the Great with Badge." Mr. Ying Ch'en Li, who Father was Vincent Ying, "a Commander of St. Gregory the Great"; Mr. Edward Zhang Huai, dean of the College of Education, was made "Knight of St. Gregory."

36 ASJA, Fu Ren News Letter, April, 1931, 3.

37 ADWM, *Fu Ren Magazine,* September, 1948.

38 ASBC, *Fu Ren Da Xue, Bulletin*, #7.

39 Ibid.

40 This letter was found at Saint Vincent Archabbey archive. This was the letter Fu Ren University sent to the archabbey when the university was trying to secure the best scholars in China for the university. All of the professors were described in detail so that the purpose of establishing the university would be achieved to be the first-rate university rather than a mediocre one in China as Archabbot Aurelius mentioned. I chose the relevant one here. This statement can also be found in Chapter Three.

41 *Beijing Shifan Daxue Xiaoshi (1902–1982)* (Beijing: Beijing shifan daxue press, 1984), 240–241.

42 Ibid. , because of the famous professors on the faculty, Fu Ren was described as "Ren Cai Ji Ji, Ding Sheng Yi Shi." (Many prominent and famous people, the greatest of the time)

43 ASJA, *Fu Ren University Bulletin*, #8, 127–130.

44 ADWM, *Fu Ren Magazine*, 1935, 158

45 Ibid., 131.

46 Ibid., 1937, 53.

47 Ibid.

48 Ibid., 1942, 18.

49 The reason for the missing records can be attributed to the administration of the university. Just prior to 1937 when Japanese troops took over Beijing and the whole northern part of China, Fu Ren had a new rector, who was a German. The administration was under the German control completely after 1941 when the Japanese attacked the Pearl Harbor. The Americans gave up their posts at the University. Some of the records were probably in Germany, or missed.

50 It has been very difficult to get the accurate numbers of the faculty throughout the years as I mentioned in the previous note. Many numbers were inconsistent in various records, such as the year 1930–1931—some records had 86, and in 1931–32, had 160. The authors sometimes combined the members from the middle school as well. After consulting other references from various archives, I decided to keep the numbers as I have them now.

51 ASBC, *Fu Ren University Bulletin*, #7, 19–30.

Notes

52 ADWM, *Fu Ren Magazine*, 1938, 58.

53 SJS *Fu Ren Da Xue, Bulletin* #1. 42.

54 ADWM, Christian Family and Our Missions, 1937, 78.

55 ADWM, *Fu Ren Magazine*, 1939, 11.

56 ADWM, *Fu Ren Magazine*, 1948, 37. This has been a long tradition at Fu Ren to go out to have exams. As early as in 1940 when 1625 applicants applied. The university had "entrance exams in six different cities: Peking 835 men and 385 women; Tientsin 190 men and 135 women; Tsinan 21 men and 6 women; Tsingdao 9 men and 17 women; suanhua 18 members of the Congregation of Disciples of the Lord; Shanghai, 5 men and 4 women." This almost became a tradition for Fu Ren University. See *Fu Ren Magazine*, 1940, 117.

57 ADWM, *Fu Ren Magazine*, 1948, 37.

58 Divine Word Fathers, Chicago, Paul Han, SVD's private collection, "Collected Historical materials of Peking Fu Ren University".

59 See Appendix A, *A Letter to Pope Pius X*.

60 ADWM, *Christian Family and Our Missions*, 1935, 119.

61 Ibid., 1935, 358.

62 Ibid.

63 ADWM, *Fu Ren Magazine*, 1947, 113.

64 While I was doing research at Saint Benedict's Convent in Minnesota, I ran into a Benedictine Sister who was Chinese and attended Fu Ren University. During the course of conversation, I came to know her and learned many things about Fu Ren University. At Women's College, she converted into the Catholic Church and decided to be a religious sister later. She joined the Benedictine order eventually. She told me that quite a few of the women from the Women's College joined the religious life and almost all of them left mainland China and came to the US prior to 1949 when Communists took over China. She was Sister Kuan.

65 ADWM, *Christian Family and Our Missions*, 1938, 478. "When the Catholic University of Peking announced the opening of a Faculty of the University for women five hundred applications were received in less than three months, clearly indicating the desirability and need of such a step."

66 ABNU, Xu Nai-qian, "Beijing Fu Ren Da Xue", 18–19. Some joined the Nationalist army and some joined the Communist army.

67 SJS, *Fu Ren University, Bulletin* #1, 43.

68 ASJA, *Fu Ren News Letter*, Februray1932, 8.

69 Ibid. , *Fu Ren Da Xue, Bulletin* #8.

70 ABNU, folder #639.

71 Ibid. , #650.

72 ADWM, *Fu Ren Magazine*, March, 1948, 13.

73 Ibid. , December, 1947.

74 Ibid. , 1948, 37.

75 ADWM, Paul Han's private Collection; *Collected Historical Materials of Peking Fu Jen Catholic University.*

76 *Geming Wenxian* (Revolutionary documents), Pre-war Era, Vol. 56. editor, Huang Jilu, 154–155.

77 ADWM, *Fu Ren Magazine*, March 1948.

78 Ibid., *Christian Family and Our Missions, 1937,* 78.

79 Ibid. , 1936. 319.

80 *China Hanbook 1937–43*: A Comprehensive Survey of Major Developments in China in Six Years of War (New York: the Macmillan Company, 1943), 384.

81 ADWM, *Christian Family and Our Missions*, 1939, 119.

82 ADWM, *Fu Ren Magazine*,1940, 239.

83 ADWM, *Christian Family and Our Missions*, 1942, 118.

84 Through the words of Madame Chiang Kai-Shek, "...the Generalissimo has not found it possible to have that law (forbidding religion to be compulsory taught in Christian schools) amended so that religious subjects may henceforth be taught in registered mission schools." This is reported in *Christian Family and Our Missions*, 1938, 279.

CHAPTER SIX NOTES

1 It is read in Chinese *Shi Nian Cheng Shu, Bai Nian Yu Ren,* a Chinese idiom that is taken from Chinese classics.

2 SJS, *Fu Ren University, Bulletin*, #5, 103.

Notes

3   *China Handbook 1937–43*. Compiled by Chinese Ministry of Information (New York: The Macmillan Company, 1943). Details on the Catholic Relief services.

4   ADWM, *Christian Family and Our Missions*, 1934, 62.

5   An organization of the elite universities' sport teams.

6   Ibid.

7   Ibid.

8   Ibid.

9   It is not to be confused with the American Football. The Chinese name for soccer is also football. In this chapter, whenever the word "football" is used in the quotations, it is meant soccer. Fu Ren University's soccer team was also called Varsity team.

10 The whole article can be found in *Fu Ren University, Bulletin*, #5, 103–4.

11 ASJA, *Fu Ren News Letter*, March 1931, 7.

12 Ibid.

13 Ibid.

14 ASJA, *Fu Ren News Letter*, May 1931, 1.

15 ASJA, *Fu Ren News Letter*, April 1931, 6.

16 ASJA, *Fu Ren News Letter*, May, 1931, 1.

17 Ibid.

18 Ibid.

19 The British Queen's Regiment was ranked as the leading foreign team in Peking; The Nankai University of Tianjin was considered the leader in the soccer world of Tianjin outside the professional class; Qinghua was the champion in the year 1930; Yenching was always strong. Fu Ren News Letter, January 1932 had full report on the championship.

20 ADWM, *Fu Ren Magazine*, 1935, 94.

21 ADWM, *Fu Ren Magazine*, 1936, 31.

22 Ibid.

23 Ibid.

24 ADWM, *Fu Ren Magazine*, 1935, 94.

25 Ibid.

26 ADWM, *Fu Ren Magazine*, 1936, 31.

27 ADWM, *Christian Family and Our Missions*, 1936, 318.

28 ADWM, *Fu Ren Magazine*, 1937, 157. Hockey team was planed and a skating rink having been projected early in the summer of 1937.

29 ADWM, *Fu Ren Magazine*, 1938, 12. The team was formed and at present only Fu Ren and the American Marines have taken up the game. It lasted until the Japanese' attack on the Pear Harbor in 1942.

30 Ibid. 1938, 165

31 SJS, *Fu Ren University Bulletin*, #2, 37.

32 Ibid.

33 Ibid.

34 Ibid.

35 ADWM, *Fu Ren Magazine*, December 1948, 53.

36 ADWM, *Christian Family and Our Missions*, 1936, 78. Cf. *Fu Ren Magazine*, 1936, 17–18

37 He was a canon lawyer, dean of the disciples of Fu Ren University, and was the Director of Fu Ren Middle School for a period of time. Details of him can be found in Chicago Archive. Paul Han, S.V.D. wrote an autobiography of him entitled *Father John Fu S.V.D.* Unpublished materials.

38 Bishop Celso Costantini established a Catholic Association in 1927 in China. Its main purpose was to encourage the Catholics to put faith into practice. Namely, to be actively involved with social service as Jesus said, "Come to serve, not to be served." Father Fu became the director of the association at Fu Ren.

39 ADWM, *Christian Family and Our Missions*.1936, 78.

40 ADWM, *Christian Family and Our Missions*, 1940, 119; *Fu Ren Magazine*, 1940, 18.

41 ADWM, *Christian Family and Our Missions*, 1938, 238.

42 Ibid.

Notes

43 ADWM, *Fu Ren Magazine*, 1938, 29.

44 Ibid. 89.

45 ADWM, *Christian Family and Our Missions*, 1940, 159.

46 ADWM, *Fu Ren Magazine*, 1940, 54.

47 ADWM, *Fu Ren Magazine*, 1941, 55.

48 ADWM, *Christian Family and Our Missions*, 1940, 159.

49 ADWM, *Christian Family and Our Missions*, 1941, 55.

50 ADWM, *Christian Family and Our Missions*, 1942, 39.

51 *China Handbook, 1937–1943,* Compiled by Chinese Ministry of Information (New York: The Macmillan Company, 1943), 778–782.

52 *Ge Ming Wenxian (Revolutionary Work)* Vol. 56 (Taiwan, central government press, 1974). Fu Ren University was one of four arts schools in the nation and was the only school that combined with both Western and Eastern Arts, 207.

53 35% of the Catholic population was rather high this year. The average was around 10% or so as I discussed the student ratio in chapter five

54 ASJA, *Fu Ren News Letter*, March, 1931, 6.

55 Ibid.

56 ADWM, *Fu Ren Magazine*, 1936, 107.

57 ADWM, *Christian Family and Our Mission*, 1938, 278.

58 ADWM, *Fu Ren Magazine*, 1936, 107–108.

59 Ibid.

60 Ibid.

61 ADWM, *Catholic Family and Our Mission* 1939, 118.

62 ADWM, *Christian Family and Our missions*, 1931, 1. "On June 20, 1931, Fr, Wang baptized Mr. Wang Shi-Ching's wife and her daughters. Mr. Wang is Athletic Director of the University, the following week eight 8 students were baptized." In 1939, "thirteen were baptized before graduation. Wang Su Da, the great painter was one of them. *Fu Ren Magazine, 1940, 53:* " Nineteen were baptized, including two middle school teachers and twelve students of the Unviersity, were baptized. Included in the group also were Mr. Liu Chen-

tung, an official of the National library here, and the families of two professors. *Christian Family and Our missions, 1941, 38:* "On the feast of Assumption, (1940) Mr. and Mrs. John Liu, both teachers at the girls school and four children were baptized." *Fu Ren Magazine, 1948, 38:* "More than 32 baptisms at the university."

63 This Catholic Action Group got into trouble when the Communists took over the university. It was considered as an anti-revolutionary organization.

64 ADWM, *Fu Ren Magazine*, 1936, 35.

65 ADWM, *Fu Ren Magazine*, 1938, 164.

66 Luke Chen was baptized in 1932. He became the dean of the Fine Art Department as a non-Catholic.

67 ADWM, *Fu Ren Magazine* 1944, 1.

68 ADWM, *Fu Ren Magazine*, 1938, 164.

69 ADWM, *Catholic Family and Our Mission*, 1937, 79.

70 ADWM, *Fu Ren Magazine*, 1938, 165.

71 Ibid., 1938, 238.

72 Ibid., 1938, 78.

73 Ibid.

74 Ibid.

75 ADWM, *Christian Family and our Mission*, 1938, 318.

76 ADWM *Christian Family and our Mission*, 1939, 358.

77 ADWM, *Christian Family and our Mission*, 1940, 198.

78 Mr. Wang, was formerly professor at Peking Art College and now is an art instructor at Fu Ren. His carvings were based largely on Western originals. He was not himself a real designer of them but used models. Cf. *Fu Ren Magazine*, 1940, 27.

79 ADWM, *Christian Family and our Mission*, 1940, 198; cf. *Fu Ren Magazine*, 1940, 27.

80 ADWM, *Christian Family and our Mission*, 1940, 199.

Notes

81 Ibid. 398. This was to show how various materials and utensils common in China may be adapted to liturgical uses. The aim of the organizers was to call attention to the beauty and adaptability of many Chinese designs and to show that Chinese churches could not only be beautified by their use, but can be equipped in this way with the necessary ornaments at a great financial saving.

82 ADWM, *Christian Family and our Mission*, 1938, 78.

83 ADWM, *Fu Ren Magazine*, 1938, 89f. More details in this regard: Dr, W. H. Pettus, Director of the Peking College of Chinese studies (protestant) long an admirer of the art of the University and a zealous promoter of Christian Art in General, delivered a lecture at the (American) Monday Club, on "Present Day Chinese Religious Art," illustrating his comments by specimens of sacred art in lantern slide form. In Shanghai, too, the T'ien Hsia Monthly has been devoting attention to exhibitions of art, mostly, however, of a secular nature, though here too Western influence on native art is being stressed.

84 ADWM, *Fu Ren Magazine* 1941, 43.

85 Ibid. , 47.

86 Ibid.

87 ADWM, *Fu Ren Magazine*, 1935, 13.

88 ADWM, *Christian Family and Our Mission*, 1935, 118.

89 Ibid.

90 Ibid.

91 Ibid.

92 ADWM, *Christian Family and Our Mission*, 1937, 478.

93 ADWM, *Christian Family and Our Mission*, 1938, 359; cf. *Fu Ren Magazine*, 1938, 170.

94 ADWM, *Christian Family and Our Mission*, 1937, 478.

95 ADWM *Christian Family and Our Mission*, 1941, 78.

96 ADWM, *Fu Ren Magazine*, 1942, 19.

CHAPTER SEVEN NOTES

1 SJS, *Fu Ren University Bulletin*, #4, 1928, 27.

2   Ibid. , Liu Zhe, the Minister of Education Ministry says, "Do what your are doing! So long as you are student, your one duty is to study. Let no other thought than that of self-improvement and the acquisition of knowledge ever occupy your minds. Above all things, you must eschew politics of any description and under any guise." The Vice-Rector, Mr. Chen Yuan also confirmed this: 'I should like, however, to draw Their Excellencies' attention to the fact that the various Departments of this University are devoted to the teachings of Philosophy Literature, and History, subjects which only attract those who seek knowledge for its own sake. Hence, I make bold to assure Their Excellencies that our Curriculum is of itself a sufficient guarantee that no budding politicians or self-appointed social reformers will seek to enter this Institution.' Archbishop, Papal Delegate Celso Costantini's address was on moral issues, entitled "Know thyself" drew attention of students two different philosophers: a Greek philosopher who summed moral teachings in "know thyself", and a Chinese Mencius who speaks of the rectitude of the soul at dawn, after a night of repose.

3   Jerome Chen, *China and the West: Society and Culture 1815–1937* (Bloomington: Indiana University Press, 1979); Jessie G. Lutz, *Chinese Politics and Christian Missions: the Anti-Christian Movements of 1920–28* (Notre Dame, Indiana: Cross Cultural Publications, Inc., 1988); Ruth Hayhoe & Marianne Bastid, *China's Education and the Industrialized World* (New York: M.E. Sharpe, Inc. 1987); Ruth Hayhoe, *China's Universities 1895–1995: A Century of Cultural Conflict* (New York: Garland, 1996); Glen, Peterson, Ruth Hayhoe, and Lu Yongling, *Educational Culture and Identity in 20th Century China* (Ann Arbor: University of Michigan press, 2001); A. Cohen & John E. Schrecker, *Reform in Nineteenth Century China*, (Cambridge: Harvard University, East Asian Research Center, 1976); Cyrus H. Peake, *Nationalism and Education in Modern China* (New York: Columbia University Press, 1932); Colin Mackerras, *China in Transformation 1900–1949* (London: Longman, 1998).

4   Cyrus H. Peake, *Nationalism and Education in Modern China* (New York: Columbia University Press, 1932), xii.

5   Jessie G. Lutz, *Chinese Politics and Christian Missions: the Anti-Christian Movements of 1920–28* (Notre Dame, Indiana: Cross Cultural Publications, Inc., 1988). He has a whole history of anti-Christian movements: its origin, its development and the result. In Chapter one, he explored the anti-Christian Tradition and the Beginnings of Modern Chinese Nationalism.

6   Jerome Chen, *China and the West: Society and Culture 1815–1937*, (Bloomington & London: Indiana University Press, 1979), 146.

7   Cyrus H. Peake, *Nationalism and Education in Modern China* (New York: Columbia University Press, 1932), xii.

Notes

8   Colin Mackerras, *China in Transformation 1900–1949* (London: Longman, 1998), 32.

9   ASBC, *Fu Ren University Bulletin* #7, 21.

10 Eric O. Hanson, *Catholic Politics in China and Korea* (New York: Orbis Books, 1980), 25.

11 Akira Iriye, *After Imperialism: the Search for a New Order in the Far East 1921–1931* (New York: Atheneum, 1969), 3. In this book, the author makes an interesting argument, which is different from the Chinese historians' views. It is not my intension to argue his point, but to point out what has been mentioned. "… Japanese expansionism, even if it did exist in the abstract, would take different forms as conditions change in the concepts, practices, and patterns of international relations. Changes in these variables, which constitute what one may term the framework or system of diplomacy, will often modify the content and expression of a policy…"p2. In reality, there is a dispute on the rights or wrongs about the Jinan Incident. *The China Year 1929–1930* has description of this and presented many documents as well, 'A serious conflict occurred at Tsinan, the Chinese and Japanese versions of what occurred are so conflicting that the only way of dealing with the incident appears to be to publish selection of documents from both sides….' 878–892.

12 Marco Polo Bridge, in many writings is also referred as *Lu Gou Qiao*. This incident, which triggered the declaration of the war with Japan, is described as "7.7 Luguo Qiao Incident" in many Chinese writings.

13 Wen Han Kiang, *The Chinese Student Movement* (Morningside Heights, New York: King's Crown Press, 1948), foreword.

14 ASBC, *Fu Ren University, Bulletin,* #7, 21. The dismissal of the students will be discussed again later in the section Fu Ren and the Nationalist Government.

15 ASVA, Fr. Ildephonse, *Letter to Archabbot*, Nov. 9, 1928, Box #4, folder #9.

16 Ibid.

17 Donald A. Jordan, *The Northern Expedition* (Honolulu: University of Hawaii Press, 1977) has detailed the whole incident in Jinan which can be found on pages from 132 to136. In fact, the whole North Expedition history: the interactions between the Nationalists and Communists have been spelled out in this book.

18 Jessie Lutz, *Chinese Politics and Christian Missions: the Anti-Christian Movements of 1920–28* (Notre Dame, Indiana: Cross Cultural Publications, Inc., 1988), 270.

19 Ibid., 271.

20 Lutz made it clear that it was not his intension to include the Catholic Universities in his book. The relationship between these two universities was rather close respectively.

21 SJS, *Fu Ren University, Bulletin*, #5, 106.

22 Wu Xiao-xin, unpublished dissertation, "A Case Study of the Catholic University of Peking" (San Francisco: University of San Francisco, 1993), 100.

23 ASVA, *Letter to Val*, October 23, 1931, Box #1, folder #5.

24 Ibid., December 2, 1931.

25 Ibid., December 17, 1931.

26 Ibid.

27 Ibid.

28 Ibid., A note on the word 'Red' which is meant to be either associated with the Communist Party or a Party member.

29 Ibid.

30 Ibid.

31 Unfortunately, the Catholic Church unwisely also recognized this special state in opposition against the Communists which cause eventual criticism from China.

32 ADWM, *Christian Family and Our Missions*, March 1936, 118. Cf. *Fu Ren Magazine*, 1936, 33.

33 ADWM, unpublished material, Paul Han, S.V.D. "Father John Fu S.V.D.", 20.

34 Ibid.

35 Ibid., 20. Cf: Xu Nai-qian, *Beijing Fu Ren Da Xue Ge Ming Shi (Fu Ren University Revolutionary History)*, (Beijing Normal University Archive). According to the record here, only in December protests alone, there were as many as 51 of Fu Ren University students were injured, and 22 were arrested by the police. No other university suffered as much as Fu Ren University. Page 6.

36 ADWM, unpublished material, Paul, Han, S.V.D. "Father John Fu S.V.D." 44.

37 ADWM, *Fu Ren Magazine*. June 1948, According to the description, in those years, 'the Chinese Dollar, the Yuan, crashed to an all time low—1,000,000 to

1 American dollar. Some 20 years ago a Chinese dollar was equality to fifty cents in our money.'

38 Ibid.

39 A note about this date: Paul Han has December 2 of this incident in his writing. Another record from Beijing Normal University *The History of Beijing Normal University (1902–1982)* had it on December 24, Xu Nai-qian, in his book *Beijing Fu Ren Da Xue* also used December 24. I use December 24 because the protest against the Americans was occurred on the Thirtieth of December as other the historical record show. The girl's name is also spelled Shen Chong.

40 ADWM, unpublished material, Paul Han, "Father John Fu S.V.D.", 44.

41 *Beijing Shi Fan Da Xue Xiao Shi (1902–1982)* (History of Beijing Normal University, 1902–1982) (Beijing: University Press, 1984), 257–8.

42 In the Petition Letter to Pope Pius X, see Appendix A, the Chinese co-founders of the university mentioned this treaty would protect the American property. American treaty was signed after the Opium War when eight countries came into China. Britain, Russia, Italy, France, Germany, the United States, Japan, Austria, all these countries could buy properties and build buildings which were protected by that treaty which no Chinese could violate that. In chapter four, I mentioned that when the Benedictine bought the property, the treaty protected it.

43 This name *Gong Jiao Da Xue* was given by Vincent Ying, the co-founder of the university and was discussed in Chapter Three.

44 ASVA, Ildephonse, *Letter to Father Archabbot*, dated August 7th, 1927. Box #2, folder #2. Cf. "The Inauguration and Registration of the School of Arts" in Fu *Ren University Bulletin #2, 1927*, has some details.

45 Ibid. , Ildephonse, Nov. 7th, 1928, Box #2, folder #2.

46 ASJA, *Fu Ren University, Bulletin*, # 8, 105.

47 Ibid.

48 When the researcher was doing research at Beijing Normal University, I inquired all the possible places would have archival materials on Fu Ren University. The Archivist Mr. Liu informed me about Beijing City Archives. I spend an entire day there to look through the materials. The materials there were pretty much the same as in Beijing Normal University. There was no reason to be given why the City Archives would have kept the materials of Fu Ren Uni-

versity. Most of them were repetitive of the ones from Beijing Normal University with the focus on the political aspect.

49 ABNU, folder #637, *Politics from 1932–1938*.

50 Ibid.

51 Ibid. , folder #637, August, 21, 1948, *Confidential Letter to the University*, from Education Ministry.

52 Ibid. , #638 folder, *Politics 1929–1948*.

53 The Nanjing Massacre in 1937 was one incident to illustrate how the Japanese treated the Chinese. Within six weeks, the Japanese killed 300,000 Chinese in Nanjing, and raped some 80,000 Chinese women and girls in Nanjing. These horrific atrocities of Nanjing massacre shocked the world.

54 ADWM, unpublished material, Paul Han, "Father John Fu S.V.D.", 27.

55 Ibid. , 30.

56 According to Paul Han's research, when the middle school was closed by the Japanese, Father Fu, the dean of the disciplines at the University and later became the director of the middles schools for a number of years, asked the students and faculty members to come to school before 6:30am, every morning to have classes behind the doors because the summer was coming soon. For the sake of the students, for their graduations, transfers or continuations, the school tried their best in case the school was never allowed to open again. Father Fu was arrested twice and was tortured greatly.

57 ADWM, unpublished material, Paul Han, "Father John Fu S.V.D.", 36.

58 Ibid.

59 Ibid. , 37.

60 Also called *Te Wu* in Chinese. Many of these detectives were Chinese who decided to work for the Japanese. In fact, many times, these defected Chinese were very efficient to help the Japanese.

61 ABNU, folder #4: *Fu Ren University developmental history. 1929–1946*, 19. The Japanese arrested many professors because of their relationships with the Nationalist Party: Shen Qian-shi, Dean of School of Arts and Literature; Ignatius Ying Qian-li, Secretary General of the University. Zhang Huai, professor, Dong Xi-fan, acting dean were arrested...By February 1944, more 33 professors from Fu Ren were arrested, along with more than 20 students, and 10 teachers from middles school. All of them were released after the Japanese surrendered in 1945.

Notes

62 *Beijing Shi Fan Da Xue Xiao Shi* (1902–1982) (History of Beijing Normal University, 1902–1982) (Beijing: University Press, 1984) 243. These four addresses are: in 1938, the President addressed: *Wu Shi Fu Xiao Shi Li Yu Ren, Wu Xi Gu Mu Qian, Wu Jian Li Wang Yi, Yong Bao Ru Ling Ming.* (When you do things, do not brag yourself and therefore lose your integrity; Do not be near-sided; Do not forget justice when bribery is offered, Keep you dignity forever." In the years 1940, 1941 and 1942, he used *Lun Yun* (Analects) to address them.

63 Ibid., 244.

64 ABNU, folder #4: *Fu Ren University Developmental History. 1929–1946,* 19.

65 ADWM, *Fu Ren Magazine*, March 1948, 14–15, the Catholic middle schools were down from 553 to 559.

66 ABNU, Xu Nai-gan, *Beijing Fu Ren Da Xue Geming Shi,* 103.

67 ADWM, Paul Auer's letter, dated on November 10, 1948.

68 Ibid.

69 ADWM, *Fu Ren Magazine,* 1947, 124.

70 Ibid., 1947, 113.

71 ADWM, *Fu Ren Magazine,* June 1948, 29.

72 ADWM, Paul Auer's letters. Dated on November 1, 1948.

73 Ibid., Paul Auer, November 1, 1948.

74 Ibid., November 1, 1948.

75 ADWM, Father Harold Rigney's short biography

76 There were no courses on religions in the core curriculum, they were probably the elective courses for those priests and the new founded Saint Thomas Institute where seminarians were, and no specific curriculum could be found in the archives.

77 Beijing Normal University archive, Xu Nai-qian, *Beijing Fu Ren Da Xue Geming shi:* (Beijing Fu Ren University: Revolutionary History), Beijing: Fu Ren alumni association), 116.

78 *Beijing Shi Fan Da Xue Xiao Shi (1902–1982)* (History of Beijing Normal University, 1902–1982) (Beijing: University Press, 1984), 262–3.

79 ADWM, Father Rigney's short Biography. More details in Xu Nai-qian's book. In order to keep the university's autonomy, Rigney insisted on the two conditions if the Church financed the university: (1) the Board of Trustees should be decided by the Church, (2) the Church has the right to hire or fire professors. Pages159–160 illustrated the details of the differences.

80 *Beijing Shi Fan Da Xue Xiao Shi (1902–1982)* (*History of Beijing Normal University*). 264. From the available materials, I find a conflicting story of Father Rigney's confrontation against the Communist Government. The Divine Word Father's Archive has one positive story of this confrontation. Father Rigney in his book *Four Years in Hell* also had some comments on this matter. As a Catholic priest and a representative of the Church, He stood on the Church's side. The *Beijing Shi Fan Da Xue Xiao Shi (1902–1982)* has a totally different version on this. In it, Father Rigeny appeared to be a bad person and was completely wrong and evil. He worked as an imperialist and an American spy under the mask of religion. Certainly, the political stands of the authors could make a great difference in describing a person or an event. Xu Nai-qian, in his book *Fu Ren Catholic University,* mentioned the struggles between Father Rigney and the Communist Party. In the later months of 1950 when the Communist took over the university, they tried to work out a deal to finance the university. Neither party was successful in the negotiations because of the uncompromising principles.

81 ABNU, Xu Nai Qian, *Fu Ren Da Xue Ge Ming Shi,* 164.

82 Ibid. , 164.

83 Father Rigney's arrest was on July 25, 1951. He was officially sentenced to 10 years in prison in September 1954. A year later, on September 11, 1955, he was released and returned to the US.

84 ABNU, Xu Nai-qian, *Beijing Fu Ren Da Xue,* 138.

85 Dison Hsueh-Feng Poe, "Political Reconstruction, 1927–1937' in Paul K.T. Sih, ed. *The Strenuous Decade: China's Nation-building Efforts, 1927–1937(* New York: St. John's University, 1970), 38.

86 Ibid.

87 Jessie Lutz, *Chinese Politics and Christian Missions: the Anti-Christian Movements of 1920–28* (Notre Dame, Indiana: Cross Cultural Publications, Inc., 1988), preface.

88 *Beijing Shi Fan Da Xue Xiao Shi (1902–1982)* (History of Beijing Normal University, 1902–1982) (Beijing: University Press, 1984), 241.

89 ABNU, Xu Nai-qian, *Beijing Fu Ren Da Xue*, has the whole history of how the communists worked secretly on Fu Ren campus and mobilized the students.

90 Richard C. Bush, *Religion in Communist China* (Nashville and New York: Abingdon Press, 1970), 70–76.

91 ADWM, unpublished article. Paul Han, "Father Fu S.V.D.", 42.

CHAPTER EIGHT NOTES

1   According to Anthony Li, *The History of Private Controlled Higher Education in the Republic of China* (Washington, D.C.: the Catholic University of American Press, 1954), there were 21 private controlled higher education institutions established between 1864 and 1911. Details are on Table II on page 7 in his book. Of course, Fu Ren University was not established yet; however, between 1912 and 1948, the numbers of all universities were varying from year to year. In 1912, there were 115 higher education institutions in total both private and public; in 1925, when Fu Ren University was established, the number reduced to 108. In 1948, there were 207 institutions. Details can be found in table IV on page 37–38.

2   Kenneth Latourette, A, *A History of Christian Missions in China* (New York: the MacMillan Company, 1929), 91–101. 'At Peking there were conversions among some of the highest officials, even including two members of the *Hanlin Academy* and an imperial prince and some members of the latter's family.' p96. The Jesuits led by Ricci had obtained permission to reside permanently in Beijing because the Chinese Emperor was interested in their work. Ricci could speak and write Chinese well which earned more respect from Chinese intellectuals. His fellow Jesuits did the same.

3   *Beijing Shi Fan Da Xue Xiao Shi 1902–1982* (the History of Beijing Normal University) accused Fu Ren "After the WWII, the American Imperialist invasion had permeated the whole world and this also happened in the University of Fu Ren. Father Rigney replaced Father Rahmann is also a sign of that..." 251. *Beijing Fu Ren Da Xue* by Xu Nai-gan accused Fu Ren, especially Rigney that used the Church to deceive people by forming a secret organization *Legion of Mary* to continue its anti-revolutionary actions...to be spies, and tried to steal the national secrets, collecting Chinese military, political and economic information for their imperialist countries...137.

4   Appendix A. *Letter to Pope Pius X.*

5   ASVA, Box #2, folder #9, *Letter to Schmit*, March 21, 1960.

6   Appendix A, *Letter to Pope Pius X.*

7   Appendix A. *Letter to Pope Pius X.*

8   SJS, *Fu Ren University Bulletin,* #1, September, 1926. See also, Appendix A.

9   Appendix B. Vincent Ying, *Exhortation to Study.*

10 Ibid.

11 Ibid.

12 ASJA, "The Catholic University of Peking", # 71–12, 6.

13 Kenneth Latourette, *A History of Christian Missions in China* (New York: the MacMillan Company, 1929), 540.

14 ASJA, "The Catholic University of Peking", # 71–12, 9.

15 Ibid. , 7.

16 Ibid. , 19.

17 Ibid. , 20.

18 Kenneth Latourette, *A History of Christian Mission in China* (New York: the MacMillan Company, 1929), 528.

19 Ibid. , 529.

20 Ibid. , 532.

21 ASVA, Box#1, folder #7, Protocol N. 1625–22. See also *Fu Ren University Bulletin* #1, 17.

22 Jessie Lutz, *China and the Christian Colleges 1850–1950* (Ithaca: Cornell University Press, 1971). He has one chapter on the history and purpose of amalgamation. 444–489.

23 ASJA, *The Catholic University of Peking,* #71–12, 17–18.

24 Appendix, A. *Letter to Pope Pius X,*

25 Kenneth Latourette, *A History of Chinese Missions in China* (New York: the MacMillan Company, 1929), 132.

26 The Rites Controversy was basically a misunderstanding of the Chinese Confucian culture by the Catholic Church. First was the use of name of God in Chinese: *Tian* or *Shang Di* which were common in Chinese language. Rome condemned theseis uses. The other one was the so-called *Worshiping Ancestors,* a ritual for Chinese to pay respect to their ancestors and to Confucius for

centuries. This was considered as idolatry by the Church and was condemned by the Pope Clement XI in 1704. See Latourette, A, A *History of Chinese Missions in China,* 132, 132–146 for details.

27 Clement XI issued a decree *Ex Iilla Ddie.* This decree "commanded obedience of all missionaries and ecclesiastical officers in China on pain of suspension, interdict, and excommunication, rejected all privileges, dispensations, or rights of interpretation that might be used to nullify or postpone obedience... When Bishop Bernardin Della Chiesa's envoy read this decree in Beijing he was imprisoned by the Emperor." see Latourette, 146–7 for details. As a result of this, the Pope and the Chinese Emperor became enemies.

28 Bob Whyte, *Unfinished Encounter: China and Christianity* (Collins: Fount Paperbacks, 1988), 160.

29 Ibid.

30 Jachques Leclercq, *Thunder in the Distance* (New York: Sheed & Ward,1958, 1958), 45–49.

31 Wayne Flynt and Gerald Berkley, *Taking, Taking Christianity to China* (Alabama:TheAlabama: The University of Alabama Press, 1997), 17.

32 Jacques, Leclercq, *Thunder in the Distance* (New York: Sheed & Ward 1957), 45.

33 Ibid., 50–51. He states that this attitude was not peculiar to missionaries to China, it was true of missionaries in other continents.

34 Ibid. , 50–51.

35 Ibid. , 56. According to Leclercq, the missionaries had a national meeting in 1914 in Tianjin to discuss their missions in China. During that meeting, the question of the Chinese priests came up, since it could not be avoided any longer: the rise of the new republic, the part played by the Tianjin Christians in deciding the matter of religious freedom, had shown that China had begun to take its place in the world as a modern nation and that the days of the "unfair treaties" were over. But after their discussion a strong majority declared for the status quo. '*Let us leave the Chinese priests as they are...*' more details on 143.

36 Ibid. , 56.

37 Appendix B, *Exhortation to Study.*

38 See Appendix A, *Letter to the Pope Pius X.*

39 ASVA, Box#7,. Donald Paragon, *Ying Lien-Chih (1866–1926) and the Rise of Fu Ren, the Catholic Uuniversity of Peking,* 192.

40   Ibid. , 192.

41   Appendix A, *Letter to the Pope Pius X.*

42   *America* (April 10, 1926), 610. See also, Saint Vincent Archabbey, Box #7, Donald Paragon, *Ying Lien-Chih (1866–1926) and the Rise of Fu Ren, the Catholic Uuniversity of Peking,* 192.

43   Thomas A. Breslin, *China, American Catholicism and the Missionary* (University Park and London: the Pen. State University Press,1980), 21.

44   Eric O. Hanson, *Catholic Politics in China and Korea* (Maryknoll, New York: Orbis Books, 1980), 22. More details of how Vatican tried to bypass French government and to establish direct relations with China, 22f.

45   ASJA, *Fu Ren News Letter,* April 1931, 1.

46   ADWM, *Fu Ren Magazine,* September 1947, 106.

47   ABNU, #678, 1931–1949.

48   *China Yearbook 1937–1943*, Complied by The Chinese Ministry of Information (New York: the MacMillan company, 1943), 562.

49   Ibid. , 373.

50   Ibid.

51   Ibid. , 384.

52   Kenneth Latourette, *A History of Christian Missions in China* (New York: the MacMillan company, 1929), 555. According to his record, by 1906, there were 64 seminaries in China with less than two thousand students. After that, no record available to know how many seminaries increased in later years. The number was certainly higher than 64 because many more missionaries came to China after 1911 after the founding of the New Republic of China.

53   Ruth Hayhoe, "Towards the forging of a Chinese University Ethos: Zhendan and Fu Dan 1903–1919" in *China quarterly,* No. 92, (June, 1982, 323–341.0

54   According to Ruth Hayhoe, "Catholics and Socialists: the Paradox of French Educational Interaction with China", in Ruth Hayhoe, Marianne Bastid, ed. *China's Education and the Industrialized World (Armonk, New York/London: M.E. Sharpe, Inc., 1987), 97–119.

55   Ibid. , According to Ruth Hayhoe, *Ma* traveled to many countries and visited many universities: Oxbridge, the University of Paris and certain distinguished American universities. He had concluded that these institutions were responsi-

ble for the prosperity of the West. 105. Elsewhere in another book Ma Xiangbo and the Mind of Modern China 1840–1939 (New York/London: M.E. Sharpe, Inc., 1996), she mentioned quite a lot about Ma's education. He was trained in French style College and studied in France earned his doctorate in Theology. He was really talented.

56 Ibid., 105.

57 Fu Ren University, Women's College was established in1932, recognized as college in 1936. Anthony Li had a different year 1938 for this recognition; Aurora College for Women was established in 1938.

58 Hua Nan College for Women was established in 1908 and was the first women college; Gin Ling College for Women was established in 1915.

59 ADWM, Frederick C. Dietz, "Education in Mission Countries", in *Christian Family and Our MissionsFu Ren Magazine, 1940,* 279.

60 According to Wu's research, many of the Fu Ren graduates became teachers or professors. Some became politicians, business people. It is also noted, the wife of the first president of China, Liu Shao-qi, Wang Guang-mei graduated from Fu Ren Women's College, as well as her sister.

61 *Beijing Shi Fan Da Xue Xiao Shi* (History of Beijing Normal University) (1902–1982), ed. History Department. 269.

Bibliography

ARCHIVES

Archives of Beijing Normal University. Beijing, China

Archives of Beijing City. Beijing, China

Archives of Saint Benedict's Convent. Minnesota, USA

Archives of Saint John's Abbey. Minnesota, USA

Archives of Saint Vincent Archabbey. Latrobe, Pennsylvania, USA

Archive of Sisters of the Holy Spirit, Techny, Illinois, USA

Archives of Divine Word Missionaries, Techny, Illinois, USA

BOOKS

English Books

Altbach, Philip G. ed. *Student Political Activism—an International Reference Handbook*. New York: Greenwood Press, 1989.

Altbach, Philip G. et al. ed. *From Dependence to Autonomy*. Dordrecht, Boston, London: Kluwer Academic Publishers, 1989.

Barrett, David & Shyu, Larry. *China in the Anti-Japanese War, 1937-1945*. New York: Peter Lang, 2001.

Bary, Theodore. Chan, Wing-Tsit. Watson, Burton. *Sources of Chinese Tradition*. New York: Colombia University Press, 1960.

Bastid, Marianne. *Educational Reform in Early 20th Century China.* Center for Chinese Studies: University of Michigan, 1988.

Bays, Daniel, H. *Christianity in China: From the Eighteenth Century to the Present.* Stanford, California: Stanford University Press, 1996.

Becker, C.H. et al. *The Reorganization of Education in China.* Montpesier, Paris: League of Nations; Institute of Intellectual Co-operation, 1932.

Bing, D. *China, Cultural and Political Perspectives.* Auckland, New Zealand: Longman Paul, 1975.

Borthwick, Sally. *Education and Social Change in China—the Beginning of the Modern Era.* Stanford, California: Hoover Institution Press, Stanford University, 1983.

Breslin, Thomas A. *China, American Catholicism, and the Missionary.* University Park, PA and London: The Pennsylvania State University Press, 1980.

Brown, Thompson G. *Christianity in the People's Republic of China.* Atlanta: John Knox Press, 1983.

Bush, Richard. *Religion in Communist China.* Nashville and New York: Abingdon Press 1970.

Cady, John F. *The Roots of French Imperialism in East Asia.* New York: Cornell University Press, 1954.

Chan, F. Gilbert and Etzold, Thomas H. ed. *China in the 1920s.* New York: New Viewpoints, 1976.

Chauncey, Helen R. *Schoolhouse Politicians.* Honolulu: University of Hawaii Press, 1992.

Chen, Jerome. *China and the West.* Bloomington, Indiana and London: Indiana University Press, 1979.

Cherrington, Ruth. *China's Students: the Struggle for Democracy.* London & New York: Routledge, 1991.

Chesneaux, Jean & Bastid, Marianne & Bergere, Marie-Claire., ed. *China from the Opium Wars to the 1911 Revolution.* New York: Pantheon Books, 1976.

Chiu, Kaiming A. *Impact of Communism on Education in China 1949–1950.* Chicago: University of Chicago. 1952.

Ch'ien, Tuan-Sheng. *The Government and Politics of China.* Cambridge, MA: Harvard University Press, 1961.

Bibliography

Chu, Michael. ed. *The New China: a Catholic Response.* New York: Paulist Press, 1977.

Cleverley, John. *The Schooling of China—Tradition and Modernity in Chinese Tradition.* Sydney, Boston: George Allen & Unwin Ltd., 1985.

Chinese National Association. *Bulletins on Chinese Education 1923.* Shanghai, China: The Commercial Press, Ltd., 1925.

Cohen, Paul & Schrecker, John E. ed. *Reform in Nineteenth-Century China.* Cambridge, Ma. And London, England: Harvard University Press, 1976.

Deng, Peng. *Private Education in Modern China.* Westport, Connecticut: Praeger, 1997.

Djung, Lu-Dzai. *A History of Democratic Education in Modern China.* Shanghai, China: the Commercial Press, Ltd., 1934.

Dom Pierre-Clesestin Lou, Tseng-Tsiang. *The Voice of the Church in China.* London: London, Green and Co., 1938.

Du, Ruiqing. *Chinese Higher Education.* New York: St. Martin's Press, 1992.

Dufay, Francis & Hyde, Douglas. *Red Star Versus the Cross—the Pattern of Persecution* London: Pateroster Publications LTD., 1954.

Endicott, James G. *Rebel Out of China.* Toronto: University of Toronto Press, 1980.

Epstein, Israel. *From Opium War to Liberation.* Beijing: New World Press, 1964.

Edmunds, Charles K. *Modern Education in China.* Washington: Government Printing Office, 1919.

Flynt, Wayne & Berkley, Gerald. *Taking Christianity to China.* Tuscaloosa: University of Alabama Press, 1997.

Fairbank, John K. & Teng, Ssu-yu. ed. *China's Response to the West.* Cambridge: Harvard University Press, 1961.

Fairbank, John K. *The Cambridge History of China, Vol. 10, Part I.* Cambridge, London, New York, Melbourne: Cambridge University Press, 1978.

———. *The Cambridge History of China, Vol. 12, Part I.* Cambridge, London, New York: Cambridge University Press, 1983.

———. *The Great Chinese Revolution: 1800–1985.* New York: Harper and Row Publishers, 1986.

Fairbank, John K. & Goldman, Merle. *China—a New History.* Cambridge, Ma, London, England: The Belknap Press of Harvard University Press, 1998.

Fay, Peter Ward. *The Opium War 1840–1842.* Chapel Hill: The University of North Carolina Press, 1975.

Flynt, Wayne and Berkley, Gerald. *Taking Christianity to China.* Tuscaloosa and London: The university of Alabama Press, 1997.

Freyn, Hubert. *Chinese Education in the War.* Shanghai: Kelly & Walsh, Ltd., 1940.

Gentzler, J. Mason. *Changing China—Reading in the History of China from the Opium War to the Present.* New York: Praeger Publisher, 1977.

Gernet, Jacques. *China and the Christian Impact.* Cambridge: Cambridge University Press, 1985.

Gompertz, G.H. *China in Turmoil: Eye-witness, 1924–1948.* London: J.M. Dent & Sons LTD., 1967

Grieder, Jerome, B. *Hu Shih and the Chinese Renaissance.* Cambridge, MA. : Harvard University Press, 1970.

Gu, Yulu. *The Past and Present of the Catholic Church Shanghai.* Shanghai: Social Science Institute Press, 1989.

Hanson, Eric, O. *Catholic Politics in China and Korea.* Maryknoll, New York: Orbis Books, 1980.

Hartnett, Richard. *The Saga of Chinese Higher Education from the Tongzhi Restoration to Tiananmen Square.* Lewiston: The Edwin Mellen Press, 1998.

Hayhoe, Ruth. *China's Universities 1895–1995: a Century of Cultural Conflict.* New York: Garlard Publishing Inc., 1996.

Hayhoe, Ruth and Pan, Julia. *East-Western Dialogue in Knowledge and Higher Education.* Armonk: M.E, Sharpe, Inc., 1996.

Hayhoe, Ruth & Bastid, Marianne. ed. *China's Education and the Industrialized World.* Armonk, New York/London: M.E. Sharpe, Inc., 1987.

Hayhoe, Ruth & Lu, Yongling. ed. *Ma Xiangbo and the Mind of Modern China 1840–1939.* Armonk, New York/London: M.E. Sharpe, Inc., 1996.

Heyndricks, Jerome. *Histography of the Chinese Catholic Church.* Leuven: Ferdinand Verbiest Foundation, 1994.

Holy Spirit Center. *Tripod.* Hong Kong: Holy Spirit Center, 1992.

Hsu Long-hsuen & Chang, Mingkai. Trans., Wen Ha-Hsiung. *History of the Sino-Japanese War 1937–1945*. Taipei, Taiwan: Chung Wu Publishing Co., 1971.

Huang, Philip C.C.; Bell, Lynda Schaefer; Walker, Kathy Lemons. *Chinese Communists and Rural Society, 1927–1934*. Berkeley: University of California, 1978.

Huang Jianli. *The Politics of Depoliticization in Republican China: Guomindang Policy Towards Student Political Activism, 1927–1949*. Bern; New York: P. Lang, 1996.

Iriye, Akira. *After Imperialism: the Search for a New Order in the Far East 1921–31*. New York: Athenueum, 1969.

Israel, John. *Student Nationalism in China, 1927–1937*. Stanford, California: Stanford University Press, 1966.

———. *Rebels and Bureaucrats*. Berkeley: University of California Press, 1976.

———. *Lianda*. Stanford, California: Stanford University Press, 1998.

Johnsen, Julia E. *China, Yesterday and Today*. New York: the H.W. Wilson Company, 1928.

Johnson, Charlmers. *Ideology and Politics in Contemporary China*. Seattle & London: University of Washington Press, 1973.

Jordan, Donald A. *The Northern Expedition: China's National Revolution of 1926–28*. Honolulu: Hawaii University Press, 1976.

Kiang, Wen-han. *The Chinese Student Movement*. New York: King's Crown Press, 1948.

Kuo, Ping Wen. *The Chinese System of Public Education*. New York: Columbia University, 1915.

Ladany, L. *The Catholic Church in China*. New York: Freedom House, 1987.

Lam, Anthony. *The Catholic Church in Present-day China*. Hong Kong: Holy Spirit Center, 1997.

Latourette, K. S. *A History of Christian Missions in China*. New York: the MacMillan Company, 1929.

Leclercq, Jacques. *Thunder in the Distance—A life of Pere Lebbe*. New York: Sheed & Ward, 1958.

Leung, Beatrice. *Sino-Vatican Relations Problems in Conflicting Authority 1976–1986.* Cambridge: University Press, 1992.

Lew, Timothy Tingfang, "The New Culture Movement and Christian Education in China" in *The Christina College in the New China.* (Report of Second Biennial Conference of Christina colleges and Universities in China), Shanghai: China Christian Educational Association, 1926.

Li, Anthony. *The History of Privately Controlled Higher Education in the Republic of China.* Washington D.C.: The Catholic University of America Press, 1954.

Li, Lincoln. *Student Nationalism in China 1924—1949.* Albany: State University of New York Press, 1994.

Ling, Oi Ki. *The Changing Role of the British Protestant Missionaries in China, 1945–1952.* Madison: Fairleigh Dickinson University Press; London: Associated University Press, 1999.

Liu, Kwang Ching. *American Missionaries in China.* Cambridge: Harvard University Press, 1970.

Lutz, Jessie, Gregory. *China and the Christian Colleges 1859–1950.* New York: Cornell University Press, 1971.

———. *Chinese Politics and Christian Missions—the anti-Christian Movements of 1920–28.* Cross Roads Books: Cross Cultural Publications, Inc., 1988.

Mackerras, Colin. *China in Transformation 1900–1949.* New York: Longman, 1998.

———. *Western Images of China.* Oxford: Oxford University Press, 1999.

MacFarquehar, Roderick. ed. *The Politics of China.* Cambridge: University Press, 1993.

MacNair, Harley Farnsworth. *China: History and Politics.* Berkeley and Los Angeles: University of California Press, 1951.

Madsen, Richard. *China's Catholics: Tragedy and Hope in an Emerging Civil Society.* Berkeley: University of California Press, 1998.

Mancall, Mark. *China at the Center: 300 Years of Foreign Policy.* New York: the Free Press, 1984.

Menzies, Marion, et al. *Notes on Educational Problems in Communist China.* New York: International Secretariat Institute of Pacific Relations, 1950.

Murphy, Murray G. *Our Knowledge of the Historical Past*. Indianapolis and New York: The Bobbs-Merrill Company, Inc., 1973.

Nathan, Andrew J. *Peking Politics, 1918–1923*. Berkeley, Los Angeles, London: University of California Press, 1976.

North, Robert C. & Eudin Xenia J. *M.N. Roy's Mission to China: the Communist-Kuomingtang Split of 1927*. Berkeley and Los Angeles: University of California Press, 1963.

Oetgen, Jerome. *Mission to America: a History of St. Vincent Archabbey*. Washington D.C.: the Catholic University of America Press, 2000.

Orleans, Leo, A. *Professional Manpower and Education in Communist China*. Washington: Library of Congress, 1961.

Peake, Cyrus H. *Nationalism and Education in Modern China*. New York: Howard Fertig, 1970.

Pepper, Suzanne. *Civil War in China: the Political Struggle 1945–1949*. Lanham, Md.: Roman & Littlefield Publishers, Inc., 1999.

Peterson, Glen and Hayhoe, Ruth & Lu, Yonglin, ed. *Education, Culture, and Identity in 20th Century China*. Ann Arbor: The University of Michigan Press, 2001.

Preston, Diana. *The Boxer Rebellion*. New York: Walker & Company, 2000.

Purcell, Victor. *The Boxer Uprising—a Background Study*. Cambridge: the University Press, 1963.

———. *Problems of Chinese Education*. London: Kegan Paul, Trench, Trubner & Co. Ltd., 1936.

Ranklin, Backus Mary. *Early Chinese Revolutionaries Radical Intellectuals in Shanghai and Chekiang, 1902–1911*. Cambridge: Harvard University, 1971.

Rigney, Harold W. S.V.D. *Four Years in a Red Hell—a Story of Father Rigney*. Chicago: Henry Regnery Company, 1956.

Rosinger, Lawrence K. *China's Crisis*. New York: Alfred A. Knopf, 1945.

Rowbotham, Arnold H. *Missionary and Mandarin*. Berkeley & Los Angeles: University of California Press, 1942.

Ryan, Thomas, F. S.J. *China through Catholic Eyes*. Boston: Society of the Propaganda of the Faith, 1942.

Sih, Paul. *The Strenuous Decade: China's Nation-building Efforts 1927–1937*. New York: St. John University Press, 1970.

Shanghai College. *The Christian College in the New China*. Shanghai: China Christian Educational Association, 1926.

Smith, Bernard T. *The Chinese Batch: the Maynooth Mission to China Origins, 1911–1920*. Ireland: Four Courts Press, 1994.

Smith, Donald Eugene. *Religion and Political Development*. Boston: Little, Brown and Company, 1970.

So, Wai-chor. *The Kuomingtang Left in the National Revolution 1924–1931*. New York: Oxford University Press, 1991.

Spae, Joseph John. *Church and China, Towards Reconciliation?* Chicago: The Chicago Institute of Theology and Culture, 1995.

Standaert, Nicolas. S.J. *The Fascinating God: the Challenge to Modern Chinese Theology Presented y a Text on the Name of God*. Rome: Editrice Pontificia Universita Gregoriana, 1995.

Stenz, G. M. *Life of Father Richard Henie, S.V.D.* Techny, Ill.: Mission Press, S.V.D., 1921.

Stranahan, Patricia. *Underground: The Shanghai Communist Party and the Politics of Survival, 1927–1939*. New York: Rowman & Littlefield Publisher Inc. 1998.

Tang, Edmond & Wiest, Jean Paul. *The Catholic Church in Modern China*. New York: Orbis Books, 1993.

Taylor, George E. *The Structure for North China*. New York: Institute for Pacific Relations, 1940.

Townsend, James R. *Political Participation in Communist China*. Berkeley: University of California Press, 1968.

Varg, Paul A. *Missionaries, Chinese and Diplomats*. Princeton, N. J.: Princeton University Press, 1958.

Wang, Xiaochao. *Christianity and Imperial Culture*. Boston & Koln: Brill Leiden, 1998.

Wang Y. C. *Chinese Intellectuals and the West 1872–1949*. Chapel Hill: the University of North Carolina Press, 1966.

Wasserstrom, Jeffery N. *Student Protests in 20th Century China*. Stanford, California: Stanford University Press, 1991.

West, Philip. *Yenching University and Sino-Western Relations, 1916–1952*. Cambridge: Harvard University Press, 1976.

Wilkinson, Endymion Porter. *Chinese History: a Manual*. Cambridge: Harvard University Asia Center for the Harvard-Yenching institute, 2000.

Whitehead, James D. & Shaw, Yu-ming & Girardot, N.J. ed. *China and Christianity—Historical and Future Encounters*. Notre Dame: The Center for Pastoral and Social Ministry, 1979.

Whitson, William W. & Chen-Hsia Huang. *The Chinese High Command: a History of Communist Military Politics, 1927–71*. New York: Praeger, 1973.

Wolferstan, Bertram. *The Catholic Church in China*. London: Sands & Company, 1909.

Wolfgang, Franke. Trans. by R.A. Wilson. *China and the West*. Columbia: University of South Carolina Press, 1967.

Woodhead, H.G. W. ed. *The China Year Book 1929–30*. Chicago: University of Chicago Press, 1930.

Woodside, A. & Elman, B. *Education and Society in Late Imperial China, 1600–1900*. Berkeley: University of California Press, 1994.

Wurth, Elmer, M.M. ed. *Papal Documents Related to the New China*. Maryknoll, NY: Orbis Books, 1985.

Yang, C.K. *Religion in Chinese Society*. Berkeley and Los Angeles: University of California Press, 1961.

Yeh, Wen-hsin, ed. *Becoming Chinese: Passages to Modernity and Beyond*. Berkeley: University of California Press, 2000.

Young, Arthur N. *China's Wartime Finance and Inflation, 1937–1945*. Cambridge, MA: Harvard University Press, 1965.

Zheng, Shiping. *Party Vs. State in Post-1949 China: the Institutional Dilemma*. Cambridge: University Press, 1997.

Unpublished materials

Lee, Sophia. "Education in Wartime Beijing 1937–1945." Unpublished Doctoral dissertation, University of Michigan University, 1996.

Wu Xiao-xin. "A Case study of the Catholic University of Peking during the Benedictine period (1927–1933)." Unpublished Doctoral dissertation, University of San Francisco, 1993.

Paul Han S.V.D. "Father John Fu, SVD" unpublished article, Chicago, Divine Word Fathers. No date.

Xu Nai-gan., ed. "Beijing Fu Ren Da Xue: Revolutionary history." Beijing Normal University Archive, 1997.

Periodicals

Chan, Gerald. 1989. "Sino-Vatican Diplomatic Relations: Problems and Prospects." *China Quarterly*, Vol. 117–120: 814–836.

Edmonds, Richard Louis. 1997. "The State of Studies on Republican China." *China Quarterly*, Vol. 149–152: 255–259.

Esherick, Joseph W. 1998. "Revolution in a Feudal Fortress: Yangliagou, Mizhi County, Shaanxi, 1937–1948." *Modern China*, Vol. 24: 339–377.

Gong Jiao Bao. Catholic News paper Hong Kong, December 10th 2000.

Hayhoe, Ruth E.S. 1987. "China's Higher Curricular Reform in Historical Perspective." *China Quarterly*, Vol.109–112: 196–230.

Hevia, James L. 1992. "Leaving a Brand on China: Missionary discourse in the wake of the Boxer Movement." *Modern China*, Vol. 18: 305–332.

Hockx, Michel. 1998. "The Literary Association (Wen Xue Yan Jiu Hui, 1920–1947) and the Literary Field of Early Republican China." *China Quarterly*, Vol. 153–154: 49–81.

Leung, Beatrice. 1998. "The Sino-Vatican Negotiations: Old Problems in a New Context." *China Quarterly*, Vol. 153–154: 128–140.

Lloyd Eastman. 1997. "The Nationalist Era in China 1927–1949." *China Quarterly*, Vol. 149–152: 282f.

Myers, Ramon H. 1980. "North China Villages during the Republican period: socioeconomic Relationships." *Modern China*, Vol. 6: 243–266.

Osterhammel, Jurgen. 1984. "Imperialism in Transition: British Business and the Chinese Authority 1931–37." *China Quarterly*, Vol. 97–100: 260–286.

Rankin, Mary Backus. 1997. "State and Society in Early Republican Politics 1912–18." *China Quarterly*, Vo.149–152: 260–281.

Rowe, William T. 1982. "The Qingbang and Collaboration under the Japanese, 1939–1945." *Modern China*, Vol. 8: 491–499.

Strauss, Julia C. 1994. "Symbol and Reflection of the Reconstituting State: the Examination Yuan in the 1930s." *Modern China*, Vol. 20: 211–238.

Xu Xiaoqun. 1997. "The Fate of Judicial Independence in Republican China, 1927–37." *China Quarterly*, Vol. 149–152:1–28.

Young, Ernest P. 1976. "A Summing Up: Leadership and constituencies in the 1911 Revolution." *Modern China*, Vol. 2: 221–226.

Chinese Books and Periodicals

Du Yuan Zai, ed. *Ge Ming Wen Xian* (Revolutionary Documents), Vol. 58– Vol. 60: During Sino-Japanese War period.

Gao Jiao Zu (Higher Education Committee), ed. *Zhong Guo Gao Deng Xue Xiao Jian Jie* (Introduction of the Chinese Higher Education Institutions) Beijing: Jiao Yu Ke Xue Chu Ban She, 1982.

Huang Ji Lu, ed. *Ge Ming Wen Xian* (Revolutionary Documents) Vol. 53– Vol. 57: Prior to Sino-Japanese War period.

Jiao Yu Zu, (Education Committee). ed. *Jiao Yu Za Zhi* (The Educational Review), Shanghai: Shanghai Shang Wu Chu Ban She, series from 1911–1952. Vol. 18, February 1926.

———. Vol. 19, January 1927.

———. Vol. 24, October 1934.

———. Vol. 25, October 1935.

———. Vol. 26, October 1936.

———. Vol. 27, October 1937.

———. Vol. 28, October 1938.

———. Vol. 30, October 1940.

Li Shi Zu (History of University's Committee). ed. *Beijing Shi Fan Da Xue 1902–1982* (History of Beijing Normal University 1902–1982). Beijing: Beijing Shi Fan Da Xue Bhu Ban She, 1984.

Wang Zhong Xin. Zhang Kai-yuan & Ma Mei , ed. *Ji Du Jiao yu Zhong Guo Xian Dai Jiao Yu* (Christianity and Chinese Modern Education). Hu Bei: Hu Bei Jiao Yu Chu Bian She, 2000.

Xu Yi Hua. *Jiao Hui Da Xue yu Shen Xue Jiao Yu* (Christian Universities and Theology Education). Fu Jian: Fu Jian Jiao Yu Chu Ban She, 1999.

Zhang Kai Yuan, ed. *Wen Hua Chuan Bo yu Jiao Hui Da Xue* (Cultural Transmission and Christian Universities). Hu Bei: Hu Bei Jiao Yu Chu Ban She, 1996.

———. ed. *She Hui Zhuan Xing yu Jiao Hui Da Xue* (The Changing of the Society and Christian Universities). Hu Bei: Hu Bei Jiao Yu Chu Ban She, 1998.

Zhang Kai Yuan & Ma Mei, ed. *Ji Du Jiao Yu Zhong Guo Wen Hua Cong Shu* (Christianity and Chinese Culture Series). Hu Bei: Hu Bei Jiao Yu Chu Ban She, 2000.

Index

American Cassinese-Benedictines, 2, 4, 5, 7–8, 14, 18, 28, 31, 40, 43, 48–56, 59–61, 63–67, 69, 71, 73–77, 83, 104, 120, 173, 176–78, 181–82, 186, 188, 190
Anti-Christian, 8, 15, 17, 36–38, 78, 90, 115, 149, 152, 159, 167–68
Anti-foreign, 8, 37, 152
Anti-imperialism, 159, 168
Archbishop Zanin, 30, 116, 141, 186
Aurelius, 8, 48–52, 55, 64, 68–75, 77–78, 132, 181–82
Aurora University, 2, 23–25, 188, 189
Autonomy, 8, 19, 23, 35, 39, 64, 151, 166, 168, 172

Beijing Normal University, 4, 10, 12–13, 102–03, 106, 118, 128, 148, 160, 173, 186, 190
Beijing University, 2, 4, 6, 9–10, 44, 72, 83, 91, 94, 100, 103, 107–08, 117–18, 172, 186–87
Benedictine Sisters, 3, 14, 32, 74, 94, 100, 191
Benedictines. *See* American Cassinese-Benedictines

Cardinal Van Rossum, 4, 48, 51, 55, 75, 176
Chen Yuan, 12, 17, 26, 29–30, 78, 81, 83, 94, 100–03, 135, 142, 148, 158–59, 162, 167, 169, 180, 186
Crossroad, 5
Cultivation, 3

Da Gong Bao, 6, 44, 101
Divine Word Fathers, 2, 8–10, 13–14, 16, 29, 63–67, 73, 77–83, 93, 100, 104–05, 120, 130, 132, 137, 164, 166, 173, 180–182, 188, 190–91

Elevation, 3
Enculturation, 3, 92

French Jesuits, 6, 23–25, 188–89
Fu Dan University, 21, 24, 128
Fu Ren She, 2, 3, 27, 42, 46, 54, 68, 70, 89, 101, 177

Gong Jiao Daxue, 2, 54–55, 61, 70, 89, 158
Great Depression, 7–8, 63, 67, 71–72, 74–75

Hautes Études, 23, 25, 189

Imperial, the,. *See* Da Gong Bao

Jiang Jie-shi, 153
Jing Mao Xue Yuan, 10

Latourette, 20, 24, 25, 37, 42, 151, 176–77

Ma Xiang-bo,1, 6, 16, 24, 26–27, 30, 42–45, 56, 59, 99–101, 110–11, 173–74, 177, 182, 185, 188–89
MacManus Academy for Chinese Studies, 3, 27, 46, 54–55, 68, 70, 89, 101, 177
Matteo Ricci, 6, 43, 182–83, 186
Modernization, 5, 10, 22, 149, 177

Nationalism, 7–8, 10, 14, 17, 19, 28, 33–34, 36–37, 63, 71–72, 78, 90–91, 93, 95, 97, 114, 131, 136, 14–154, 157–160, 164, 168–169
Nationalist Government, 10, 22, 36, 55, 149, 157, 159, 161, 167, 169

O'Toole, 4, 41, 43, 48–49, 53–54, 60, 73–74, 77, 176, 182, 185

Politics, 6, 10–11, 15–17, 26, 32, 34–36, 38–39, 41, 47, 66, 90, 117, 146–49, 152, 156, 166–67, 171, 179, 183, 191
Pontifical university, 2, 4, 51, 99–100, 188
Pope Benedict XV, 48–49
Pope Clement XI, 186
Pope Pius X, 1, 4, 42–43, 46, 48–49, 59, 79, 100, 110, 174, 186, 195
Pope Pius XI, 48–49, 63, 79, 100, 186
Preservation, 3

Puppet government, 8, 33–34, 150, 162

Qing Hua University, 4, 94, 107, 153

Ren Da, 10
Rigney, 34–35, 83, 156, 165–67, 179, 182
Rome, 4–5, 7, 14–15, 27, 35, 41–43, 46–52, 55, 58–59, 63, 65, 67, 73, 75–79, 87, 111, 138, 141, 166, 173, 175–77, 181, 185–86, 204
Rudolph Rahmann, 14, 162, 171

Saint John's Abbey, 8, 13, 64, 76–77
Saint Vincent's Archabbey, 8, 13, 50–51, 53, 64–65, 68, 77, 101, 181–182
Shanghai, 2, 23–24, 44, 78, 108, 127–129, 13–140, 150, 153, 162, 165
Sino-Japanese War, 8–9, 11, 14, 17–19, 29–30, 32, 34, 79, 81, 107, 113–15, 118, 125, 130, 135, 150, 161, 168–69, 172, 178–80, 187, 188
Sisters of the Holy Spirit, 3

Tianjin College of Industry and Commerce. *See* Hautes Études

Vincent Ying, 1–2 5–6, 16, 26, 42–48, 51, 54–56, 58–59, 65, 78, 87, 89, 94, 99, 100–01, 110–11, 173–77,180, 182–85, 189

Wai Guo Yu Xue Yuan, 10
Westernization, 5, 10, 37, 177

Yan Jing University, 4, 8, 32–33, 70, 78, 94–95, 103, 114, 150–53, 161, 186
Ying Lian-zhi,. *See* Vincent Ying

Zhang Kai-yuan, 23, 38
Zhang Zhi-dong, 22
Zhang Zuo-lin, 7, 27, 72, 90, 132, 150, 153, 157–58
Zhendan University, 21, 26. *See* Aurora University

For Product Safety Concerns and Information please contact our EU representative GPSR@taylorandfrancis.com
Taylor & Francis Verlag GmbH, Kaufingerstraße 24, 80331 München, Germany

www.ingramcontent.com/pod-product-compliance
Lightning Source LLC
Chambersburg PA
CBHW061437300426
44114CB00014B/1729